Teaching
14–19

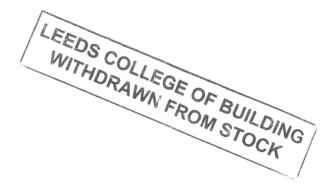

Also available:

In at the Deep End
A Survival Guide for Teachers in Post-Compulsory Education
Jim Crawley
1–84312–253–7

Leadership in Post-Compulsory Education
Inspiring Leaders of the Future
Jill Jameson
1–84312–339–8

Mentoring Teachers in Post Compulsory Education
A Guide to Effective Practice
Bryan Cunningham
1–84312–316–9

Teaching in Post Compulsory Education
Policy, Practice and Values
Anthony Coles
1–84312–233–2

Teaching Business Education 14–19
Martin Jephcote and Ian Abbott
1–84312–254–5

Teaching 14–19

Everything you need to know
about learning and teaching
across the phases

Georgina Donovan

 David Fulton Publishers

David Fulton Publishers Ltd
The Chiswick Centre, 414 Chiswick High Road, London W4 5TF

www.fultonpublishers.co.uk

First published in Great Britain in 2005 by David Fulton Publishers.

10 9 8 7 6 5 4 3 2 1

Note: The right of Georgina Donovan to be identified as the author of this work has been asserted by her in accordance with the Copyright, Designs and Patents Act 1988.

Copyright © Georgina Donovan 2005

British Library Cataloguing in Publication Data
A catalogue record for this book is available from the British Library.

David Fulton Publishers is a division of Granada Learning, part of ITV plc.

ISBN 1 84312 342 8

Typeset by FiSH Books, London
Printed and bound in Great Britain

Contents

Figures and tables

Figures

Tables

Preface

The 14–19 phase presents professionals with exciting opportunities as well as many challenges and threats. It is a work in progress and this book reflects the provisional nature of the area. My attempt to provide some information, to gather some views and to pose some questions is in itself a response to the pressures and the appeal of the current rapid movement in policy.

I appreciate the renewed emphasis on the individual which appears to be emerging as new structures and approaches are established. The incorporation of values into more aspects of the curriculum and the wider recognition of the whole person are also welcome moves.

I became actively involved in working across the sectors and in the 14–19 phase as a result of a combination of circumstances and choices. Like many others I had watched post-compulsory PGCE students increasingly migrating to secondary education as they were drawn by enhanced opportunities and incentives. There was a growing demand for training and support in response to the increasing signs of reform across the sectors and the identification of a new phase. I was always interested in working with 14–19 ITE but did not want to place students in new contexts without providing real opportunities for genuine cross-context working and for genuine professional development.

The original mixture of optimism and trepidation I experienced in anticipating imminent reform was dissipated to some extent by the pre-election decisions earlier this year. However, the powerful effects of the real shared vision and agreement among so many of the major stakeholders in favour of a unified overarching diploma continue. Support for the Tomlinson proposals was measured and at times qualified but almost unanimous and the prospect of more radical reforms in the future remains live.

The assumption that there would be a coherent provision and a more joined-up approach led to a move to take the joint approach, involving key bodies and agencies including the TTA, DfES and FENTO/LLUK, and the decision to aim for a dual-qualification model. As it transpired, this proved to be a unique pilot course and the small team at Canterbury Christ Church University College found itself pioneering in the field. The benefits were widespread support and interest, genuine constructive criticism from partners and externals, learner enthusiasm and success, and a steep learning curve for those of us involved. The intensity and pressures of establishing a new programme were repaid by the opportunity to be involved in the creative cross-sector partnerships and developments.

My thanks to all those involved in the creative team-working, and to the trainees and learners whose efforts continue to reward us all.

Gina Donovan
June 2005

Introduction

This book outlines the background to current 14–19 policies and initiatives, and their effect on educational environments, learners and professionals, providing detailed information for professionals involved. It is intended mainly for those who require an overview along with recent, clear information on the key areas and concerns. It attempts to provide answers to more frequently asked questions. The fears and criticisms of some are acknowledged and explored as are the hopes, achievements and innovations of others. Finally, perspectives for future directions are included.

While it is not a text for teaching, the book does seek to provide some background information on the history, theory, politics and economics of the phase in question. It is not a reader, but it does refer to some of the major voices within the current debates and it seeks to open the field and extend this important discussion by providing an accurate picture of this fluid, confused and often contradictory area of educational enterprise. Neither is it propaganda, though there is an inevitable concentration on explaining and illustrating as much as criticising the contemporary scene.

This is a hugely significant time for education. While statements such as this have been repeated every year for many years there is surely more justification for the statement now than ever before. The long-awaited White Paper in response to the extended period of consultation and structural change has finally produced some firm pronouncements. They may be broad and general but closer study does give a real sense of the future directions.

The 14–19 Education and Skills White Paper, published on 23 February 2005, contains the government's vision for reform across the phase. There are many stakeholders who feel disappointed that the opportunity for full root and branch reform has been lost. Yet the White Paper claims to keep on the track established in the Tomlinson Working Party Final Report. A levels and GCSEs have been retained and this vote for the academic status quo has provided predictable headlines and confirmed the worst fears of those who, like Sir Mike Tomlinson himself, had warned against 'cherry-picking'. The focus is still on targets relating to post-16 retention and the basic skills of school leavers entering employment directly. There is also the same concern for young people who are 'not as fully stretched as they could be' and for the unacceptable size of the group of young people termed 'NEET' (not in education, employment or training), currently standing at over one million, of whom a shocking one in five have no GCSEs.

> We propose therefore a radical reform of the system of 14–19 education – curriculum, assessment and the range of opportunities on offer. The White Paper sets out the government's proposals for an education system, 'focused on high standards and much more tailored to the talents and aspirations of individual young people, with greater flexibility about what and where to study and when to take qualifications'.
>
> (DfES 2005a)

The central difficulty for many professionals lies in the government decision to retain the existing 'gold standard' qualifications while claiming that the elitism within the academic/vocational divide can be addressed and ultimately removed. They contend that only a completely fresh start has any chance of achieving this goal.

The key proposals within the White Paper include measures to:

- Allow young people more choice, both of what to study and where to study.
- Motivate young people through a curriculum which allows them to learn in a style that suits them and to achieve qualifications as soon as they are ready, rather than at a fixed age.
- Support all young people to succeed in the basics.
- Remove the focus on 16 as a crucial point – as more young people accelerate, more take longer in order to achieve higher standards and virtually all remain in learning to 18 and beyond.
- Increase the flexibility within the system so young people can mix theoretical and practical styles of learning.
- Ensure confidence that the qualifications achieved form a coherent package for further progression in education and into the workplace.
- Improve vocational education and qualifications – offering interest and variety to many more young people and new routes to success.
- Stretch all young people to achieve – whether by accelerating to higher levels of learning, increasing the breadth of their studies or by pursuing greater depth in the subjects they are learning – so that all are learning and doing their best.
- Increase the drive to re-engage those who are currently switched off by school.

Both new and experienced professionals are faced with the constant challenge of shifting curricular emphasis and phase boundaries. While veteran enthusiasts were claiming prior to the White Paper that, if implemented, the proposed reforms would be the best thing to happen since the lost initiatives of the 1980s, detractors used the same examples in a completely different tone to support the opposite cause. One certainty, following publication, is that without real understanding and acknowledgement of the actual contexts concerned there can be no effective implementation of any new policy.

In fact, such debates have been taking place nationally at all levels and over many years. When attempting to consider the 14–19 question as something separate, one of the most difficult questions is when did it begin? Perhaps it is relevant to recall that it is over sixty years this year since the 1944 Education Act gave us free education for all and raised the school leaving age to 15. It is worth noting that the tensions evident today between education in a general sense and the world of work are still as apparent. Prior to the Act, education for the majority of this age group was not work related but ended as work of one kind or another began. Since the 1902 Education Act and alongside the inception of the LEAs, there had been choice for the post-13 secondary student between vocational and technical education. Grammar and technical schools gave formal structure to the educational divide still apparent in the UK.

Tackling the skills-shortage gaps is not a new endeavour; successive governments have sought solutions through education for decades. Curriculum relevance, with its range of meanings, and vocational training, with its range of purposes, have been repeatedly employed in the quest for a generation of skilled workers.

At the heart of many disagreements are fundamental differences in defining the aims of education. For some the emphasis on knowledge is linked to an elitist past that does not reflect a real learning-based culture, which empowers individuals to find meaningful and profitable roles in twenty-first-century society. For others the current skills mantra speaks from a hollow machine driven by blind functionalism where all critical and creative initiative is crushed.

At the launch of the Final Report of the Working Group, '14–19 Curriculum and Qualifications Reform', Mike Tomlinson told a press conference that reforms would 'result in far less atomistic and mechanistic learning and allow a far greater passion for a subject' (www.education.guardian.co.uk/1419education/story). The report recommended radical reduction in public examinations and a shift towards higher-status vocational education within a coherent new diploma framework. The hope for reform is that the trend of pupils dropping out of education at 16 and below, with limited or no qualifications, can be reversed.

Origins and context of policy

It is generally assumed that an advanced, globally focused, industrial economy requires a highly educated, flexible and mobile workforce. The acceptance of this link as an established fact by governments is clearly demonstrated in both rhetoric and legislation across the major economies. The focus is strong on both competitiveness and qualifying the workforce. These new economic realities confirmed by international comparisons and experiences are driving the policies of all Western economies. As first manufacturing and then service industries shift their operations to take advantage of cheaper labour, infrastructure and new markets so there are new pressures and demands upon national economies to respond wisely and rapidly to the changes.

The present government has incorporated targets into policy designed to create a more responsive workforce with higher-level skills into their employment and education policy. Improving skills in business and raising productivity are connected aims addressed directly through the LSC's workforce Development Strategy and indirectly through the long-term strategies for the future workforce embedded in 14–19 policy:

> While qualifications are still integral to personal success, it is no longer enough for students to show that they are capable of passing public examinations. To thrive in an economy defined by the innovative application of knowledge, we must be able to do more than absorb and feedback information. Learners and workers must draw on their entire spectrum of learning experiences and apply what they have learned in new and creative ways. A central challenge for the education system is therefore to find ways of embedding learning in a range of meaningful contexts, where students can use their knowledge and skills creatively to make an impact on the world around them.
>
> (Seltzer and Bentley 1999)

One of the questions asked is whether more qualifications are necessarily the most efficient and effective approach to achieving skills improvements in the population. The Demos report cited above makes the point that detailed knowledge is not in itself of value in an economic and social environment that places a premium on the new and on flexibility. It is the development and application of ideas in new situations that counts.

The report's writers do not believe that qualifications are the best indicator of appropriate skills and their views are not that controversial. Many politicians, employers, parents and professionals in education strongly believe that the qualifications we have are incapable of reflecting real levels of skill or ability. What this means is that while we continue to exchange certificates as currency and claim to be attached to them, they are employed as gateway tickets and there is widespread lack of confidence in their actual value. The coexistence of demands on the system for genuine upskilling and increased pressure on all providers to produce results in the form of qualifications is described in the report as 'The Skills Paradox' (www.demos.co.uk/openaccess).

The huge expansion of education has exacerbated this situation, and the steady and consistent improvement in student attainment resulting in the 'A grade norm' situation has led to an annual ritual of questioning the worth of the qualifications gained. As a result, education systems are trying to deliver a wider range of outcomes than ever before. Emotional, parenting and relationship skills, citizenship and civic virtues, business and enterprise skills, problem-solving and analytical skills, motivational and leadership skills are all called for, while the pressure to achieve in traditional subjects remains as strong as ever.

This paradox leads us to two main conclusions. The first is that, to meet escalating demands, the education system itself needs a greater capacity for innovation and creativity. Maximising the effective use of resources, creating and applying knowledge in new ways, these aims are as important to education as to any other sector. Second, we must recognise that innovation partly depends on being able to leave behind established assumptions and educational methods, which may have outlived their usefulness. The education system will be unable to innovate effectively unless it can create a new space in which to do it. Simply adding to the list of requirements and outcomes, even with increased spending, is not enough if we are looking for education to deliver different kinds of outcome.

To some, the politicians seem to be ignoring history and therefore to be doomed to repeat past mistakes. It is 18 years since the Higginson Report advised the Thatcher government to increase the breadth of study at A levels. Of course the 'gold standard' of A level was famously preserved at that point through the personal intervention of the Prime Minister. Subsequent attempts to address the same issues through Curriculum 2000 have produced many new problems to outweigh the gains. It is very difficult to achieve ambitious aims with piecemeal approaches.

The political capital invested in these issues is huge but it is sometimes difficult to judge where the advantage lies and, as a result, this area of policy is hotly contested. Recent manifesto announcements by the Liberal Democrats show a move into the reform territory as they promise a new diploma to combine the academic and vocational. Sounds familiar? It will certainly be sure of friendly support in many quarters. The bandwagon moves on.

Before leaving her ministerial post, Estelle Morris had underlined what seemed to be the government's dedication to wholesale curriculum and qualification reform in the February 2002 Green Paper. The statements were brave and unequivocal: 'for too long, vocational studies and qualifications have been undervalued', and the follow-up appeared to preface radical change. Working Group consultation supported root and branch reform and with widespread professional and industry support the stage seemed set.

On 17 February 2004, exactly one year before the publication of the 2005 White Paper, the School Standards Minister David Miliband welcomed the publication of the interim report from the Working Group on 14–19 Reform as a standards-raising element in the government's reform agenda: 'Curriculum reform is the next part of the reform process to raise standards and is part of our drive to make education personalised around the needs of young people.' Even with the sense of withdrawal from radical reform visible in the White Paper decisions on what the present government will implement following the Working Group's final report, ministers would claim adherence to the four key tests for reform set out in 2004 by the then Secretary of State, Charles Clarke.

The government used the following key tests to measure the Tomlinson proposals:

- Excellence – does it stretch the most able young people?
- Vocational – does it address the historic failure to provide a high-quality vocational offer that stretches young people and prepares them for work?
- Assessment – does it reduce the burden of assessment?
- Disaffection – does it stop the scandal of our high drop-out rate?

Many decry the lack of courage evident in the missed opportunity to go for election on a ticket of sweeping reforms for education in the 14–19 phase. But the unified framework of more appropriate qualifications was not destined to arrive in this way. Whatever the reasons – opinion polls, fear of providing the popular press and the opposition with too many hostages to fortune or just the last-minute trepidation of a new minister at the scale of the undertaking – permission to go ahead with the full reform package was not forthcoming.

What remains? The language of the Working Group Report is recognisable with stretch, breadth, individual choice, reduction of assessment, removal of barriers and increased status for vocational routes and qualifications all very evident as recurring themes but the structures designed to carry the principles through are not so visible. Diplomas survive, though they are limited to vocational learning. With the retention of existing academic qualifications the core recommendation of a single overarching diploma has been put aside. Personalised learning has remained intact though the interpretation has been altered by the compromises, and the key move towards greater internal assessment has not materialised.

Ideally, a real framework, incorporating not just qualifications and curriculum but organisational and professional relationships, may still be developed from the prolonged consultation and legislation. Evolution is still a possibility over the long term. Until the balance between partners is equalised and the boundaries are made more fluid, then tensions and counter-productive competition will continue to subvert the real efforts of many parties to achieve improvements.

14–19: policies and initiatives

The '14–19 Education and Skills' White Paper is twinned with the 'Skills: Getting On in Business, Getting On at Work' White Paper (DfES 2005e), and this link in itself demonstrates the nature of the agenda and provides insight into underpinning government philosophy. Whether they approve or not, those involved in education in any capacity must understand that it is now defined in terms of its function as an arm of the economy. The focus on individuals of all ages – their creativity, talents, attitudes and aspirations – is a focus on their potential contribution to national growth and wealth creation.

On 3 April 2005, in the final budget before the election, the Chancellor Gordon Brown announced an extra £12 billion for schools and colleges. Most of the key points for education in this budget were expected since, in spite of the ministerial changes, there has been a relatively consistent approach to policy spending over two Labour terms. Education spending in England will grow by an annual average of 4.4 per cent in real terms so that by 2007–8 spending will be £7.4 billion higher than in 2005–6. This will bring education spending in the UK to 5.6 per cent of GDP, with the increased spending directed at continuing to raise standards and pursuing the skills agenda.

The vision for the 14–19 phase that all young people should reach the age of 19 'ready for skilled employment or higher education' is constantly promoted. The strategy and funding to support this is, in spite of the reduced scale of change, referred to as 'reform' and reflects the sense of shifting education to serve and develop the potential of all individuals but with national economic and social interests uppermost. This generation of 14–19-year-olds are the first to receive such treatment and their choices, experiences and destinations will be the test of these twenty-first-century policies.

What did the White Paper finally unveil?

'Today's teenagers are tomorrow's parents, entrepreneurs, public servants and community leaders.' Ruth Kelly laid a dual emphasis on social and economic aims in the Foreword to the White Paper, '14–19 Education and Skills' (DfES 2005a).

Stakeholder disappointment has been mentioned, as has the Secretary of State's insistence that the White Paper was a genuine and potentially effective response to the challenges issued in the Tomlinson Final Report. So what full-policy picture did it propose?

In brief, the White Paper (DfES 2005a) offered the following:

- Retention of GCSE and A levels as 'cornerstones' of a new system
- New 'general' diploma for 5 GCSE grades A*–C (including English and maths)
- GCSE English and maths to include compulsory functional skills test
- New specialised Diplomas in 14 subject areas, with apprenticeships entering the framework
- Diplomas to be designed with SSC and employer input
- Pilot 14–16 programme based on E2E scheme to be made available to 10,000 young people from 2007

Across all sectors of education, the learner was given increased attention at the expense of learning, and the 14–19 phase is no exception. The White Paper as a whole emphasised the individual and set out the new 'personalised' and 'tailored' phase.

Moral and economic imperatives seemed linked in the White Paper though there was no doubt where the main emphasis lay. There is an extensive section (Chapter 2) dealing with the economic background, all set in the widest international context. Less prominent but still present is the following:

> In this context, the need to offer every young person the opportunity to become educated and skilled is not only an economic imperative, but a moral one. Young people who do not have a good grounding in the basics and the right skills and knowledge for employment will not have much prospect of making the most of themselves in life and at work. If young people leave full-time education without well-respected and recognised qualifications, then they are unlikely to be able to gain employment and then cope with the changing context of work through their lives. And the ongoing social and technological change that affects our world demands that more young people are prepared not only with transferable skills but also to adapt and learn throughout their lifetime. In simple financial terms, as Figure 1.1 shows, those who achieve higher levels of qualification will earn more.
>
> (DfES 2005a)

At the broadest level the proposals claimed to:

- tackle low post-16 participation – with participation at age 17 to increase from 75 per cent to 90 per cent over the next ten years;
- ensure that every young person has a sound grounding in the basics of English and maths and the skills they need for employment;
- provide better vocational routes which equip young people with the knowledge and skills they need for further learning and employment;

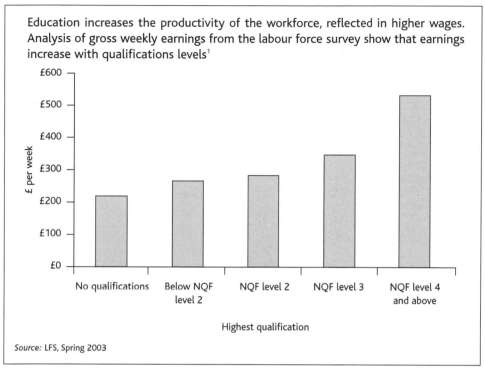

Education increases the productivity of the workforce, reflected in higher wages. Analysis of gross weekly earnings from the labour force survey show that earnings increase with qualifications levels[1]

Source: LFS, Spring 2003

Figure 1.1 The impact of qualifications on wage potential

Source: DfES 2005a

[1] Levels refer to National Qualifications Framework (NQF) levels. Level 2 is intermediate level (equivalent to 5 or more A*–C grade GCSEs); level 3 is advanced level (equivalent to 2 or more A levels); level 4 is equivalent to first degree level.

- stretch all young people; and
- re-engage the disaffected.

High hopes for the social impact of education reforms were also evident in some statements, reminding us of the enduring central place of education in New Labour policy. The citizen employee of tomorrow is to be shaped in the redesigned system of today. The White Paper highlighted the correlation between truancy and offending behaviour in both male and female populations extending into their later life. The issue of disaffection has also been placed firmly in the foreground:

- There is a strong and well-documented association between poor attendance and behaviour at school and later anti-social behaviour and criminality, as Table 1.1 shows.

Table 1.1 The correlation between offending behaviour and truancy

	Males		Females	
	12–16 % offender	17–30 % offender	12–16 % offender	17–30 % offender
Truant at least once a month	47	21	30	9
Occasional truant	13	16	18	3
No truant	10	8	4	2

Source: YLS 1998/9 HO RS 209 – note 12–16-year-olds were asked about truanting in the last year. Those aged 17+ were asked about truanting in their last year of school.

Source: DfES 2005a

■ If we are to have a healthy society of responsible, active citizens, well-prepared to take a role in our democracy and the international community, then our education system provides us with the means of achieving that. (DfES 2005a, p. 14)

What are these reforms designed to achieve?

The reforms have been designed to ensure:

■ a reduction in the amount of prescription in the Key Stage 4 curriculum, providing more scope for schools to support catch-up in English and maths;

■ an extension of the Key Stage 3 Strategy to improve classroom practice, so that it provides support across secondary schools;

■ the expectation for more teenagers to achieve 5 A*–C grade GCSEs including English and maths and the introduction of a general (GCSE) Diploma to recognise those who achieve this standard;

■ a revision of the GCSE Achievement and Attainment Tables, showing what percentage of young people have achieved the Diploma standard, i.e. 5 A*–C grade GCSEs including English and maths. The existing 5 A*–C measure will be phased out by 2008;

■ the provision that no-one can get a C or better in English and maths without mastering the functional elements. Where a young person achieves the functional element only, it will be recognised separately.

The drive in the proposals is obviously aimed at fuelling improvements in achievement of functional skills in English and maths before and during the 14–19 phase. These skills are deemed essential to support learning in other subjects and for employment. Achieving level 2 (GCSE level) in functional English and maths is placed at the heart of the reforms. More opportunities and incentives are to be put in place for teenagers who have not achieved level 2 by 16 to do so post-16 and support them in achieving level 1 or entry-level qualifications as steps on the way. Below this there is a welcome recognition of the importance of Key Stage 3 with an emphasis on developing a strong base in the 11–14 phase. So the increased choice of the 14–19 year should in theory rest upon a sound foundation built in the preceding years.

The following proposals express this plan to:

- retain all of the core and foundation subjects within that phase, but review the curriculum to improve its coherence in subjects where there are problems. Reduce prescription so that schools have space to help those below the expected level to catch up and to stretch all their pupils;
- support and challenge schools through the Secondary National Strategy and the New Relationship with Schools to use the new flexibility well;
- strengthen the emphasis on English and maths, in particular by expecting schools to focus systematically on those who arrive from primary school without having reached the expected standard in the Key Stage 2 literacy and numeracy tests, continue to publish national test results and introduce a new on-line test of ICT skills;
- introduce models of moderated teacher assessment in the other compulsory subjects, providing professional development for teachers to support their skills in assessing young people, which will help to raise standards across the curriculum; and
- emphasise the importance of achievement at age 14 by recording in a 'Pupil Profile' for each young person and their parents, achievement across the curriculum.

These proposals aim to increase the numbers of young people achieving National Curriculum level 5 in English, maths, science and ICT, and to stretch achievement across all subjects.

Policy and policy-makers

New Labour, new vocationalism: in over seven years of government the two concepts have come to seem inseparable but the future for the policies is still not guaranteed. Although many plans have been laid to push forward the education for employment agenda, the final direction to be taken depended upon the outcome of the 2005 general election. In order to understand the policies in question a wider view of the government's agenda is required. What is the vision? Individuals, especially it would seem in education, are far less important than the strategic driving forces. In the past four years there have been no less than four different ministers at the head of the DfES.

For better or for worse, politicians have become convinced that our economic advantage requires a significant vocational upgrading of the workforce. Skills gaps, competitiveness, and the notion of the 'skills crisis' as an accepted fact are all factors that contribute to the current vocabulary and the new orthodoxy. The new beliefs do not fall into a single group yet there is much consensus.

The 14–19 phase, its related policies, projects and new legislation cannot be viewed in isolation. There is a wider context and this will, to a large extent, influence the success or failure of policies at the implementation stage. The opinions and attitudes of professionals and the wider workforce to any new proposals will inevitably have an impact on delivery. Those responsible for putting policy into practice across all agencies and institutions involved have long and sometimes painful memories of earlier initiatives. Unless they can be persuaded to support the new policies, there is little chance that these will succeed.

Not all the new skills are easily defined and recognisable, like spoken English or ICT competence. Nor are their applications so obvious in an economic sense, like call-centre work or web-based companies. The 1990s produced and popularised such terms and concepts as 'the knowledge economy' (Neef 1998) and intellectual capital. Having developed different ways of reading our social and economic structures there is a growing sense among policy-makers of the importance not only of traditional notions of knowledge as the key to new products, services and markets but as a business asset to be bought, sold, audited and developed.

One outcome of this tendency has been the attempt to embed intangibles into education. From creativity and imagination to responsibility and general problem-solving skills, the issues of how to define let alone teach and assess these skills and attributes have been exercising the minds of teachers and lecturers for some time. Wurzburg (1998, p. 39) identified some important management strategies evident in the best uses of the new 'knowledge workers'. Among these he included the employment of multi-skilled people who could operate in self-managed groups and were 'responsive'. It is these flexibilities, which have become so desirable, and their effect on the teaching and learning of the pre-work cohort that will be discussed in detail in Chapter 2.

Having pointed to the 2005 election as a decisive point, it is worth remembering that there is considerable cross-party agreement on many of the fundamental principles driving current policy. In addition there is a degree of inertia in all major enterprises so that once instigated there will be a tendency to allow the policy implementation to play out its course with minor amendments.

In a recent policy announcement the Conservative Party planted a flag of their own in 14–19 territory with the promise of £1,000 for every 14–16 student studying on vocational options. This could be used for the direct purchase of training places. The method might be different but the commitment to the phase in terms of extending choice and supporting increased vocational training is clear.

Industry is supposedly at the heart of the new debates and is given voice through the new organs like the Sector Skills Councils as well as existing employers' bodies, vocational examining boards and the CBI. We are told that the employers have identified a dearth of skills appropriate for industry and that companies perceive the UK to be at a huge commercial disadvantage compared to partners and competitors within and beyond Europe.

The whole learning and skills sector is central to wider government policy. Schools had a high profile as standards were driven up and the pre-school years continue to receive attention but the 14–19 phase is now playing a major role across sector boundaries. The progress planned is intended to be a generator of economic prosperity and a mechanism for improving social equality and driving forward the social-justice agenda. 'Success for All', launched by Charles Clarke in 2002, began the process of increasing the achievements within the learning and skills sector and subsequent changes and initiatives are driving the movement forward.

The '14–19: Opportunity and Excellence' document (DfES 2003a) outlined the government's vision for young people. It was in this policy document that the staged reform process, skills for life and work and personalised learning for young people were set out but the consultation and Working Group that followed were always focused on the long-term view. In spite of the criticisms of the White Paper's conservatism there are still many elements recognisable from the initial development phase.

On 1 October 2003 the new Chief Executive of the Learning and Skills Council said, 'We must continue to focus on 16–18 participation and to drive up skills.' There is still a mid-phase divide explicit in the focus of responsibility but increasingly partnerships are being encouraged, established and fostered as the realisation grows that it is impossible to achieve anything from 16–18 without incorporating 14–16 in the strategy at the very least. For many, even this younger emphasis is insufficient and they believe it should be extended to Key Stage 3 and below. There is considerable support for giving Key Stage 3 far greater importance, on the grounds that much evidence identifies this stage as pivotal in the development of the young person.

New structures

Department for Education and Skills

The DfES has begun a major restructuring process to streamline the Department and its Non-Departmental Public Bodies (NDPBs). By 2008 the workforce will have been reduced by 31 per cent along with savings in the wider education and skills sector and reductions in the costs of Ofsted's school inspections. These and other efficiency gains should enable the Department to focus resources on strategic leadership of the system, on delivery mechanisms for education and other priorities.

The Learning and Skills Council

In April 2001 the LSC was launched, replacing the Further Education Funding Council and the Training and Enterprise Councils, to assume responsibility for a very broadly defined Post-Compulsory Education and Training sector. The LSC is responsible for all post-16 education and training apart from that within universities and aims to understand, to define and then meet training and education needs in the sector. The use of the word training is a key to understanding its focus though its remit is very wide and covers the management, planning and funding of Further Education Colleges; school sixth forms; work-based training for young people; workforce development; adult and community learning; information, guidance and advice for adults; and education–business links.

The LSC has a central role in the development of the work in the 14–19 phase but a clear division still operates at the 16 marker separating 14–16 and 16–19 as parts of a phase. In policy-implementation terms, the LSC is tasked with meeting the aims of the government's 'Learning to Succeed' White Paper. Some of the national targets set by this illustrate the overlapping agenda for the phase:

■ To raise the number of 16–18-year-olds in education and training from 75 to 80 per cent

■ To increase the number of 19-year-olds attaining a level 2 qualification from 75 to 85 per cent

■ To raise the number of 19-year-olds attaining a level 3 qualification from 51 to 55 per cent

From its national office in Coventry, the Council operated with a (2003–4) budget of over £8 billion. This has already risen from an initial £5.5 billion and is set to rise substantially over the present government term. There are 47 local LSCs across England. The Council consists of four directorates for Learning, Skills, Finance and Corporate Services, which are supported by a Chief Executive's Division and a Communications team. On the National Council are 15 members and representatives of employers, trades unions, community groups and learning providers. There is an Adult Learning Committee and a Young Persons' Learning Committee, which provide direction for provision to the specific learner groups.

The LSC works closely with a number of key organisations to build effective collaboration in order to understand and meet training and education needs. In addition to the schools, colleges and training providers, these include Connexions/Careers, National Training Organisations within LLUK and the Small Business and Employment Services.

Lifelong Learning UK

Lifelong Learning UK (LLUK) is the Sector Skills Council (SSC) set up by the sector employers to lead the professional development of all staff involved. One of its key roles, to be discussed further in Chapter 7, is the establishment of durable partnerships between employers, providers and other stakeholders.

Working together to form the Sector Skills Council for Lifelong Learning are a number of partners all involved in various ways in the support and delivery of post-compulsory education and training. Those involved include:

ALP	Association of Learning Providers
ENTO	Employment National Training Organisation
FENTO	Further Education National Training Organisation
HESDA	Higher Education Staff Development Agency
isNTO	information services National Training Organisation

LLUK was formally licensed and began operating from 1 January 2005, having been recommended as the SSC for Lifelong Learning by the Sector Skills Development Agency in December 2004. Its board consists of representatives from higher and further education, the voluntary sector, work- and community-based education, employers involved in development initiatives and major 'blue chip' public and private employers with special arrangements for the area of library and information services.

The very new SSCs have been given considerable influence over learning in the sector and it remains to be seen how their relationship with those currently planning and delivering in the field unfolds. The skills agenda through the Skills White Paper is supposed to place employers in a position to address the shortages and weaknesses they have identified for too long. Development of other Sector Skills Councils (25 licensed) is continuing. At this stage some bodies are more established:

- CITB-Construction Skills (www.citb.co.uk)
- e-skills UK (www.eskills.co.uk)
- Skillfast-UK (www.skillfast-uk.org)
- Skills for Logistics (www.skillsforlogistics.org)
- Skillsmart (www.skillsmart.com)
- Voluntary Sector National Training Organisation (VSNTO) (www.voluntarysectorskills.org.uk)

Effectively replacing and extending what was the Further Education National Training Organisation (FENTO), LLUK will represent over a million PCET employees. Their remit is to raise standards of teaching and learning. This means involvement with workforce development across the sector through its relationships with employers and employees. The emphasis is on employer needs, the development of workforce for economic purposes and the importance of meeting national skills targets. The future for the 14–19 phase can only be fully understood in the context of the kind of vision expressed in the LLUK mission statement:

> To fulfil the needs of employers by developing a skilled workforce and a nationally recognised set of standards and qualifications which have full employer relevance and 'ownership' and support the delivery of national skills targets.
> (http://www.lifelonglearninguk.org/aboutus/aboutus_index.html)

The standards and specifications for these areas of training and development were previously under the auspices of the relevant National Training Organisations and now answer to LLUK. They include the following:

Community Development Work

English for Speakers of Other Languages

Family Learning Practitioners

Governors and Clerks

ILT standards

Learning, Development and Support Services

Literacy and Numeracy

Management

Social Inclusion

Support Roles

Teaching and Learning

Teacher Training

Work with Parents

Youth Work

Clearly, the scope of the work is wide and many of the areas such as youth and social inclusion demonstrate the relevance of such changes for the new focus on 14–19. This is intended to usher in a new era of 'joined-up thinking' in line with other multi-agency approaches in, for example, family policy. Consistency across the professions and support roles and in management and organisation will provide a sense of common purpose and direction. If new policies are to be successfully implemented the effective building of real functional partnerships is absolutely essential.

Standards Verification UK is the new, wholly owned subsidiary of LLUK that takes over the endorsement and approval of initial teacher training formally undertaken by FENTO. They will assume increasing responsibilities over time for other forms of workforce training and development and expand their services to meet these new needs.

What went wrong with previous reform attempts in this phase?

Further detail relating to some of the more important attempts at radical change will be explored in later chapters but here the specific history is less relevant than the general principles to be extracted from the cases in question. One shared factor of previous failed attempts must certainly be the lack of a broad-based support and understanding. Without a shared vision the parties concerned across very distinct and separate sectors will not be able to operate effectively in truly functional partnerships. This is not a funding or training issue but rather a matter of joint vision and of partners working within real coherent frameworks.

The Nuffield feasibility report on reviewing 14–19 education in October 2002 (Raffe 2002) expressed the conviction that the only way to guarantee effective innovation or reform was through a long-term process 'comprising a series of incremental changes over several years'. In this kind of statement we can find the seeds of the Tomlinson final report 24 months later. Several of the key participants have been instrumental and influential in the latter process. In addition, the Nuffield report addressed the problem of research. There had been considerable research undertaken in some parts of the 14–19 area but key empirical questions remained unanswered. Much better evidence and greater participation from all stakeholders was needed as well as long-term commitment and rigorous evaluation, if the desired reform agenda was to be successful.

Policy-makers have clearly tried to address the issues identified in 2001 at the Nuffield seminars. As expressed in the feasibility report, the characteristics of past reforms, the surrounding debates and the causes for failure seem clear:

- They are not informed by a clear, explicit and shared vision of 14–19 education and of its values and purposes. One theme of the seminars was the need to identify such a vision, and that it might be expressed in terms of an entitlement.

- Effective innovation or reform is likely to be achieved through a long-term process, probably comprising a series of incremental changes over several years.

- Despite substantial research in at least some areas of 14–19 education, key empirical questions remain unresolved.

- The full range of stakeholders, and especially 14–19-year-olds themselves, tend to be inadequately represented in debates about 14–19 education.

- Finally, there is a desire not to repeat the experience of past reform processes which failed to break the cycle of policy change in Britain, characterised by short-termism, rapid policy turnover, the lack of continuous strategy, a deficit approach to reform, a reluctance to consider policy options on their merits, a failure to base policy on evidence and in particular a failure to learn from the outcomes of past reform attempts.

Following this, and with the exception of sufficient research to improve the evidence base, the aims of a constructive reform process seem to have been achieved. What remains to be seen is whether the policy decision and implementation phase can fulfil the expectations raised throughout the period of development and debate.

2001: 'Schools: Achieving Success'

In the wake of the Green Paper 'Schools: Building on Success' which set out the intention to reform education for 14–19-year-olds, the White Paper 'Schools: Achieving Success' really opened the whole debate on developing the new phase. Its main contribution was the identification of key components for the phase, including creating space in the 14–16 curriculum to allow students to pursue their talents and aspirations while maintaining a strong focus on the basics. The strategy is intended to address issues at different ends of the achievement spectrum from 'stretch' and challenge for those already destined for success to new means for engaging the disaffected and failing learners.

Table 1.2 A brief chronology of recent policy

1999		Establishment of Learning Partnerships (101)
2000		Learning and Skills Act Education Act
2001		White Paper 'Schools – achieving success' – started the debate on developing a coherent 14–19 phase
	2 April	Launch of Learning and Skills Council
	26 July	LSC introduces the Centre of Vocational Excellence programme for FE Colleges
2001	2 April	Learning and Skills Council launched as national organisation to plan and fund all post-16 education other than the university sector. Replaces Training and Enterprise Councils (TECs) and the Further Education Funding Council (FEFC)
	26 July	Centre of Vocational Excellence Programme launched
	29 November	New generation Modern Apprenticeships is launched to deliver work-based learning options for young people – target is to increase entrants over three years in order to include 28 per cent of under 22-year-olds
2002	February	'14–19: extending opportunities, raising standards' DfES Green Paper
	14 May	69 FE colleges moving towards CoVE status
	12 July	Pathfinders Entry to Employment announced supporting the implementation of the Modern Apprenticeship Advisory Committee Report (The Way to Work)
	23 August	LSC guarantees to fund every 16–18-year-old in Further Education
	8 October	'Golden Hello' scheme introduced. Recruitment in eight shortage subject areas in FE to be supported by new lecturer payments of up to £4,000
	November	'Success for All' published – quality transformation programme (DfES and LSC)
	14 November	Launch of Workforce Development Strategy to tackle poor skills in the workforce
2003	21 January	'14–19 Opportunity and Excellence' published in response to the consultations on a coherent phase for 14–19
	10 February	LSC publish the Skills in England 2002 Report providing a national survey of research identifying skills gaps for business and warning that skills gaps posed a serious threat

	March	Working Group on 14–19 Reform established
	2 April	First 20 FE college Pathfinders selected on a 'reducing bureaucracy' remit including 'light touch audit' regime
	24 April	Launch of 'The Great Skills Debate' as the LSC in conjunction with the British Chambers of Commerce begins the process of gathering employer and business views on the skills crisis
	8 May	Entry to Employment E2E scheme launched designed to target the 16–19-year-olds most disengaged from education
	9 July	Government Skills Strategy launched by Charles Clarke
2004	2 February	National Employers Skills Survey results published for LSC in partnership with DfES and the Learning and Skills Development Agency – identified the scale and impact of skills shortages in England
	11 June	Extension of 'Trust in FE' pathfinder to include a further 97 FE colleges
	July	Five-year strategy for children and learners
	10 May	Apprenticeships reforms announced by Gordon Brown and Charles Clarke to improve take up and achievement
	September	Education Maintenance Allowance introduced
	18 October	Final Report of the Working Group on 14–19 Reform.
2005	February	14–19 Education and Skills White Paper

2002: '14–19: Extending Opportunities, Raising Standards'

In the Green Paper '14–19: Extending Opportunities, Raising Standards' the government built on the White Paper proposals and outlined their vision for more coherence in the wide 14–19 phase. The consultation on this ran from February to May 2002 and was one of the most extensive ever undertaken by the Department. There were 4,000 responses from the young people consulted and 2,000 written responses and this level of direct discussion on the proposals was unprecedented. It was then for the QCA and the Working Group to take matters on and develop a more flexible curriculum and qualifications framework.

2002: 'Success for All'

The proposals set out in the discussion document 'Success for All' were developed by the Department for Education and Skills and the Learning and Skills Council in order to extend social inclusion and economic prosperity. It was designed to transform quality by improving responsiveness throughout the newly defined post-16 learning and skills sector, including school sixth forms. 'Success for All' was launched in June 2002 with a consultation over the summer and a published response in November 2002. A number of documents are available to support this, including the Standards Unit Teaching and Learning Frameworks. The four themes are:

1   Meeting needs and improving choice:
   - Strategic Area Reviews
   - Review of Provider Missions
   - Centres of Vocational Excellence
   - Three-year Rolling Capital Programme

2   Putting teaching, training and learning at the heart of what we do:
   - Standards Unit, New Teaching and Learning Frameworks
   - Expansion of e-learning

3   Developing the leaders, teachers, trainers and support staff of the future:
   - Initial Teacher Training
   - Qualifications
   - Continuing Professional Development
   - Leadership
   - Professional and Occupational Standards
   - Lifelong Learning Sector Skills Council
   - Pay, recruitment and retention
   - STAR awards

4   Developing a framework for quality and success:
   - Three-year development plans, including headline improvement targets, plan-led funding (including three-year funding agreements), Learning and Skills Beacons
   - New measures of success, Support for Success, supporting quality improvement
   - Minimum performance levels for providers, recognising and rewarding achievement

Implicit in the themes is the drive towards Embedding Equality and Diversity across Success for All.

The 14–19 phase, as it is now being defined, is a product of this way of thinking. Success is defined in terms of economic effectiveness and workforce performance. Success is measurable and the indicators show a clear emphasis is on skills acquisition and application, the growth and development of vocational routes, and improving the retention and achievement of those in this phase.

2003: '14–19: Opportunity and Excellence'

The policy document '14–19: Opportunity and Excellence' outlined in more detail the long- and short-term actions necessary to transform the phase. The key steps include:

- Putting student needs at the centre of 14–19 provision
- Providing greater flexibility at Key Stage 4 by reducing statutory requirements to the minimum essential for future progression and personal development
- Encouraging students to progress at a pace consistent with abilities and interests
- Providing a range of appropriate opportunities, including promoting modern apprenticeships, individually focused programmes on entry to employment programmes (for those not ready for apprenticeships) and student apprenticeships
- Encouraging a much higher level of collaboration and partnership between schools, colleges and work-based training providers, to offer all individuals the widest possible range of opportunities
- Promoting high-quality teaching and learning through a range of guidance and frameworks
- Increasing and improving employer involvement
- Funding 14–19 pathfinder projects to try out new ideas
- Providing financial support (e.g. Education Maintainance Allowance) to encourage young people to stay in education and training

The long-term reforms are placed in the following three areas:

- A much stronger vocational offer with a firm underpinning of general education
- Ensuring assessment within programmes is fit for purpose
- The development of a unified framework of qualifications suitable for young people across all abilities

The key challenges set out here still remain though it could be said that the structures which might have supported changed attitudes to vocational education and genuine new, high-status options across the sectors have not followed.

2003: Working Group on 14–19 Reform

It was in March 2003, that the independent Working Group on 14–19 Reform, chaired by Mike Tomlinson and comprising a wide range of experts from all relevant sectors, was set up, as a direct result of the DfES paper '14–19: Opportunity and Excellence' (annex 6), to advise the government on the long-term future shape of reforms. This 14–19 Working Group worked very closely with the key organisations like Ofsted, the Learning Skills Council and the QCA, and was charged with issuing an interim report within one year and a final published report in 18 months. The group's remit covered the following strands:

- 14–19 assessment arrangements
- Coherent 14–19 learning programmes
- Unified framework of qualifications

What was finally understood or required of a coherent set of learning programmes and a unified framework of qualifications by different interested parties has been central to subsequent events.

E-initiatives

Of all the elements proposed in the Tomlinson report and widely accepted by both education and employment sectors, the e-agenda seems destined to survive. All subsequent developments have indeed preserved this area of strategy. The White Paper (2005) deliberately avoids detail and prescription in this area, which it calls 'the ongoing development of technologies that support learning', and concentrates instead on setting out 'the changes in curriculum and qualifications that will improve what is available to young people'.

Among the many roles and responsibilities of the new Standards Unit is that of e-learning development. Knowledge in this area is now labelled 'the new currency', reflecting the fact that the learning of ICT has long been privileged in terms of funding. As new infrastructures for lifelong learning provide evidence of attempts to meet the perceived needs generated by local and global economic movement, the potential of the e-learning environments become increasingly tempting. Where there appear to be huge economies of scale and solutions to issues relating to delivery of learning, there will inevitably be serious investment.

Initially the e-approaches targeted the adult learner and pioneers like the Open University benefited from the advances just as they coped with the difficulties. The whole field opened up as all phases of learners were involved and in some senses primary education has proved more creative than other sectors in its integration of technology to learning.

Debates, which should have preceded developments, are only just taking place and those in the forefront of e-learning and teaching are trying to explore the real implications for all learners as new approaches are implemented. The implications for the 14–19 sector are quite serious as the first generations of such learners will be subject to the most experimental schemes. Attracting and retaining these learners, tracking their progress, and recording and transferring their credits, are all components that should be accommodated in the planning for reform. Social mobility and genuine education for work and for personal development are apparently at stake.

In the Final Report of the Tomlinson Working Group on 14–19 reform there was a clear move towards emphasising the importance of ICT. Becta present the developments as they relate to this area as follows:

- ICT is fundamental to the effective delivery of all of the proposals in the report, with particular reference made to the e-assessment and 'functional ICT' as core components. The impact of ICT on motivation and learning remains tacit throughout the report, with occasional prompts, such as the blanket recommendation that electronic learning and assessment should be extended.

- Assessment is seen as the key element of learning and one way to give students a voice. ICT is presented as an essential tool for e-assessment and to satisfy the implications of the report's proposals for learning, tracking, recording and reporting, particularly where these occur across institutional boundaries. The user-interface of this system is the 'e-transcript', a clear document mapping a person's achievement in what is hoped will become the lingua franca of the framework.

- The e-transcript should be the gateway to obtaining the details of programme content and references. The report recognises 'the need for a national ICT infrastructure that permits the transcripts to operate in the ways we have described'. It continues: 'The capacity and technology for e-assessment is developing rapidly', requiring, as with many of the proposals in the report, 'extensive research and piloting'.

- ICT – Information and Communications Technology – is the term used throughout the report, except in the summary. There it becomes 'computing', sometimes prefixed as 'functional ICT' and sometimes suffixed as 'ICT skills'. What remains common is that, as with all vocational qualifications, the content of a particular ICT qualification 'can only be determined in consultation with end-users, including HE, employers and community groups ', and that the Sector Skills Councils (SSC) will have a crucial role to play.

The key questions for many practitioners arising from such developments concern the definition and nature of 'functional ICT'. What will this mean in real terms for a 14–19-year-old studying on a new or established programme? One thing that is now clear is the recommendation that 'electronic learning and assessment in 14–19 should be extended'.

The Interim Report from the working group had already placed ICT at the core of the reform proposals:

> ICT skills are central to many aspects of modern life. Their place must be assured within the 14–19 cohort, we would propose discrete learning and assessment. However, this is a fast-moving area. We believe that the nature of ICT development should be kept under review, as young people should increasingly acquire these skills earlier and faster than their predecessors. Within the ten year time frame for implementation of our proposals it may be that ICT skills will have become a standard tool that the vast majority of young people take for granted by age 14. In this case, most learners would not need to give these skills specific attention within their 14–19 programmes. Arrangements will still be necessary for those who do.
>
> (Working Group in 14–19 Reform 2004)

Pathfinders' work was evaluated for the DfES by the Universities of Exeter and Leeds through their first academic year (2002–3). Also useful for reference is the

Becta document, *Using Technology to Support the 14–19 Agenda*. This document outlines the ways in which ICT can support the implementation of cross-sector 14–19 education.

Background to policy development

Tomlinson: 14–19 curriculum and qualifications reform

In the wake of a generally constructive set of responses to Tomlinson's final report, one of the major fears for a section of those who will implement and deliver the reforms has been the spectre of a diluted and weakened working version. Some of the initial reactions from the politicians who commissioned the consultation and report caused so much concern to the writers and supporters that they provoked debates around the dangers of selecting preferred elements and missing the opportunity for radical reconstruction within the sector. The publication has confirmed many of the worst fears of this group (see Chapter 9 for details of the responses).

It was very tempting for ministers to appease the immediate concerns of the general public and of particular stakeholders in the early stages of release and under the scrutiny of intense press coverage. Rather than allow headlines mourning the passing of the A level as the gold standard so beloved by parents and universities, there were instant and fairly simplistic denials. This tended to obscure the fact that the report is multi-layered, supports phased yet radical change and contains a complex new set of structures that are essentially interdependent. To some extent the complexities and promise of the reforms are lost in a relatively crude debate centred upon the survival or demise of one component qualification. There were indeed debates but to some extent these missed the main points.

The most useful debates have in fact been taking place nationally at all levels and over many years. When attempting to consider the debates, one of the most difficult questions is where do they begin? It is 60 years since the 1944 Education Act provided free education for us all. What is not widely realised is that vocational education within institutions began long before this, developing initially in the early Mechanics' Institutes from the early part of the nineteenth century. As ever, investment and funding were the key and only the support of industrialists and the perceived economic need ensured the spread and success of this particular brand of vocational education. In the twenty-first century, as in the nineteenth, what kind of education, what curriculum and who teaches remain the key questions linked with policy decisions. At the heart of many disagreements are fundamental differences in the definition of the aims of education. For some, the emphasis on knowledge is linked to an elitist past that does not reflect a real learning-based culture. For others, the vocational, skills-based curriculum disregards the inherited value of knowledge and culture and fails to develop any real critical faculty.

The implications of all this change for teaching and learning will be explored in more detail in Chapters 2 and 8. From a political rather than a teaching point of view the most interesting and potentially damaging aspects of the current situation are the battle lines being drawn upon the topography of the educational landscape. Who will own the new territories of vocational provision? Who will draw down the huge amounts of funding promised to accompany the surge in skills upgrading, first for the young pre-workers and workers, then for the continuing lifelong strategies? The answers to these kinds of questions will give a different meaning to the much heralded notions of partnership. Competition in the old sense may be being buried but though there is a real drive towards strategic educational business partnerships under way, it would be a delusion to assume that there will be no winners and losers.

What were the Tomlinson plans for stakeholders?

The reception for the Tomlinson reform proposals was surprisingly favourable in many quarters. The most significant criticisms were not of the principles behind the proposals but rather of the hollowness of the resulting framework. Inevitably there is less matter than outline and structure in the plan. It was always intended to be the bones for something with a long-term gestation and existence rather than a fully fleshed entity.

While the final report could not exactly be accused of trying to be all things to all people, its emphasis on 'evolution not revolution' did result in some carefully considered compromises and, perhaps most constructively though also controversially, an incremental and developmental approach designed to allay the worst fears of key stakeholders in areas of greatest sensitivity. This was supposed to limit the worst of the potential for outright rejection of the reforms yet it laid the report writers open to predicable accusations that they have sold out on some key issues and in the end the main argument for the overarching diploma was lost for the present.

However, the issues surrounding the original proposed reforms have been thoughtfully addressed over time. One of the proposals' strengths with regard to implementation was certainly the way in which they combined both principle change and recognition of the difficulties inherent in altering an existing set of structures on a practical level. The nature of the four-part diploma was intended to enable flexibility and a broader view and this seems to have pleased a majority right across the very diverse range of providers and other stakeholders in 14–19 education. FE colleges have always struggled with the tensions of delivering choice and maintaining quality and financial viability in a rapidly shifting market. Many vocational qualifications have insufficient recognition to be accepted as credible currency by those involved. Even where employers and industry lead bodies are signed up and instrumental in the design, delivery and assessment, parents and learners may remain unconvinced or transferability is always an issue. There was a broad acknowledgement that, in spite of some weaknesses, Tomlinson has met these key challenges head on.

The Working Group report emphasised this complexity and proposed a new consistency without rigid uniformity. To many veterans of previous campaigns to raise the status of vocational education without devaluing existing academic standards, the present climate is one of considerable and almost forgotten optimism. However, warning notes are frequently sounded and a degree of cynicism is not uncommon. Most significant in this case were the concerns surrounding ownership of the proposed systems. Who would drive it all? Would there be real local, professional and learner ownership?

The fault-lines inevitably lie as always along the old phase divisions and the White Paper does not alter this situation. Many would claim that it will exacerbate the complex problems and tensions. After all, you cannot expect to generate and promote competition, poaching and harsh implementation of business approaches throughout education for years and then to swing all concerns into idealised and harmonious partnerships. Those schools currently in a position to make choices inevitably keep the pupils who will achieve at the higher levels, leaving FE as a repository of the excluded, disaffected and vulnerable. Whatever the political standpoint of the stakeholders, there is fairly general agreement that for the status of vocational education to improve, a radical shift in such attitudes must take place. This would require more than small movements in the qualifications' goalposts. Schools have the powers to compel attendance, and teachers and managers in schools have the advantage that they work within the relative stability of a more fixed long-term population of learners so that culture and relationships can have a stronger impact on their learning over time.

Over recent years, even taking account of dissatisfaction, it is widely felt both outside and within the teaching profession that salaries, support and resources of all kinds have improved under the government's education agenda. Any reforms must be appropriately resourced and given a long-term commitment on the part of government for their success to be assured. If the school and FE sectors are to work in partnership then the long-term differences in pay, terms and conditions must be addressed.

What were the responses to Tomlinson from the various stakeholders?

A recent *Times Educational Supplement* poll (30 December 2004) showed that most head teachers support total rather than partial reform, giving a figure of seven out of ten in favour of full implementation of the report. Only one in five backed a compromise retaining the GCSE and A-level titles within a new diploma and only 15 per cent supported the status quo. Immediate responses from the main school, industry and higher-education spokespeople were very supportive and positive. Dr John Dunford, General Secretary of the Secondary Heads Association, said:

> Secondary school leaders will strongly support the Tomlinson recommendations. We see A level and GCSE courses as the building blocks of the new Diploma system, which will create a stronger, more coherent qualifications structure, raise the esteem of vocational awards and reduce the burden of external examinations.
>
> The proposals for chartered assessors are particularly welcome in placing more trust in the professional judgement of teachers to carry out internal assessment to external standards.

This is a long-term reform programme that will benefit from the consensus that Mike Tomlinson has built around his proposals and I look for support from all political parties, as well as universities and employers.

Delyth Chambers, Chair of the Russell Group of Admissions Officers said:

The Russell Group of Universities welcomes the publication of the Tomlinson report with its firm recommendations for changes to the school curriculum and 14–19 qualification structure.

We would hope that the diploma proposals, and the structuring of 14–19 as a single phase, if implemented, should improve the motivation, engagement and confidence of a wider range of young people to achieve to their best abilities and, where appropriate, to progress to higher education.

(14–19 Working Group Press Notice, 18 October 2004)

Michael Geoghegan, Director and Chief Executive of HSBC plc said:

HSBC supports the principles in the thinking of the Tomlinson Working Group on 14–19 reform. HSBC endorses the need to develop not only the intellectual capacities of young people but also their competencies and skills and acknowledges the fact that learning takes place through classroom teaching and also through practical projects, activities, work experience and community involvement.

(For the reactions to the actual White Paper publication, see Chapter 9.)

It remains to be seen whether the longer-term reactions and developed responses to implementation in whatever form will remain so constructive. There is already a view that the proposed structures give little real sense of the final nature of a reformed phase and certainly none of the practical implications of radical change.

New National Assessment Agency

Centre and periphery – new independence or divide and rule?

A common assumption is that school heads have gained ample autonomy to respond to the challenges and opportunities presented. The reality is that many do not feel that they have sufficient control over key areas of finance. The Chancellor's recent plans to hand over more budgetary control to heads and to reduce the powers and influence of LEAs are being welcomed. In conjunction with the adjustments to the Ofsted processes and other measures designed to cut red tape in schools, there is a sense that beyond Tomlinson there are shifts, which could potentially improve the lot of the head teacher and, through this, school performance and morale. Whether the implementation of the measures in question will confirm the optimists' belief in a 'new relationship' with schools remains to be seen.

Detractors of the new moves in finance for schools are particularly anxious about the tendency for greater centralisation and would fear the consequences of any move away from the regions and LEAs to a Whitehall-driven model. Whatever the weaknesses of the present model, they believe that there are many potential problems inherent in the proposed changes. Further decoupling of schools from existing systems and relationships, they claim, will just leave some struggling to cope. Wheels of interaction would have to be reinvented at the cost of wasted time and resources.

FE has always perceived itself to be a financial poor relation with relatively less political power. On the other hand FE can be seen to gain from its reputation for an inclusive mixed environment where the emphasis is on learner freedoms and a far broader range of options, resources and links. It seems to escape the constraining elements of a national curriculum and the responsibilities for children. In fact the truth is more often located somewhere between the two. Schools have received a far higher unit of resource over recent years but the targets set have been extremely demanding and costly in terms of increasing the pressures on staff. The profile of schools may indeed be higher but mistakes are equally very public and some schools have suffered from this.

The constraints upon FE colleges have been equivalent. Targets are not a new phenomenon nor are under-16 learners, and the pastoral elements of college provision have been steadily increasing over time. As institutions whose role has always been to meet the needs of a huge variety of learners at all levels, the FE colleges are best placed to appreciate the benefits, which should accrue from the new developments.

Widening participation has long formed a part of the FE brief and redesigned levels from entry through foundation and intermediate to the new extended advanced will surely assist with success in this area.

The Association of Colleges supports the idea of wider college registration of 14-year-olds on vocational courses. This full 'ownership' of significant numbers of the 14–16 cohort is the next step beyond partnership and differing levels of participation. In addition they support the government's significant commitment to young apprenticeships for this age group. Named Diplomas will be work related and there are so many areas that the choices should provide significant increases in the options across the whole 14–19 phase.

The qualifications debate

Huge investments of time, resources and professional capital have been ploughed into the existing system. This means that from individuals there are strong responses and a highly critical approach to the potential new framework. As mentioned before, the A-level issue has produced a keen debate and the questions have been met by the most diplomatic and guarded of answers. Just prior to the Working Group Final Report, the DfES position could be read in the following extract from the 'Qualifications' section of their website:

> Will A levels be replaced in reforms of 14–19 education?
>
> The Working Group on 14–19 Reform, Chaired by Mike Tomlinson, has not yet decided what changes it will recommend but has identified some broad proposals around a

balanced curriculum and a new diploma framework. It may be that some of the components of the diploma might be like the GCSEs, A levels, NVQs or other courses; other components may need to be designed specifically. However, reform will not be rushed and A levels will continue in the short and medium terms. A levels continue to be valued and prized qualifications.

(http://www.14-19reform.gov.uk)

This now seems prophetic and, at the time, in spite of the optimism from some advocates of the full diploma across all levels, there were many who could see the writing on the wall as well as in the political speeches.

Even from a relatively early stage in the consultation process (DfES 2003a), it was emphasised that any change to a radically new qualification framework would be a very long term agenda matter. In this the Tomlinson report concurred and maintained the softly, softly evolutionary approach. When the report was first published the earliest government response from Tony Blair and David Miliband gave the strong message that whatever new system emerged from reform they wanted the 'gold standard' reputation of the existing named qualifications to remain. This attitude triggered further debate and, having said that 'cherry picking' of proposals would sabotage the possibility for real improvement, there seemed to be the potential for serious controversy.

When asked about the prospects of government support in the forthcoming White Paper for the Working Group proposals, Mike Tomlinson gave the following response: 'I don't think there will be an answer on that, given the timescale over which the reforms will occur and the fact that the diploma would be the final piece of the jigsaw. I don't think one needs a decision so soon.' The extended time-frame and the initial importance of the implementation of a strong basic skills core are being emphasised over and above the detail of individual qualifications.

The post-White Paper qualifications situation will be further explored in Chapter 8.

What was the impact of the Tomlinson Final Report on 14–19 Education?

It was called 'the most radical shakeup of exams in England for 60 years' (*The Guardian* 2004). On the day the Tomlinson report was published, Tony Blair gave a speech to the Confederation of British Industry in Birmingham emphasising the evolutionary nature of any proposed reforms: 'As Mike Tomlinson and Charles Clarke said, GCSEs and A levels will stay, so will externally marked exams. Reform will strengthen the existing system where it is inadequate, there will be greater challenge at the top for those on track to higher education.' Finally, and with no real surprises remaining following 18 months of consultation, private and public sector discussion, the working group on 14–19 returned its findings. The profile of the event was high, with both headlines and extensive coverage and analysis throughout the media.

As expected, the Tomlinson final report caused waves, though, due to the extensive consultation process, much of its content was predictable and had been designed to meet the needs of a variety of interest groups. This was no short-term plan. If it had been fully implemented, the diploma would not have been fully delivered until 2014. This ten-year development span was an acknowledgement of the scale and difficulty of the endeavour. The committee called it 'evolution, not revolution', and the issues addressed were indeed ambitious. Fears were expressed that the diploma heralded the death of the A level and GCSE but Tomlinson himself was reassuring on this front, preferring to describe a situation where these are components in a larger structure. In the end, such careful use of language did not swing the decision in favour of the diploma.

The question remains one of stakeholder viewpoint. Where some commentators have chosen to reflect on the radical terms of the new designs for a qualifications framework, others prefer to play down the change agenda. The differences in view and position taking are characteristic of the political nature of this debate.

What did Tomlinson set out to do?

The Group sets out proposals for a new diploma framework to establish a structure for reform that would:

- be more rigorous than the current system;
- place literacy and numeracy at its centre;
- stretch and challenge all young people;
- reduce the burden of assessment;
- offer high quality vocational education; and
- encourage more people to stay in education and achieve highly.

Key aspects of the proposed new diploma were the four levels; the compulsory core skills; the breadth of options; the vocational bias; extra-curricular projects; teacher assessment and external testing; and additional differentiation in the top grades.

All kinds of metaphors have been applied to the new 14–19 scene, from landscape to canvas, and from battleground to new dimension, but now that the final recommendations are published what are the responses and repercussions?

The National Association of Head Teachers were firmly behind full implementation as were the Secondary Heads Association, and the Chief Inspector of Schools, David Bell, who espouses the complete replacement of GCSEs and A levels.

Support from universities appeared fairly solid: vice-chancellors were openly in favour of widening participation opportunities and the new top grades for highest achievers.

Independent schools gave more low-key and qualified approval and the Institute of Directors remain unconvinced of the economic and social benefits of the diploma route. A central question for employers is whether more will be gained than lost through the re-organisation of 14–19 qualifications.

Most welcome to many was the emphasis on the reduction of the assessment burden on the learner though the jury will remain out on questions of rigour and resource in this area until the detailed arrangements for funding teacher assessment and for providing appropriate external examinations are unveiled. The then Education Secretary Charles Clarke acknowledged these significant elements and public sensitivities when he assured his audience 'Assessment must and will continue at all levels on the basis of rigorous, trusted and externally marked examinations.'

Area inspection for 14–19

Area inspections assess the quality of training and education provision in areas for 14–19-year-olds. As such, they are a key element in the government's drive to raise standards. To some extent, the areas are defined by local LSC/LEA boundaries, though adjustment is made where factors dictate that external economic or regional issues are having an impact that should be taken into account. The area inspections were introduced originally in 1999 and initially only covered the 16–19 phase of learning. Jointly run by Ofsted and the Adult Learning Inspectorate, they were extended in 2003 to cover 14–19 learning. The intention was that the findings from these inspections would provide information on the quality of 14–19 arrangements to support local and national development.

Inspection of the provision of non-HE education and training as directed by LSCs, LEAs and their partners has been carried out by Ofsted and the Adult Learning Inspectorate (ALI), though, following the 2005 budget announcement, the plan is for ALI to merge with Ofsted. These inspections are scheduled for completion in at least a part of each LSC area by the end of 2006. Every effort is being made to co-ordinate the timing of the area inspections with institution and service inspections of colleges, Connexions/careers service, pupil referral units and other partners, and with thematic surveys.

The process involves an initial analysis of all recent relevant reports and documents and their consideration along with an LSC/LEA joint Self Evaluation report in order to produce a formal pre-inspection analysis. Following discussion and confirmation of arrangements an inspection week takes place. There are sample visits to a range of 14–19 provision, from schools and colleges to voluntary and work-based training provision. While they do not make direct observations of teaching and learning, inspectors will meet with managers, governors, employers, parents, staff and learners at all levels.

Finally, a report is published in which judgements are made and grades fixed against the following headings:

- Strategy for education and training (14–19) in the area
- Achievement
- Access to and participation in education and training
- Quality of education and training (14–19)

- Guidance and support
- Leadership and management

Summary grades reflecting the efficiency and effectiveness of area provision in relation to learner, employer and community needs are then published with a three-year time-frame for re-inspection in the case of unsatisfactory area provision. These reports are useful maps of available provision, partnerships, strengths and weaknesses in the field. They are available on the Ofsted site (www.ofsted.gov.uk). The code of conduct that applies to this inspection process is contained within the Common Inspection Framework for Inspecting Post-16 Education and Training. This should ensure a focus on the 'best interests of learners'.

Following an area inspection, the Learning and Skills Council, along with the LEA, should lead the local partners in the development of an appropriate and robust action plan to address any issues identified, both negative and positive, and to ensure high-quality provision for all learners. Both the LSC and Ofsted have produced guidance to support the new framework. These include a published supplement to the Common Inspection Framework for Area Inspections and revised departmental Advice on Post Area Inspections as well as the LSC Advice and Guidance for Area Inspections.

Changes to inspection and the impact on 14–19

The use and adaptation of existing structures and systems runs throughout the 14–19 phase, resulting in both good and poor quality outcomes. In the case of Ofsted inspections, where there were already concerns emerging about notice, complexity and flexibility being raised in relation to the general inspection regime, 14–19 raises further issues. The modifications to the process are set to continue as part of the continual improvement drive and the new relationship with schools but this should also include a shift in the relationship with multiple partners and stakeholders in the increasingly complex 14–19 environment.

Procedures assessing quality within the new subject inspections and vocational provision in schools and colleges are highly significant in terms of the development of a newly defined phase in 14–16 education. They must take account of the special conditions surrounding vocational and other provision and the very individual nature of the problems surrounding the area. Without a fundamental understanding of how relationships across the sectors evolve and how new programmes and structures have an organic growth and reproduction cycle similar to a dynamic business trajectory, the chances of new policy and funding generating a really constructive period of development and change will be severely reduced.

What are the implications of new policies for the training of teachers and lecturers?

Training debates, to be discussed in Chapter 3, are being addressed through changes to the legislation and to the partnerships, infrastructure and funding, especially in the Learning and Skills Sector. Traditionally, this has been post-16 but the reforms and the responses to them across all countries in the UK are identifying and defining new requirements, and attempting to create appropriate solutions. Routes for entry into the teaching profession have multiplied over recent years and, if all three phases are included, number well over twenty. When we consider the increasingly complex network of support systems and staff it is hardly surprising that the training map can seem very confusing both to new entrants and for those wishing to undertake a professional transfer and to access useful professional development opportunities.

The whole endeavour of making 14–19 something worthy of special focus and attention is based on assumptions related to the acceptance that education is a key factor for transformation in the economy. It is not a precursor for change in subtle and long-term ways; it is rather an actual current and short-term aggressive driver. Among the social and educational perspectives being addressed by the reforms are: young male underachievement; 14–19 retention and progression; citizenship and behaviour modelling; and the values and ethics debate.

What differences are there in 14–19 provision throughout the UK?

The wide range of approaches to issues that in many ways are common presents an interesting study. Lessons can be learned from the experiences, even where the context and conditions are very different. The value of the opportunity for comparison of pilots and initiatives is somewhat offset by the complexity of structures and systems being established in such close proximity. It is certainly true to say that the autumn 2002 exam crisis reinforced the reform camp case. The National Assembly for Wales had announced its own consultation with major 14–19 stakeholders in 'The Learning Country: A Paving Document' in 2001 and its progress has been extensive. By contrast, the other UK countries have worked at a slower pace. In both Northern Ireland and in Scotland there are more phase divisions and difficulties with clear identification of a 14–19 stage.

Learning and Teaching Scotland is a national public body sponsored by the Scottish Executive Education Department. LT Scotland was set up to provide support staff development and resources to improve pupil and student achievement and the general quality of education in line with the commitments laid out in 'A Partnership for a Better Scotland' (May 2003), and the subsequent review of principles, framework and curriculum.

In Northern Ireland 14–19 education responsibility is shared between the Department of Education and the Department for Employment and Learning. The former covers the schools sector and the latter all further education, training providers and higher education.

Wales, the self-designated 'Learning Country', has established Learning Pathways within its 14–19 agenda. The key issues sound familiar: parity of esteem, increased entrepreneurship and creativity, and a focus on personal and social skills. There are some significant new ideas, which demonstrate that policy in Wales has travelled further and faster than elsewhere in the UK. Learning coaches are a new concept being piloted here and the 14–19 phase is clearly identified as separate without the division at 16. In addition there is real joint emphasis on the 3–7 phase as a deliberate twin-pronged attack to deal with perceived social and educational development issues.

The Welsh Baccalaureate is up and running with evaluation under way, though numbers of candidates expected to complete are a little disappointing. It is designed to have a high degree of flexibility and can be taken in a conventionally academic or vocational configuration, and both elements can be combined. It has been a revolutionary change, the more so since it has emerged in advance of any wider UK developments.

It is claimed that the Credit and Qualifications Framework for Wales will 'enable anyone to climb on the learning ladder' and that, as a result of the planned initiatives, learners of all ages in all situations will be 'banking learning credits'.

At this early stage there are 24 colleges participating and the Baccalaureate has been allocated 120 UCAS points. There is an Intermediate one-year qualification, which should pick up those who fail to gain GCSEs at grade C and above. In support of these changes the 14–19 networks are being established across Wales. Students will receive a National Certificate of Educational Achievement in order to provide a full picture of the learner. By 2005 the new Credit and Qualifications Framework should be in place and this follows the new directions and encompasses informal learning of all kinds. It does not formalise the position of community, commercial and voluntary work learning experiences but it does attempt to acknowledge their value. Both the Welsh and English models stop short of a formal accreditation for these different types of achievement. The hope among advocates of a wider more radical approach must be that these moves are a precursor of future developments.

Holding key aspects of these ventures together in order to ensure that the needs of employers are met is a priority of LLUK. There are other stakeholders involved and three national and five regional Performance Officers will take responsibility for the operational agenda on behalf of all concerned. At this stage the transition from separate National Training Organisations to the single Sector Skills Council is still proceeding. Education has been seen increasingly as a means to improve the success of international global economies. The strategies may be given long-term time-frames but the current phase of students is still the focus of intense attention and debate.

What is the 14–19 phase? The pupils and students have always existed and been taught, so why do we suddenly require a new set of policies and initiatives? Any answers in the recent White Paper relate to the English system, though it does contain elements which have implications for Wales, Northern Ireland and Scotland. There are some shared qualifications and the development work will entail close co-operation. The next stage will involve the QCA and other regulatory authorities collaborating to ensure a reasonable degree of coherence and compatibility.

Conclusion

The stated aims of the new LLUK highlight the issues that beset the policy-makers. Even as the White Paper emerges, the ideal outcomes already seem beyond reach. If simplification and new coherence in the field of curriculum and qualification through 'a nationally recognised set of standards and qualifications' are to be achieved to any extent, the four-nation differences have already ensured they will be a series of compromises.

CHAPTER 2

Teaching and learning 14–19: approaches and structures

Politicians and educationalists have always argued about the purposes of education and its scope, in particular about the relative value of depth and breadth. The fortunate and able few can opt for the International Baccalaureate, which offers both breadth and depth. Otherwise, the non-vocational choice in England has seemed to be between the depth of A levels and the breadth offered by an 'English baccalaureate'. The Welsh Baccalaureate is a current practical illustration of an alternative and comparable model.

It now appears that the A levels we know so well will be with us for a long time to come and that they will be made even more stretching. But Mike Tomlinson's interim review and final report on 14–19 education in England was about attempting to square a circle by offering breadth as well as stretch. The Working Group was also adamant that all students, whatever else they studied, must achieve competency in number, communication and IT.

In rejecting the recommendations for an overarching diploma while retaining existing academic qualifications, and introducing new vocational diplomas, Ruth Kelly has ensured criticism from both camps. Conservatives and reformers are both dissatisfied with the outcomes and she has acknowledged the sense of disappointment but stressed the need to listen to all stakeholders. The proposals will be discussed in more detail throughout but it is evident there are some fundamental issues emerging, more as the result of compromise and omissions rather than of elements included.

Crucially, the reformers had argued that qualifications should be unhooked from age bands, allowing more scope for early achievement and later development. Much attention was paid to the benefits of personalised learning, not only as a route to improved standards but ostensibly as a means to develop the individual's skills, attributes and ultimately choices. The White Paper does contain proposals relating to these areas, in particular the removal of the fixed assessment point at 16 but with GCSEs retained detractors can easily claim that the system will not allow the individual learner to experience real flexibility in terms of ability and pace of learning rather than age. They believe that only those already in more privileged, personally tailored settings by virtue of class or income will continue to benefit from customised approaches.

Of course, the argument is that individual schools or colleges find flexibility hard to achieve but partnerships have made it possible. In different ways, schools and colleges are already committed to the overlapping and occasionally contradictory agendas for increasing diversity, widening participation and accelerating learning for the gifted and talented.

Tomlinson echoed the commitment in the government's skills strategy for unitisation of accreditation with the aim of improving opportunities for a broad education. But unitisation is no panacea. To pick up credits as you study implies more frequent exams or continuous coursework, the opposite of what most of professionals and students want. And unitisation does not suit subjects where understanding is cumulative and progress in the early stages can seem slow. The recent Smith review of mathematics education summed up the Curriculum 2000 reforms, which launched AS level maths as an utter and complete disaster, resulting in a 15 per cent fall in maths entries. The hope always was that the Tomlinson committee's final report would acknowledge that different subjects need different approaches to accreditation as well as to teaching. This has proved to be the case.

It is an irony that as the significance of content and knowledge diminishes in education, the claim is increasingly made that we inhabit a society that can be described as knowledge based. Kathryn Ecclestone has said, 'Questions about class have all but disappeared from debate about public policy and education' (2004: 134). Knowledge through an appropriate education was once a ticket to a kind of economic and social elevation.

It will be interesting to see how many of the contemporary accepted 'credos' of post-compulsory education and training will migrate into the 14–19 agenda. It would seem that many already have. The vulnerability and fragility labels currently attached to many of the learners entering education as returners are taken for granted and are applied to younger learners. The debates relating to the reality of 'self esteem' and the validity of therapeutic education are too seldom aired. The same situation can be found in the schools sector where those who are not achieving are provided with an alternative curriculum. The question remains whether the redesigned framework is an acknowledgement of the failings of the statutory system or a real attempt to shift attitudes and provide new opportunities for all.

Party politics cannot be left out of the equation although there is a need for coherent long-term approaches and the collaboration of those concerned. As has been said, in the re-organisation of the system, most stakeholders are involved in a discussion of the issues and the evolution of the services provided for students. No government can afford to establish a brand new system without extensive consultation simply because, in spite of legislation and regulation, the power to force compliance does not really exist.

What are the professed aims of the new teaching and learning?

Understanding what lies behind the new initiatives sheds the sharpest light on the reasons for the new directions. Whether or not we accept the underlying rationale, it is necessary to acknowledge the potential impact of the reforms. In 'Learning: The Treasure Within', a UNESCO report by Jacques Delors, there was a clear emphasis on a particular view of the place and nature of learning within societies that reflects a version of what might now be called a new orthodoxy.

Of four identified core functions of learning, learning to know and learning to do are classed as vital in economic terms. The other two – learning to be and to co-exist – are equally important for the individual. We are told we need a learning society and, further than this, that education should be concerned with facilitating students to learn how to learn so that they can continue to adapt and respond to the rapidly changing needs of the economy.

The talk about changing environments and improving behaviours has resulted in extended options and attempts to enhance relevance and these developments are central in the proposed reforms. Without appropriate advice and guidance this can seem based on a belief that there is a system which can deliver everything and that the individual students are equipped to make appropriate choices. With sufficient planning and committed partners there can be increased opportunities for students.

If we look at the innovations being piloted through the Skills Academies many of the supposedly radical approaches to teaching and learning seem quite familiar. For example, increased group work, peer assessment, students directing their own learning pace and the embedded use of learning-styles approaches within the institutions' curriculum planning provide some examples of this. Critics will, of course, immediately point to the lack of real innovation being displayed here and it is true that the majority of these methods, far from being new, can be found in a wide range of contexts across the sectors.

Under the heading 'Examples of Innovation', the DfES Standards Site refers to the way that staff at the Unity City Academy in Middlesbrough 'incorporate different learning styles (Visual, Auditory and Kinaesthetic) into their topics and learning sessions' (www.standards.dfes.gov.uk). This involves storyboarding for media tasks and the 'freedom and responsibility to go within the school grounds and take their photos'. If this truly were innovative teaching and learning for any phase, including primary students, there should be even more serious concerns for education than currently exist. The jury is still out on the city academics whose results will be viewed as the real evidence.

What concerns are being expressed about the effects of new directions on teaching and learning?

The General Secretary of the Association of Teachers and Lecturers, Mary Bousted, speaking at the annual conference, linked the new teaching and learning approaches and goals to the 'technical schools' and class-related vocational and academic divides of the second half of the twentieth century:

For all the talk of inclusion, the supposition that half the cohort is well served by GCSEs and A levels and that we need a better vocational diet for the rest is incorrect, deeply divisive and wasteful of the nation's talent. The clear intent to create a 14 plus selection is stunningly retrograde.

(www.education.guardian.co.uk)

Her interpretation of the intentions and means of implementing the policy set out in the White Paper is not accepted by those in favour of the reforms but it does express some serious and widespread popular fears. The anxiety is that by making 14 the new dividing line where significant options are chosen one will just introduce another point at which middle-class children will be divided from others as they follow an academic rather than vocational route.

Concerns that the pace will never really suit the individual, that we will just have a new set of rigid routes with even earlier selection and labelling, are strong in some quarters. Advocates of a broad vocationally focused curriculum can seem to pursue their goals with an almost evangelistic enthusiasm. For some, these concerns go deeper. There is talk of a return to academic selection under cover of the wider 'specialist school' structures. For some, this would not be a problem nor would it be divisive, just another route. If, as is now the case, every school aims to establish itself as a specialist school working to strengths, developing them and collaborating with others locally as a means of sharing them, then academic excellence becomes just another strand. This model, in line with all developments, would require a school to demonstrate that it was catering for reasonable proportions of children from disadvantaged and other diverse backgrounds. Opponents of such aspects of policy claim it will simply reinforce existing distinctions and advantages.

What view does the White Paper take on teaching and learning?

National entitlements for learners form the heart of the vision. These are built on the existing set of entitlements, extending the reach of learning and the support for it into social and personal environments.

Professionals will be expected to teach to these aims and the inspection of schools and colleges will ensure quality in these terms:

- Effective teaching and learning in the 14–19 phase should be supported by good-quality formative assessment throughout
- More robust teacher assessment can enhance the professional judgement of teachers and contribute to better teaching and learning

What do learners in the new phase need in workforce terms?

In the present system, 75 per cent of 17-year-olds participate in post-compulsory education. The target is to increase this number to 90 per cent within the ten-year

---

National entitlements

Our education system already provides:

- a broad and balanced compulsory curriculum until age 16. Key Stage 4 requires students to study English, maths, science, citizenship, RE and sex education; and to learn about careers and experience work-related and enterprise learning;

- a further entitlement for all 14–16-year-olds to study a modern foreign language, design and technology, a subject from the humanities and one from the arts;

- an entitlement to continue learning until age 18; and

- an entitlement to study functional English, maths and ICT to level 2 until age 19.

We will build on those with new entitlements.

Our new entitlements	Whey they will start
There will be an entitlement to financial support for young people in learning aged 16–19 who live in low income families	This year
We will create an entitlement to study a science course at Key Stage 4 that will lead to the equivalent of two GCSE qualifications	2006 or as soon as legislation can be passed
We will ensure schools and colleges make all 14 specialised Diplomas available to all young people in every locality	First 8 Diplomas by 2010, all 14 in 2015
We will create an entitlement for all 14–16-year-olds to experience 2 hours of high-quality sport or PE	2010
We will ensure that objective and individualised advice and guidance is available at key points in the 14–19 phase	We will set out our plans in due course
We will introduce an extended project at level 3 and examine how to develop a national entitlement to it	Pilots will begin in 2006

And we will expect all schools and colleges to emulate the best by:

- making functional English and maths their priority, so that all young people who can, achieve level 2 functional skills before they leave learning; and

- tailoring the curriculum to motivate all young people, stretching the brightest and supporting those who are falling behind to catch up.

Figure 2.1 National entitlements for learners

Source: DfES 2005a

period set for implementing reform. It must be remembered that the population in this age group is actually set to fall and this affects the total numbers. It is a quality and training rather than simply a quantity issue. Actual staffing numbers have been increasing in both schools and colleges, and this includes rises in support staff and in those involved with work-based learning, whose numbers are nearly equal to the full-time equivalent college teachers figure. The group set to increase most in support of policy implementation is the secondary-school support staff. There is no anticipated need for large additional numbers of staff actually based in schools because the learning in the vocational lines will take place more off site than on.

These figures have been carefully considered for cost effectiveness. The following analysis is made in the White Paper:

> The demand for extra vocational courses in FE colleges will largely be offset by the fall in the number of 14–19 year-olds in England. However, there will need to be additional staff to deliver the types of courses we want to offer these learners. We will bring more specialist professionals with relevant expertise from business into colleges and training providers. The new 'passport to teaching' module being developed as part of the Success for All reforms will be available to equip them with the skills and knowledge required to teach.
>
> (DfES 2005a: 77)

The total increases in staff numbers in schools and colleges needed to implement reforms will be of the order of:

- 1,250–1,450 support staff in schools and colleges to help manage collaborative arrangements and provide teaching and learning support; and
- 1,000–1,250 college staff in teaching roles, mainly made up of people with relevant specialist business experience.

There is a sense in which the relatively low additional staff resource needed is an advantage but it may also mean that hard-pressed existing, experienced staff in colleges are made to shoulder the extra burden. The difficulty with the scale of the new work is that although numbers are low the range of entitlements and options is high, and each local area must provide these within travelling distance for individual students.

Who will be teaching the phase?

In broad terms, significant new practice already exists within 14–19 education. The answer to this question increasingly appears to be a team. The current situation will, we are told, be allowed to evolve in different areas to suit needs as the local partnerships begin to respond to national policy. The most obvious, efficient and cost-effective way to address reforms which involve increased choice, improved specialised skills and require large numbers of students across a five-year age band to move between schools, colleges and workplaces is surely to deploy existing learning professionals, enhance support and build an appropriate set of structures to plan, deliver, manage and monitor the learning. This means that learning will be the result of team efforts. Those involved will perhaps be tutored and tracked by a trained teacher with specific understanding of the needs of the individuals, the nature of the phase and its demands, and the options and routes through what will be a reformed 14–19 phase.

Partnership is usually a term employed to indicate institutional contacts and formal arrangements but for high-quality delivery it should extend downwards to all stages of learning relationships: individual teachers liaising with careers and youth-service personnel; technical support staff with access to current vocational experience providers to ensure relevance in the skill acquisition and up-to-date industry practice; support staff of all kinds who understanding the specific challenges of the students in the 14–19 phase as they move across the provision.

One of the most significant features of 14–19 teaching following new reforms will be the increased use of teams. In terms of teaching teams, the experience, facilities and knowledge are likely to be lodged in different locations. From the learner perspective the shift to teacher and e-assessment, to e-learning, extended projects and personalised learning opportunities, to apprenticeships and mixed academic and vocational routes, are all approaches that rely upon greater learner autonomy. If this empowerment of young learners is to succeed there must be considerable investment in the structures supporting and guiding learners and in the development of effective teams dedicated to 14–19 learners.

This is not to say that there should be segregation within the phase. Separate labels and a distinct identity might be useful in some respects and are inevitable if the reforms are to become mainstream as their designers hope. However, it will be even more important to retain the strengths of the employment and education contexts involved in the learning contracts. One of the dangers inherent in such radical reforms, anticipated by the working party, is the piecemeal nature of partial implementation. These proposals and the pilot work already under way demand a truly integrated model, and would lose all coherence without the full-scale commitment called for by advocates.

In order to preserve high-quality learning experiences for the 14–19 phase, there is a pressing need to develop the role of the specialised teacher as manager and monitor of students' progress. In education environments where learning professionals are becoming an increasingly diverse group there will be even more changes. It will certainly not be appropriate for students to have contact only with the conventional teacher. This remains a very sensitive area but there are issues here that will certainly come to the fore in the 14–19 phase delivery.

Where will 14–19 teaching and learning take place?

Schools and colleges working with this age phase are supposed to become professional learning communities. The Department for Education and Skills has expressed the following: 'We want school and college leaders to lead a shift in culture and practice and to use the remodelling agenda to make the best use of teachers' time.' This seems to mean that the educational institutions will somehow act as brokers and advisors rather than as repositories of special and valued knowledge. In a future version of such a model, teaching would involve specialised advice and consultation; facilitation and liaison; and the expertise in accessing knowledge systems through ICT and the application of the information to 'real' situations.

Schools, FE colleges and workplaces are just some of the settings students in this phase might find themselves and the combinations involved will depend on the structures and partnerships within a region. In this sense, changes will not be that noticeable at first. The local schools may well have been developing a broad range of vocational choices and will have considered the needs of their own pupils. Many colleges and schools are already participating in established partnerships.

What are the pressures on resources and accommodation?

Like almost everything else in this phase the answer is that the picture varies across the sectors and individual providers. The pressures are very high for some struggling providers while others are enjoying excellent facilities. Nor can we assume that it is only schools who are suffering from a lack of specialist accommodation or well-developed resources in the new vocational areas. On the contrary, although this is true of many schools and the problems will multiply as options become entitlements, there are examples of schools, like city academies and specialist schools, that possess hugely impressive workshops, ICT labs, media and art studios, and other newly built, state-of-the-art facilities.

Equally, for all the colleges with excellent resources and accommodation in certain subject areas, there are counterparts working against the odds in old, inadequate buildings with unsuitable and dated equipment. Partnerships work best, not always by providing better facilities but also by injecting different practice in delivery. For example, an FE course might take students out far more to compensate for insufficient resources in house. Students then spend considerable time in a workplace and so get hands-on experience with current ICT, customer practice, health and safety, community art or a working manufacturing environment.

There are considerable capital funds going into new building for schools and the PCET sector is now being promised increased funding across the board, so it would be heartening if there was greater consideration of the new phase and programme flexibility in the forward planning of any developments. There are numerous courses being delivered in unsuitable environments and while all professionals respect the need for compromise and understand the constraints that exist, they are badly disadvantaged when they do not have a base, storage facilities or basic equipment for a demanding new programme.

Many schools are still making use of poor resources and there has not been sufficient central support in this area. Specialised subject texts for teaching vocational programmes, especially to 14–19 learners, are practically non-existent and although there are some good websites and centres, the provision of resources and support in this area is still uneven.

The contexts for teaching and learning certainly make a difference and in this phase it is important for all those involved to understand this diversity. Attention frequently falls on challenges of the real contrasts between the environments but as partnerships develop the shared elements of best practice can also be given an opportunity to emerge. More detail on learning contexts and qualifications will be found in the relevant chapters but an introduction is given here. In order to answer this question, the nature of the sectors concerned must be understood by those involved in joint planning and working.

What is post-compulsory education and training?

Chapter 6 provides more detail on the nature of the sector and the learner experiences available but in broad terms there are fundamental features of this area which have proved attractive to those seeking to fulfil the new aims. In particular, the following areas appeal most to reformers:

- links and established placements with real work situations
- simulated work-related environments and practices (studios, workshops, equipment)
- staff with commercial and industrial qualifications and experiences
- technician support
- knowledge of health and safety
- long-term experience of vocational qualification delivery and curriculum design

The sector provides education, training and community activities for a huge range of post- and now pre-16 learners. At its best, the PCET sector operating within and beyond more than 400 FE colleges will be delivering quality programmes and individual training to young people, adult returners and third-age learners; supporting community outreach projects; fulfilling specialised needs for local industries; educating prisoners and people in work; and providing access to HE and personal development opportunities. There are many excellent texts outlining, criticising and exploring the history, present scope and future direction of PCET (for example, Armitage *et al.* 2003 and Coles 2004).

Androgogy and pedagogy distinctions are commonly drawn to illustrate the different approaches to teaching and learning between post- and pre-compulsory sectors but there is a strong tradition within PCET of teaching younger learners using more adult-focused approaches. There is a view that rather than adjusting the teaching to suit younger learners, these learners should benefit from their own adjustment to the context and to the wider social and working contacts they develop.

Teaching and learning approaches

There is a great deal of emphasis on new collaborations in teaching. Coaching and mentoring have been seen to be effective in both educational and youth/leisure settings and we can expect to see the 14–19 sector develop and extend such approaches to support learning in new contexts.

The engagement of all learners and the re-engagement of those already switched off learning or in danger of reaching this point during Key Stage 4 have been placed centrally in the policy aims. The White Paper also places a welcome emphasis on the significance of Key Stage 3 in the process. In order to achieve engagement, all kinds of approaches have been researched and discussed within education and in the wider social, political and economic context. There is broad consensus that partnership and team working, effective liaison with advisers and experts, and continuity and consistency in dealing with individual learners are all necessary to achieve improvements in the area. The scale and nature of multi-agency collaboration is the subject of more debate, especially the issues of who leads teams, decides strategy and runs an operation.

To illustrate the issues raised, the developing Skills Academies provide some interesting cases. Along with colleges, some work-based learning providers and specialist schools these could take a lead role in local collaboration. Given the latitude they can command over curriculum, organisation and direction, the fear is that the principle of equitable, comparable opportunities for all students regardless of background or location may be somewhat compromised from area to area.

A further issue will certainly be the education system's ability to provide real expertise in teaching for the new vocational routes. There are already shortages which reflect the lower status of the occupational areas themselves and these will certainly affect the ability of the learning and skills sector to make high-quality vocational education available to all without considerable new resources and, perhaps more importantly, very well-planned management and organisation.

The 'Success for All' programme was designed to pioneer new teaching and learning approaches and specifically to support strategies for vocational education. This process will be continued in parallel with the introduction and establishment of the new qualifications and the development and adjustment of those retained.

The argument that practical and applied routes will be almost exclusively used by the lower achieving students steered by existing prejudices and expectations is put forward in different forums with varying degrees of intensity. At the recent conference, the General Secretary of the ATL (Association of Teachers and Lecturers) called the proposals 'stunningly retrograde' and went on to say:

> The last thing we need in the 21st century is to go back to grammar and technical schools. There is a danger when you divide at fourteen of narrowing young people's opportunities. Perpetuation within the education system along class lines is also a danger. Middle class children will follow academic courses as long as they are perceived to be valued.

> (www.education.guardian.co.uk)

In this view of reform only the full overarching diploma introduced across the 'so-called' academic/vocational divide with all existing qualification brand names removed would serve the stated purposes.

Which is best, teaching 14–19 exclusively or mixing the populations?

The methods employed in colleges for teaching at 14–19 derive from the practice and experience evolved through working with mixed groups though there are areas where the age group is taught exclusively and this certainly occurs with 14–16 groups on more occasions. This separation can be one of the solutions to the problems of satisfying schools on issues of safety of all types, control and carefully planned learning situations. A segregation approach reduces some of the risks and when there are work placements in the frame such matters are high on a head teacher's list. For some participants in multi-site, cross-phase working, action to limit the number and scale of the variables gives a perception of increased security. For others the loss of some of these perceived risks is also the loss of advantages, challenges and key aspects of the learning situation.

The use of work-related materials, direct experience and examples on programmes are central to vocational courses. Both real and simulated environments are employed and staff background is vital in selecting, designing, monitoring and interpreting the experience. Staff, lecturers and others often teach through drawing their previous or current work experience into teaching situations. This can be far more significant than it first sounds to those unfamiliar with the settings. After all, don't all teachers bring in stories and examples from their experience? This type of staff approach, which brings other working environments closer to learners, is very different in nature. A college chef will be running a college restaurant and possibly another business; the hairdressing and beauty, building and construction, motor vehicle and even art and design, music and media areas will all have staff involved in other commercial activities.

A college art and design lecturer, for example, is often a practising, exhibiting artist and encourages this in students. This has meant that students of all ages have been involved in, for example, significant community arts projects with all the wider learning opportunities this implies. The result is that students can be drawn into planned community projects, serve in the facilities in colleges which are open to the public from gyms to travel agencies. This is a part of the learning experience. In terms of approaches the following are most often mentioned:

- Use of case studies is often central to work in vocational subjects
- Peer and self assessment
- Emphasis on student research and study
- A new emphasis on enterprise activity has been embedded within the planned educational framework
- Practical work in real/realistic settings
- Autonomy in approaches to study

Formal and informal learning

If the new approaches are to be implemented as fully as reformers desire, then there must be far more emphasis on integrating formal curricula with informal learning through recognition, acknowledgement and encouragement of learner development across all their experiences and interests. One issue related to the development of the individual through personalised learning is the need for educators and curriculum designers to broaden their understanding of learner profiles and aspirations. For learners to make the choices being proposed, their critical skills and ability to exercise informed judgement will require development.

There is a move towards taking the influence of the education process well beyond the realms of the formal classroom. However important the work-based learning and experience is to current political aims, there is still a focus on the widest possible engagement with learners in all contexts. A number of the innovations follow Working Group recommendations to extend and enrich learning opportunities and to draw the learner's interests and talents into a wider social and educational environment. These will include opportunities for sport, drama, voluntary work and the use of aspects of such activities and projects in formal learning and as a part of overall learning experience.

Are new teaching and learning materials required?

The DfES view is strongly in favour of new materials and there has already been considerable development in the area. The centralisation of materials production for teaching and learning rather than just for assessment is often criticised by professionals, especially where the aims of teaching support the growth of the individual learner. The employer-led nature of the new vocational Diplomas means that they and the Sector Skills Councils will be closely involved in the process of setting content and creating materials. This is facilitated through the transformation programme managed by the Standards Unit.

The type of materials produced include lesson plans and activities as well as CPD material for trainers, teachers and assessors. They will be made available on the National Learning Network and the transformation programme will continue from April 2006 under the auspices of the Quality Improvement Agency for Lifelong Learning (QuILL).

The e-learning agenda is very active across all sectors and 14–19 is no exception. The range of exciting new technologies are important in there own right within specific sectors and in a more general sense they are viewed as a powerful tool in the drive to integrate several learning contexts. The new e-learning champion for the Skills for Business network will advise the Sector Skills Councils on this rapidly developing area (e-skills UK).

A central element of national planning for ICT involves the establishment of an infrastructure linking schools, colleges and other providers. According to Professor

Stephen Heppell of Ultralab, the research institute advising the Tomlinson Working Group, such a network would provide, 'some form of common system of student identity'. This would cover the management of progress and qualification tracking, all records and proposed individualised e-portfolios personal to the student. In addition, there are ambitious proposals for e-assessment, which face far more opposition and logistical challenges.

What did the Working Group 14–19 recommend for teaching and learning?

The momentum driving change can be unstoppable and the reform agenda was adamant that 'the status quo is not an option'. Unification is the agenda and 'piecemeal changes' are to be avoided. Above all, and there is much support for this position, there was a strong desire to bring about a step change in education which touches each learner and has a powerful impact on the economic and social indicators. In pursuit of this agenda, the report refuses to make 'the traditional distinction between vocational and academic learning' but prefers to emphasise personalised learning opportunities and programmes relevant to the needs of industry and higher education.

The following report proposals are central to teaching and learning:

- To raise participation and achievement
- To improve basic skills across the phase
- To strengthen vocational routes – increasing the numbers taking advanced vocational qualifications
- To increase the extent of stretch and challenge
- To reduce the overall assessment burden
- To improve and clarify the system as a whole in order to enhance accessibility

Tomlinson had a ten-year time-line with an evolutionary rather than a revolutionary approach. Its stated aims were to encourage partnership and building on existing strengths. In an ideal post-reform world, the individual student should be operating within a supportive structure of schools, colleges, community, guidance and industry partnerships.

While the majority of the report is occupied with the unifying framework, the additional elements are in some ways more interesting. If the report had been fully translated into reality there would have been significant changes in the delivery of learning for this phase and some key elements of this will still occur. With the concerns surrounding the needs of this group of learners, the variety of approaches is likely to be quite wide as many different solutions are currently being piloted and the number is set to increase.

New teaching and learning – what is set out in the White Paper?

Different aims for teaching and learning are changing the nature of work within the system. There is a very strong emphasis on employability and progression through career routes. Early choice and specialisation is encouraged and there is a tension between this and the provision of breadth, with allowance for learners who really are not best served by a tight, functional focus.

One of the key elements of the new 14–19 approach is the insistence that there should not be a clear dividing line between vocational and academic learning. Examples from higher education and professions like law and medicine provide obvious high-status illustrations of the difficulties inherent in rigid distinctions. The real integration of the theoretical and practical has become a priority for the phase with an emphasis on practical learning and the application of theory. The seduction of lively, active work-based learning contexts has driven many of the decisions apparent in the policy: 'An engineering course focused on teaching young people how to use high-tech equipment, taught by a professional engineer in the workplace, is likely to be a very attractive experience for many' (DfES 2005a). This attraction is certainly a positive factor but duplicating such experiences in shortage areas for large numbers of learners is a far harder enterprise.

Opening up new experiences involves increasing the locations and contexts for learning. The Increased Flexibility Programme has enabled schools and colleges to work together on wider curriculum choices for their students with new vocational GCSEs forming part of the more practical and relevant options on offer. It is clearly acknowledged in the White Paper that in order to make vocational education a high-quality, rather than second-class, route there must be general recognition of the new qualifications and they must have equal status with existing provision. In order to maintain the advantages of the international acceptance of A levels and GCSEs they are preserved as a 'cornerstone' of 14–19 learning.

Where do the new Diplomas fit?

The new Diplomas are described in Chapter 8, but change will be about far more than just new exams and certificates, and the long-term, ten-year, perspective on reform proposed by the Working Group still features. There is also an interesting 2008 interim point which for many suggests the possibility for revisiting some of the more radical ideas again. The message regarding teaching and learning is that even without a complete overhaul of the full range of qualifications there is a genuine interest in 'raising the bar' for achievements, missing the academic and vocational, bringing education, work and other life situations and experiences closer together.

One of the more directional aspects of the new Diplomas is that they will be employer designed. If this is the case then it does take government-led vocational education a stage further than previous models. It is an attempt to reconcile the conflicting demands of stakeholders for relevance to work and a clear centralised framework. There will be considerable interest in the detail of this process of design, decisions and implementation.

What is not so clear and is certainly not to be resolved in the short or even medium term is the fundamental tension between stretch and breadth which insists on emerging in all areas of curriculum discussion:

> There are those who argue that we should challenge our A level students further by demanding breadth in the curriculum as well as stretch. We understand and appreciate these arguments, but there is no clear consensus amongst pupils, parents, employers or universities on whether or how it should be done. We also believe that so soon after Curriculum 2000, stability is important.
>
> In the short term, we will be piloting new ways of stretching students at advanced level. We will also examine the positive experience of schools which are offering students the opportunity to take the International Baccalaureate as a means of increasing the breadth of study.
>
> In the light of these developments, we will discuss with employers and universities whether their needs are being met and the case for introducing greater challenge and breadth alongside A levels.
>
> (DfES 2005a: 45)

The whole set of issues relating to this have been set aside for research and consultation, and will be reviewed in 2008, a point many anticipate with renewed hope.

Will students gain flexibility and progression?

One key element is the movement between the routes so that, in addition to enabling students to mix both high- and lower-level elements and vocational and academic at one stage, they will also have the freedom to transfer from a predominantly academic level 2 base to a vocational level 3 Diploma or from a level 2 Diploma to A levels. The promised removal of a fixed point at 16 will occur over time as appropriate teaching in the 14–19 phase develops. Rather than moving the qualification structure, the proposals shift the onus onto the profession to accelerate learners as appropriate so that a proportion will have reached and attained full level 2 qualifications well before 16 years of age, while others, perhaps due to early barriers, may require longer or just achieve more highly and add breadth to their study.

How will acceleration and 'stretch' affect teaching and learning?

Acceleration and individual learning plans and programmes will have a significant effect on teaching and learning in schools and colleges. Since young people are likely to be attending school and or/college and other providers/collaborators, the new arrangements for this could prove to be a logistical headache. The danger of course is, as was apparent with the less complex Curriculum 2000, that vocational provision revolves around the alternative curriculum, the extension of partnership work with training providers and employers, and the development of student and modern apprenticeships. The use of individual plans and much wider offers of vocational programmes are among the key instruments for extending the 14–19 curriculum.

Pathfinders recognise the importance of tackling the current perception that vocational learning pre-16 is for the less able. The most clearly developed plans for work-related learning are in pathfinder areas where historically there have been effective partnerships with local industry and commerce. Status and an improved profile for vocational education is a key factor and much time and effort has been invested in these early pilots.

Among other aspects of the initiatives, Pathfinder projects have been piloting the use of ILPs. If individual approaches and increased choice are to be successful then reliable and good-quality record keeping is a vital component. Enterprise activity in pathfinders ranged from researching the needs of their local business community to organised enterprise-activity sessions. Pathfinders are tackling social exclusion including through 'alternative curricula' for the disaffected and disengaged, in some cases removing young people from schools completely.

The implementation of online learning infrastructures to enable shared teaching and learning resources is a developing area. E-learning is growing as an area for debate to extend the choices available to young people, providing a solution to accessibility problems in isolated rural areas and greater flexibility in areas where geographical isolation is not an issue. The pedagogy of this area is only just opening out and while much progress has been made there is still a great deal of room for advancement.

What is the current news on HE for 14–19-year-olds?

FE does offer HE level work and this is one of its strengths. Young and older students tied to the local area for whatever reason can be supported to progress directly to higher-level study in a familiar institution. This has certainly helped further the widening participation agenda and assisted many individuals facing barriers to learning to extend their experiences and achievements. The issues within schools are usually quite different but, in a climate so dedicated to individualised planning for learning, to stretch and engagement, it is hardly surprising to find this proposal on the table. Included in the Education Bill, subject to parliamentary approval, are changes to permit schools to offer HE modules across academic and vocational subjects.

Coursework

The Working Group reflected a widely held critical view of coursework when they drew attention to the duplication and resulting over-assessment to be found in the current model. Apart from the inefficiency this represents, it is a real 'turn-off' for all learners. Those who are finding courses too easy become increasingly bored and disengaged while those who are struggling with work waste time they can ill afford and are more likely to fail overall. A QCA review is addressing these issues and revisiting coursework in the light of sound assessment for learning principles so that it contributes to rather than detracts from learner progress.

What is the extended project?

Introduced to stretch, interest and prepare learners for degree-level study, the notion of a project is generally welcomed and seen to be an imaginative and very positive innovation. QCA are piloting versions of this in terms of both learning benefits and teaching management issues. In conjunction with HE and employers, they will develop an overarching framework and detailed specifications. Good practice elsewhere in the field, such as the extended essay within the International Baccalaureate and the BTEC National Diploma projects, will be taken into account. This project will be available to students on the level 3 Diploma and may even be made a requirement in some cases.

The role of guidance in teaching and learning

The recent drive to increase choice and flexibility places major demands on the advice and guidance services. According to the Tomlinson Working Group, there should be a key role for the best possible integrated, professional services for young people to provide the high-quality support required in a new curriculum and qualifications framework.

An issue for the designers and directors of any new system is the transition from existing routes and practice and the potential confusion resulting from the change process itself. The introduction of Tomlinson-based reform would generate major shifts across sectors and the intended outcomes could be jeopardised by lack of strategic planning in the provision of coherent support. It can be argued that a modified version such as that proposed in the White Paper (2005) will be more disruptive in the long term due to the compromises it forces and its failure to address the root causes of educational inequality.

The latest Youth Green Paper will address related issues and provide a blueprint for the integration of agencies and sectors involved with this group. The specialists concerned include the British Youth Council, the National Association of Youth Partnerships, the National Institute for Careers Education and Counselling, the national Association of Connexions Partnerships and the National Youth Agency. After all, without genuine development of high-quality partnerships between the practitioners and those who make policy, real integrated, vocational solutions to economic and social issues are unlikely to arrive. The most radical are likely to impact on the Connexions service as it becomes divided between the new integrated youth service and careers work in schools and colleges.

The new Standards Unit

At the start of 2003 the Standards Unit was set up to support and facilitate the drive to improve quality. It was based within the DfES and charged with developing training and resources to support staff in certain specific areas where need has been identified. To further the unit's aims specialist groups have been established to work on the best, most effective learning and teaching strategies. The unit is also responsible for e-learning strategy development.

Who may lose from the new entitlements and flexibilities?

Increasing some options results in decreasing others and there is expression of concern regarding the subjects and approaches seen to be the victims of the current focus on the vocational and relevant to the world of work. Advocates of traditional subject teaching or conventional forms from English literature to mathematics and from modern foreign languages to history and RE have much to say. The new approaches have many serious detractors in both colleges and schools.

FE colleges, however, just provide vocational programmes and basic 5 GCSE packages but innovative and highly academic A-level options, including subjects like law, government and politics, and philosophy. They see themselves as offering a wide range of subjects to the broadest community of learners and this makes them much more than institutions designed to turn out workers to meet the needs of local and national industry. The wider missions of colleges ensure that new flexibilities are not uncritically welcomed and that their cost in curriculum terms is as carefully counted in FE as in schools.

Who pays?

The resources required for the new directions are not as clearly defined as many would like. FE colleges find that the cost of providing vocational education is comparatively large as it involves higher staff–student ratios and additional support, more expensive specialist accommodation, consumables, administrative and capital equipment, and registration and examination fees which are higher than for general courses. As a result FE colleges maintain that, in spite of additional IF funding, programmes are frequently unsustainable as they are not cost effective.

Recent developments in schools have led FE colleges to see the sector as gaining unfair competitive advantage by virtue of its access to exclusive ring-fenced sources of funding. Capital funds have been made available to technology schools and centres of excellence to support EAZ and other initiatives.

This situation is exacerbated in some school settings by the uncertainty regarding the consistency of income streams to support new developments. While there are areas of the new vocational work which are well supported there is a strong perception that other elements are under-resourced. Staff development is one of these, and the training issues go beyond the financial implications since availability of quality provision is more of an issue. The development of CPD in conjunction with ITE is one such area.

For areas not already acclimatised to local collaboration, Increased Flexibility for 14–16-year-olds Programme (IFP) funding had provided the first impetus for a co-ordinated approach across this area and 14–19 Pathfinder funding was perceived as the vehicle for developing collaboration further.

Is 14–19 really a separate phase?

The debates surround more than the standard 'What is education for?' question. They are rooted in the separate development of the phases and can be complex and contradictory but the ownership battle is one of the hardest to be fought. The hope of reformers is that there will be a spirit of co-operation.

The potential difficulties between schools and colleges; questions about adolescence and adulthood and the location of the best-quality teaching, training and learning have been more obvious in the early days. However, it is worth noting that there are other views. While many practitioners and theorists emphasise the differences between learners, contexts and ideal models of training across the phases, David Hargreaves has recently argued against the commonly held notion that lifelong learning is somehow fundamentally different from school education. In many ways this is a radical attempt to shift established patterns of thought and to reassess approaches to learning in the face of many new challenges.

Theories based on acceptance of the concept of andragogy have dominated post-compulsory-sector approaches to teaching for many years. Yet there have always been teachers crossing the phase boundaries in both directions and those whose careers and personal circumstances resulted in part-time working in schools and colleges. For these and for theorists less convinced by the prevailing orthodoxy, the methods and approaches never appeared so clearly divided.

Rather than focusing on teaching and learning strategies, perhaps attention should be turned to the distinctions between teaching and training and the effects of this on learners. Such distinctions currently exercise the minds of many educators, employers and politicians. Whatever the outcomes of these debates, there is at present a new consensus that significant change is inevitable.

One of the new realities far more evident in the vocational context is the prevalence of teams consisting of very different contributors to the learners' progress. In workshops and other practical environments there are significant physical and personnel issues:

- The person managing learning – team or programme leader
- Multi-skilled teaching teams – possibly from different sections and including both part- and full-time staff. Some team working is complicated by cross-department or section staffing
- Technicians and instructors

- Trainers, mentors and other personnel in the workplace
- Learning Support Assistants
- Volunteers and visitors

The tensions and debates are not simply sets of issues raised by the demands of new qualifications, nor is there a single national answer. In fact across the UK the response to the shifting social and economic demands is varied. Scotland, Wales and Northern Ireland have taken full advantage of the devolution effect and are carving out their own pathways in this territory. The system in Scotland has always been separate but the individualisation of approaches now progressed and they are ahead of England in terms of having tried and tested a form of new qualifications. Wales has talked about the Welsh Baccalaureate quite extensively and, following consultations, has been honing a simplified version. For some, the issues are raised by the transition of Western societies to the 'so-called' knowledge-based phase. All the usual terminologies are bandied around, from globalisation to the spread of new information and communication technologies.

What is new in teaching and learning?

The stated intention of new initiatives is to increase curriculum flexibility and, as local partnerships increase the range of 14–19 learning opportunities available, students will need to make complex decisions about what courses to begin in year 10 and to set their intended progression and goals at 19. These decisions require an awareness and experience of the learning and assessment relating to different courses. The implications for Integrated Advice and Guidance and for ICT are major. Support for pedagogy is available through the National Strategies and 'Success for All'.

Assessment

As the coursework burden is reduced especially at the GCSE/level 2 stage, the suggestion is that there could be a positive impact not only on students, with external pressures minimised, but on teachers, who because they would assume some additional workload in the form of teacher assessment would benefit from redirected funding. The report points out the potential for shifting the £60 million currently spent on the examination entries to the institutions involved with teacher assessment. In terms of advancing teaching and learning the assessment-related proposals attempt to address the over-examination of learners with all its associated disadvantages, repetition, missed opportunities for depth and a failure to challenge learners. (Chapter 8 explores White Paper proposals for the area in more detail.)

What did the Working Party mean by core and main learning and are any of the recommendations retained?

The e-learning components, mentioned before, are not specified in the proposals but they are given a central position. ICT is to have an impact on delivery and to form one of the seven components of the core that must be followed by all students.

The core aims to ensure that all individuals develop the knowledge, attributes and skills necessary for life and work. Mathematical, communication and ICT skills are emphasised and will be compulsory until the achievement of level 2 (by 16 years). What many teachers may take issue with is the very strong link of the three components above-mentioned to the workplace. This very specific 'functionality' has its critics and the curriculum-related debates in teaching around the nature and purpose of skills and knowledge is set to continue. There is no doubt whatsoever which side the Working Party espouses.

According to the report, the content of any ICT qualification 'can only be determined in consultation with end users, including HE, employers and community groups', and the SSCs, the new Sector Skills Councils, are an integral part of this kind of consultation. As the three most significant of the core components are fast-tracked and proposed as the earliest to be implemented, the emphasis is once again placed on consultation towards functionality. The elements must be based on 'An understanding shared between stakeholders, about what constitute common requirements for informed citizens, effective learners and a wide range of workplaces' (DfES 2005a). The main learning equates to the existing examination courses in academic and vocational qualifications. There will be opportunities to make individual choices and to pursue a mix of subjects and subject types either in specialised lines or in an open diploma.

Education professionals express more concerns over this area than some others on the grounds of complexity and current practice. Subject and qualification offers are particularly hard to timetable, to develop and build and to run. The more vocational they are the more they tend to require additional resources, accommodation, staffing, work placements, careful tracking and so on. While these are the very features that make such lines attractive and successful, they can also be barriers. Even Curriculum 2000, which was a far more modest proposition, stumbled on the obstacles presented by attempts to broaden choice. Since this earlier initiative proved difficult within institutions, then the partnership options, though they could provide real opportunities, will certainly face substantial difficulties across the phase.

As the description of the new qualification offer shows (Chapter 8), there are many elements from the recommendations incorporated into the new framework. What many professionals either fear or expect to happen, depending on their attitude to reform, is that the status quo will continue. Schools and colleges will continue to offer the kind of curriculum they provide now but the labels and some of the processes by which students qualify will change.

What will become of the Working Party demands for personalised and extended elements?

The idea of increased challenge and individual learning was most pronounced in the extended project or personal challenge element of the proposed diploma. This was quite widely welcomed as being a more creative angle on what is often perceived to be a fairly mechanistically assessed phase. It should be something that can be described as 'a substantial piece of work'. The exact specification is not specified though the spirit of the approach seemed to encourage openness and individual choice rather than tight prescription. This idea has been included in the proposals set out in the White Paper though once again this is a concept rather than an actual specification. For the extended project to fulfil its creative promise there will certainly need to be more thought and support for students and staff in the phase.

The personal review, planning and guidance elements would require a great deal of preparation. Teachers and advisors will need to provide support to enable students to make 'clear and meaningful choices' in a new set of structures and over issues like appropriate vocational lines. This approach should enhance the learning experience for students but may well add to the workload of staff unless careful planning and CPD is in place for professionals.

Supporters of this kind of move hope that pitfalls such as over-prescription and failure to give real credit will be avoided. It still promises high levels of flexibility especially if students are permitted to submit videos, artifacts or written pieces as long as they fulfil the requirement to demonstrate the individual's knowledge, skills and understanding. The proposal is that these personal pieces will engage learners in a broader way and encourage research and greater depth of study.

Assuming that appropriate resources follow the revised framework, teaching for this element will prompt more individual personal tutorials and should draw the students' preferences into the wider programme. For some teachers, the adoption of more vocational qualifications and lines of learning combined with this sort of research and personal challenge work will mean significant changes are required. The conventional school day might well need radical adjustment and the notion of students having study and work time, and meeting less in large classrooms and more in small groups and in other learning contexts will present a considerable challenge.

How will wider activities fit with the teaching and learning?

Wider activities like sports, arts and community work will be drawn into the new framework. The enhancement of personal development is clearly one of the aims as the whole learner is the focus. There are also links with the citizenship elements of the curriculum. Experience and practice will be the real defining factors in this area of the curriculum. For some, the creative and imaginative aspects of extending approaches to reach and engage learners at all levels were founded on notions of the interrelatedness of the student's personal and social life, study and work. They do not view wider activities as peripheral but as the key bringing the curriculum to life for young people.

What will happen to CKSA post-Tomlinson?

The development of Common Knowledge, Skills and Attributes as proposed by the Working Group on 14–19 Reform is continuing. The DfES is working with the QCA on an outline description of these skills based on the Working Group's ideas and on existing National Curriculum guidance. The skills and attributes are not limited to individual subjects but cross the curriculum and the age groups. Once again they emphasise employability alongside learning:

> Young people also need to develop their personal skills and a set of thinking and learning skills. Personal skills are those that give young people the ability to manage themselves and to develop effective social and working relationships. Thinking and learning skills mean knowing how to learn independently and adapt to a range of circumstances. Together these skills are essential for raising standards, further learning, employment and dealing with a range of real-world problems. We have worked with QCA to develop an outline description of these skills, building on the notion of Common Knowledge Skills and Attributes (CKSA) developed by the Working Group on 14–19 Reform, and on existing National Curriculum guidance.
>
> (DfES 2005a: 39)

How will teaching work within a new framework?

In some cases schools have agreed with sixth-form and further-education colleges that prior attainment of units or modules of advanced-level qualifications can be built on in pupils' post-16 programmes. School and college cultures, structures and teaching approaches will certainly come under scrutiny as there is more transfer and cross-phase working. The new accountability framework is designed to monitor the quality of collaborative working. The challenge here will be to identify the most productive approaches for learners and to develop and share these without slipping into the easiest of poor-quality compromises. We have certainly all seen examples of the problems of one sector being pushed elsewhere and ignored.

Much has been made on both sides of the advantages and disadvantages of the cultures within FE, workplace settings and schools. It is often claimed that single features are not transferable; that the experience of college must contain all the diversity of age and background so problematic for those who advocate the increased entry of 14-year-olds into FE. The freedom from school-style restrictions comes at a price and, in any case, can be something of a myth.

Learning in adult environments is an aspiration for some 14–19 students who find this kind of mixed-age learning context especially stimulating. In order to capitalise on the benefits of such experiences, teachers, instructors and other staff do need the training and support to ensure both general safety and risk management and to ensure that the needs of all learners are being met in appropriate ways.

There would inevitably be alteration in approach if 14-year-olds were included in some classes or workshop situations. This is not necessarily a disadvantage but issues would be raised. Adults might feel inhibited in sharing experiences which might otherwise have contributed to their learning as a group. For example, where the majority have encountered family or carer responsibilities or perhaps experienced financial difficulties they may feel that problems or personal disclosures are inappropriate in front of younger students.

On the other hand, the assumptions made about younger students can be inaccurate and the reality of learning interactions and the negotiations concerning sensitivities and boundaries within groups can be valuable for all in spite of, and perhaps because of, this kind of constraint. The decisions about levels of integration of the 14-16 cohort will be one of the most interesting aspects of the unfolding reforms.

Some learners need high levels of attention in the initial stages of learning in new contexts. This clearly has significant cost implications and can mean one-to-one support initially, so the teaching across phase and institution/workplace is by no means a cheap option. As progress with both highly motivated but inexperienced and demotivated learners improves, the investment begins to pay off. Learners do become much more independent and tend to form good relationships and to establish themselves in work linked to their training. This development process forms part of a very constructive route to adulthood.

How do students in the 14–19 phase overcome barriers to learning?

The recruitment, retention and achievement of these learners are extensively quantified in the statistics of the school and post-compulsory sectors. There is keen interest in means by which such students can be attracted, engaged and supported towards their achievements. As Tomlinson has emphasised, the role of vocational advice and guidance is essential, though there is already a great deal of expertise in the field and some of the effort would be well spent in integrating available systems so that new learners will benefit across the phases.

In a similar way to adult learners, there are often many more independent living issues encountered by this group and these can be compounded by the relative youth and inexperience of the people concerned – a younger person who is homeless or encountering financial difficulties or suffering abuse is often more vulnerable. The post-16 drop-out rate in the UK was one of the worst in the developed world (ranking 27th out of 30 leading industrialised countries, behind all but Mexico, Turkey and Greece), and the introduction of the EMA has had a significant effect on this.

Education Maintenance Allowances

Over 250,000 students aged 16-plus have received the EMA payments since the scheme to provide financial support for these learners was introduced by the DfES in September 2004. The £500 million scheme seems to have been successful at reducing drop-out rates across the 56 local authority areas involved in the pilot study. The drop-out rates were reduced across England as a result of providing regular payments in return for attendance. Students aged 16–18 who want to stay in education, from families with an income of £30,000 or less, are entitled to payments of between £10 and £30 per week. The recent budget announcement increased this sum by £45 to £75 per week and added the additional benefit that these students will be able to access cheap rentals on computers to help them with their studies.

A fixed allocation of £70 per EMA claimant will be awarded to all schools and colleges with ten or more EMA students. This is intended to be a contribution to the implementation and administration costs of the first year of the scheme. Students taking vocational courses like NVQs, as well as those on A-level courses in school or college, can apply at any time during the academic year.

The scheme has since been made available across England and evaluated in a major study by the Centre for Research into Social Policy and the Institute for Fiscal Studies. The findings of the study were very positive, providing evidence of significant improvements in motivation, attendance and attainment levels, as well as increased year 12 participation (5.9 per cent) and improved retention in year 13.

What external issues impact upon the 14–19 learner?

For the professionals dealing with the 14–19 phase, this kind of evaluation finding and the confirmation of the importance of financial factors is particularly interesting. It confirms the opinions of many experienced practitioners that teaching and learning at this level are beset by external influences and that, while classroom and work-based strategies are significant, they are not the sole factors in determining success.

Where, in all these innovations, is the voice of the 14–19 learner?

One aspect of the purposes and values of 14–19 education, emphasised in the Nuffield Feasibility Report (2002), is 'a respect for the aspirations, values and perspectives of 14–19-year-olds themselves'. There are some accounts but far more qualitative research is required. This age is a crucial time for development and growth. The very functional and instrumental approaches may open up certain types of experiences and opportunities but others can be closed. The learners who take longer to explore their aspirations and capabilities and who are less mature but no less able are likely to be disadvantaged in a very focused system with formalised progression routes from an early age. However much we attempt to incorporate breadth and transferability, there will be losers who do not fit with the schemes and who are impressionable when faced with intense advice and guidance.

Conclusion

One view of new policies reflects not so much the separation and distinctiveness of new phases but rather a central vision directing the shape of future teaching and learning. From early years to lifelong learning there is a drive to introduce more specific economic and social behaviour training into the curriculum. This lies behind the return to the language of values and is embedded in definitions of citizenship, core skills and relevance to work. The interesting dimension of certain versions of new teaching and learning is their widespread acceptability to a broad spectrum of stakeholders. It is surprising how few voices are raised in criticism of the principles behind the approach though there are differences of opinion regarding pace and scope.

CHAPTER 3

Training and quality issues

It used to be possible to train in a phase-specific way and to assume that the career choice would be fixed but increasingly teachers are being required to develop the skills to work flexibly across a range of contexts. Throughout the debates and discussions on reform, training has been identified consistently as a key area in future strategy. It is significant as a means to drive forward both social and economic agendas and to ensure continuing flexibility in new mobile and adaptable workforces. These developments are clearly far wider in scope than just one phase but for the 14–19 age group there is a real need for change and the opportunity to construct a new model. Throughout Europe, issues relating to this phase are being addressed and, though approaches may differ, many of the aims are common.

In spite of the generally high level of new entrants to teaching as a career, shortages in certain areas have always been an issue in both schools and PCET. Almost 35,000 individuals began mainstream teacher training in England in 2004–5, the highest number in twenty years. If the employment-based routes were included, the number would be almost 7,000 more and this is the sixth successive increase in the number of ITT entrants. Producing trained teachers in adequate numbers does not necessarily address the supply issues. Subject specialisms, location and housing costs, sector training, and needs and preferences for part-time working are all factors that have an impact on the workforce.

The subjects and broad curriculum areas in short supply do vary though there are some, like maths and science, common to both sectors. FE has recently needed far more appropriately trained basic skills staff than the market could provide though new programmes and in-service training are beginning to address this. As always, support in the form of timely provision and easily accessed resources to meet changing training needs is the real key to successful responses to the sector requirements. Having said this, some problems can be solved fairly rapidly by conversion courses, and increased employment incentives like the training bursaries and the 'golden hellos', but others are more intractable and are linked to other issues like the shortages of qualified engineers or science graduates. These latter require the application of long-term strategic approaches and to some extent they are being tackled.

There are currently well over twenty different routes into teaching and a clear need, for the sake of all concerned, to establish a more coherent system. New candidates for the profession need to know the most appropriate route and, while guidance is provided, the potential for switching, deferring or accelerating training to suit individual circumstances is not high. Existing professionals need more flexible options to extend their development, employment and promotion opportunities. The 14–19 focus is only one of several reasons to expect a future rise in demand for increased mobility in the workforce.

What is the expanded remit for the TTA?

The requirements for training and for the new workforce will be overseen by the TTA (renamed the Training and Development Agency – TDA – with an extended remit from the Secretary of State for Education and Skills in December 2004) and by LLUK. It has been given a remit to build on recruitment and training success through expanding its role into the wider workforce to include comprehensive development and training for all school support staff through the School Workforce Development Board. It will be a key partner in the new strategic networks required by 'Every Child Matters' (http://www.everychildmatters.gov.uk), representing all staff working with young people. Finally, it will strengthen its contribution to teachers' continuing professional development.

What will the White Paper mean for training?

The breadth of choice set out as an entitlement in the White Paper will trigger increased demand for new staff and continuing staff training.

> We will support the workforce to deliver. We will ensure that the right staff are in place, including those who have the necessary experience of the workplace to deliver vocational education, and that they have the professional development, qualifications and support that they need.
>
> ■ We will make sure that we continue to have a properly trained workforce, by offering training and support to existing and future teachers, lecturers and others in the workforce; and
>
> ■ We will manage the effect of these changes on the workforce, and ensure that schools and colleges are able to deploy staff.
>
> (DfES 2005a: 25)

This list of promises, like much else in the political world, may sound straightforward on paper but will surely prove a very tall order to fulfil in the real world. The areas in question are the very vocational areas where existing shortages are proving problematic for industry and, even with some incentives and innovative programmes (e.g. 'Teach First') to attract high-flying recruits and retrainers, significant difficulties remain. If the government is to address this problem successfully in the new order, they will have to provide security, prospects, parity and status for the profession – a key debate best addressed elsewhere but central to the success or failure of the reforms on the table.

What does training the wider workforce mean?

Teachers, lecturers, managers and heads are only a proportion of the workforce of the future. Technicians and learning support assistants, instructors, coaches and volunteers all form part of the teams of people who will have contact with learners and be involved in their guidance, training and assessment. If the learning and training contexts are to be extended to 14–16-year-olds then there must be a corresponding focus of attention on the development of the individuals concerned. Central to these efforts is the new TDA with its wider workforce and continuing professional development responsibilities and LLUK.

If employers are to become so significant is there not a case for providing higher quality and more structured training. In the past this meant some assessor training for an interested but perhaps under-recognised or under-rewarded individual in a local company. The need is surely for schemes that blur the boundaries of education and employment. Perhaps we could see the 'secondment' of key individuals, some principally teachers, others industry-sector workers/managers, whose time crossing from education to employment is valued and credited in both arenas rather than being seen as a potentially detrimental career shift. Developments like this are risky if training and development structures are not put in place but if they are then the rewards, in terms of creative cross-phase and sector opportunities, could be significant.

The education sector already benefits from voluntary and supported 'buddy' and mentoring schemes that provide learners with help and motivation from very valuable experienced and enthusiastic individual role models. Any extension and formalising of this is a powerful tool enabling industry to loan its best talents on profitable terms and, ultimately, for both sides of the exchange, especially the learners, to reap the rewards.

What will be done to provide this skilled workforce for 14–19?

Due to the demographic trend which means a reduction in 14–19-year-olds is on the way, there will not be the demand for very large numbers of new staff in either the school or the PCET sectors. There may be a pool of trained teachers numbering around half a million but they are not all working actively in teaching (PIT: Pool of Inactive Teachers): some are only on temporary contracts and move in and out of the profession, while others are close to retirement. The picture is far from clear since school rolls are falling visibly in primary schools with the secondary sector following, and this coupled with retirements will provide career opportunities.

However, there is still a need for a shift in training to adapt the existing and growing workforce to new requirements. The changes in teaching and learning will involve the following challenges for the workforce:

- Offering a new range of tests for teacher assessment at Key Stage 3. We want to support teachers to make best use of the national bank of tests.

- Introducing the extended project. Teachers will help learners select their project; they will monitor and guide learners' progress.

- The QCA review of the Key Stage 3 curriculum will lead to changes in the programmes of study. Changes to some GCSEs will have implications for how they are taught. We will provide CPD and support teachers through the Secondary National Strategy.

- Introducing new qualifications, including the new Diplomas. We will support teachers and trainers to deliver these courses and assess parts of them.

There will be a pressing need to train existing staff to cope with new and different structures, contexts, skills and materials. The bodies involved in supporting staff include the Teacher Training Agency, the Institute for Learning, Lifelong Learning UK and other key partners who will develop high-quality training and development for teaching staff. In September 2004, it was announced that from 2007–8 an additional £70 million would be invested in workforce development for the post-16 sector, including £30 million for initial teacher training.

'Success for All' requires not only that all new college teachers must be trained to teach but that by 2010 all existing teachers must be trained as well. In terms of 14–19, the new Lifelong Learning Skills Council and LLUK are working with the TTA (TDA) to ensure that those carrying the responsibilities and challenges of catering for the majority of these learners are fully trained and supported. The training agencies in their new forms and the Lifelong Learning Sector Skills Council are playing a central part in working jointly to implement change. For example, modules are being developed for the FE lecturers and work-based trainers involved with 14–19 years, and in 2004–5 the TTA allocated 400 places for the training of teachers for vocational subjects.

'Success for All' also included information on the investment of a further £14.4 million through 2003–6 to support the Centre for Excellence in Leadership to improve leadership and management skills in the post-16 sector. This should produce better leadership, greater diversity and increased progression of staff into leadership posts. The National College for School Leadership and the Centre for Excellence in Leadership will work together on leadership development and support to equip head teachers, FE principals and work-based learning providers to work effectively in collaboration and ensure that all their staff are trained in the necessary skills. For those leaders involved in collaborations between institutions, the Networked Learning Communities Programme may prove valuable. In the future, the NLC cohorts could include networks drawn from school- and college-sector organisations.

Why is training significant?

Training, in whatever form, plays a key role in the process of generating and maintaining productive partnerships for learning and is more than a side issue in this context. The quality of teaching and learning is, among other factors, very dependent on the quality of staff, and with the pace of change and new demands, significant identified weaknesses in staffing and a fragmented environment presenting difficulties for delivery, the inspection and training become even more important.

The lack of a coherent set of structures, as well as not having a shared history and therefore the ability to understand one another, are among the existing problems faced by those trying to implement policy. There is now a real need for the rapid development of partnerships and staff across institutions. Experience of shortages and a lack of staff skills, knowledge and age-group experience in both sectors demonstrate the pivotal role of staff recruitment, development and training and of collaborations for the success of the new phase.

What follows ALI?

The Adult Learning Inspectorate (ALI) was created in 2001 under the provisions of the 2000 Learning and Skills Act (http://www.ali.gov.uk). Its responsibilities included a wide range of government-funded learning, including work-based learning for those aged 16 and over and the learning for 19 plus students in FE colleges, adult and community learning, 'learndirect' work and Jobcentre Plus 'welfare to work' programmes like New Deal. The FE college provision was shared with Ofsted under the joint inspection framework.

After 2001 ALI's remit was steadily extended. They took the lead where the majority of learners were adults and also shared responsibility for inspections in prisons and young offender institutions. By 2004 this Inspectorate had its full complement of 150 full-time inspectors and 650 associate inspectors and it seemed set to continue developing from its Coventry base. Future plans had included the commissioned inspection of government departments and private organisations' training. It was to have had a central role in the improvement of national workforce quality.

The Common Inspection Framework had supported the first four-year cycle of operation and seemed set to be retained for a second. However, in March 2005 the Chancellor Gordon Brown announced plans that would, effectively, merge the Adult Learning Inspectorate with Ofsted and cease its independent operation: 'The Government will consult with employers on the future of the Adult Learning Inspectorate with the expectation that, by 2008, it will also be part of this single inspectorate for education, children's services and skills' (www.tes.co.uk, 25 March 2005).

Ofsted and ALI have both developed through sharing joint responsibility for the quality of professional training, management, and learning issues across many sectors and cradle to grave with learners. The announcement means that ALI will be subsumed into Ofsted which will assume responsibility across this huge range. For 14–19, this restructuring is designed to ensure the development of links and improvements in secondary and post-compulsory teaching and training. The rise in school standards reflected in Ofsted inspection results over ten years has been cited as the justification for using this successful approach as a model for future quality improvement of 14–19 teaching and learning in all its contexts.

What is the new accountability framework?

The framework is intended to support development of the emerging 14–19 phase and plans to:

- include vocational qualifications in Achievement and Attainment Table measures and ensure that inspections challenge schools to offer the full range of curriculum and qualifications;
- focus on the basics through continuing to publish tables showing performance in English, maths and science at Key Stage 3; and toughening tables at 16 to measure the Diploma standard: 5 A*–C GCSEs, including English and maths;
- encourage stretch for all teenagers through giving schools credit in the tables when they achieve success in higher-level qualifications. Through the New Relationship with Schools, hold schools more strongly to account for the progress of all their students; and
- encourage institutions to focus on improving retention rates by introducing progression targets; and crediting schools for the achievement of young people completing Key Stage 4 later than the normal age.

Is there such a thing as a new phase and if so does it need a new kind of teacher?

While it is true that both secondary trainers and post-compulsory trainers have been working with the sectors and trainees involved for many years and rightly see themselves as experts in their fields, they have not generally collaborated. Less than half of secondary teachers are involved in KS4 post-16 and equally only a very small proportion of post-compulsory teachers work with 14–19-year-olds. Everyone agrees that the 14–19 phase must be a shared responsibility and careful planning is needed to avoid the dangers of replicating poor practice. If the students sent to FE are perceived as failures and the FE pathways as second-best alternatives to the academic curriculum then the chances of raising achievement and reducing disaffection in the target group will be poor.

One growing feature of current training is its assumption that there is a less fixed future; in its place is an emerging need for acquiring a range of specific skill and knowledge sets. These have often less to do with student–teacher interactions in school or college and more to do with qualification and curriculum structures, modes of delivery, professional demands and the management of organisational operations. Whether you train as a subject specialist or as a generalist, your programme and practice will comprise quite a high proportion of these shifting areas. The increasing rate of innovation and the complexity of the options available in the 14–19 phase have exacerbated the issues for training where it impacts on this group.

It is argued that the focus in training should remain broader and that generic training related to a single context, either school or college, should remain the norm. It is also argued that in terms of school delivery the strong subject focus of a teacher must be retained for the sake of preserving quality and, indeed, Ofsted/ALI inspections within FE have highlighted what they term significant inadequacies in the area of teachers' subject knowledge (Ofsted 2003). Clearly there is a case for claiming that to prepare trainees to deliver a high-quality educational experience requires the development of both the necessary depth and underpinning knowledge.

Whatever model is adopted ultimately, teaching and training for the 14–19 phase must take account of the 19-plus learners. The very benefits desired by reformers reside in contexts inhabited by a broad range of learners. Some of the attractions, especially of vocational training, can be retained in settings exclusively designed for the 14–19-year-olds but many cannot. The arguments which assert the necessity for teaching 11–16, 18 or 19 in an integrated way also hold true in PCET and, in fact, the mixed-age groups so common to the FE and training environment furnish much potential research material.

Where might future training take place and who would be involved?

There are many who believe that the best place for professional training is within the profession. This employment-based training approach involves basic core modules delivered in the work situation alongside mentorship and a developing practice as hours increase and the trainee moves towards qualification. An increasing number of schools who would once have taken PGCE trainees have moved towards the school-based training route.

It is certainly possible for high-quality training to take place in a school context and there are many advantages. Trainees are closely supported on a daily basis, they engage with pupils and staff in a whole-school context for a longer period, benefit from more established relationships and from an accepted status. PGCE programmes can and do break the process whereby a student is embedded into their training context. The same advantages apply to the in-service training in colleges and for the trainee who fits their institution there may well be a straight transition to part- or full-time employment. However, as in so many learning situations, there are disadvantages to this total immersion. The most obvious is the lack of opportunity for distance, objectivity and for cross-context comparison, though this is not always fully addressed on pre-service training and indeed it can be an key element of some in-service training programmes. The HEI role in training has been the focus of much heated discussion on account of changing policy and its impact on the schools and colleges.

This removes training from the HEI context and locates it firmly in the workplace. The shift has been quiet but it is hugely significant and the UK has, once again, been a pioneer in a public sector revolution since the establishment of school-based teacher education in 1992. The drivers behind the current 14–19 reform recommendations were already being recognised and acted upon a decade ago when this was described in terms of 'schooling for the success of international global economies'. Now, all eyes are on the various new approaches to see how they perform in terms of recruiting, fitting and delivering a competent and effective workforce within acceptable costs.

The other advantage of the use of ITE as a lever for change from a policy-makers' point of view is the direct access this provides to the new teacher. Experienced teachers are involved but they are rightly driven by the immediate, medium- and long-term needs of their own pupils/students and the wider school. For good or ill, the perspective of other educators and academics is lost. Younger or new staff have fewer preconceptions about the sector they are entering and will tend to immerse themselves more readily in an existing environment if there are no external reference points.

Employment-based training has many advantages, some of which will be explored further elsewhere, but in the often pressured work context the significance of theoretical, comparative, historical and political perspectives can recede as planning, strategies, schedules and, indeed, important professional relationships and interactions take precedence.

Should teacher education remain in universities?

For some, the boundaries between sectors have already become blurred as the teachers and lecturers from various phases involve themselves in training and research, and HE education professionals see the value of closer links and active involvement with practice. The fear is that changes are motivated disproportionately by short-term economic factors rather than quality, sector and learner needs. Elements of the HE sector have taken a defensive stance in the face of what they perceive to be a significant threat to well-established and successful programmes.

If the case for HEI concerns needed to be put more strongly, then recent closures of several major education faculties would stand as a stark illustration of the speed and potential impact of changes in modes of training. 14–19 with its vocational dimension is more of a target for innovative training approaches. After all, if society needs the employer and the influence of the workplace to become directly involved in learning, then there are training and extension implications for the learning delivery team. The constituents in this mix could well be very diverse as could the teaching management directing the learning process. If the question then becomes, 'Is an HEI-based programme the most appropriate vehicle for training?', for some the answer must be that only HEI involvement can introduce some critical distance into the partnership equation and ensure impartiality, inclusion and the examination of values. Clearly other partners work from a similar value base but the existence of their own organisational agendas and vested interests is a factor.

Naturally the possibility of radical change in training modes and even location has already exercised the minds of stakeholders in teacher training. As the pace of change increases the concerns of those within education are rising. The role of the HEI in teacher education may change in terms of the delivery and assessment of learning but there is great potential for it to continue its development as a source for critical external expertise and as a resource for the initial and continuing development of all partners within new networks.

How could the employment-based routes work for 14–19?

The employment-based routes (EBRs) are teacher-training programmes that allow trainees to work in a school and follow an individual training programme leading to QTS. This has been the preferred route for increasing numbers of graduates who do not wish to enrol on the one-year PGCE programmes perhaps because the income is too low for someone changing career. There are also those who have gained employment or have part-time experience. In addition, some trainees have already qualified to teach in the post-compulsory sector and are transferring via this route.

For the Graduate Teacher Programme (GTP) trainees must have a degree or equivalent; for the Registered Teacher Programme (RTP) they must complete the degree while they train; and for the Overseas Trained Teacher Programme (OTTP) an equivalent to a UK degree is required. These flexible programmes are contributing to increased recruitment which, to some degree, supports the 14–19 sector but they cannot usually provide the cross-context experience so essential for training a professional to teach in the new sector.

Who would be affected by changes to training?

At present, sixth-form and FE colleges have much greater freedom regarding the employment of teaching staff than schools. They can employ staff without teaching qualifications although in a sixth-form college the preference would usually be for QTS and without this, the individual would be paid on the instructor level and in the case of an NQT arrangements might be made for an induction year in the college.

In FE at present there is a two-year time limit for full-timers and four years for part-timers to gain an appropriate teaching qualification.

What are the key demands of the stakeholders?

The DfES conducted extensive consultations at all levels in June 2004 and the following views emerged:

- Teachers in the learning and skills sector want parity of esteem and of professionalism with schoolteachers
- That effective machinery is needed to implement the reforms

- That adequate funding is essential
- That time should be provided for quality reforms without piecemeal changes (http://www.dfes.gov.uk/consultations)

The responses, that largely mirror those of heads surveyed recently in the *TES*, show concerns about the level of commitment from government, cross-phase parity, time and other resources but are generally very supportive of the proposals.

Where do professional bodies fit in?

The need for common standards and for effective professional body representation has been raised in many quarters. In the context of the Scottish Executive consultation on the need for a professional body for staff in colleges, Professor Gordon Kirk argued most convincingly for a coherent approach to this issue. He suggested that a single body for FE might be divisive and awkward in the light of 14–19 phase reform. The wider relevance of this is clear though – once again, UK education does not always benefit from the experience and knowledge of all its four countries: 'Higher education institutions are currently engaged in establishing the HE Academy, which will discharge several functions relating to the professional accreditation of teaching staff' (Kirk *et al.* 2004). In an ideal world, representation and control of standards would be both straightforward and integrated in a consistent system to span the sectors: 'Is it altogether too fanciful to envisage all of those involved in the promotion of learning, from nursery school to university, deriving their professional authority and accreditation from a single body?' (ibid.).

New infrastructures for training and quality

The DfES Standards Unit considered placing all initial teacher training for the learning and skills sector under the management of the TTA and the GTC along with the schools sector. This was rejected on the grounds that it was not generally welcomed by those within the sector; the TTA responsibilities were already being significantly extended to cover the whole school workforce and the experience of the huge diversity within post-compulsory education and training in a multitude of settings was located elsewhere.

The development of LLUK provided an appropriate and representative body in which the experience and connections could be combined. Links and systems previously residing in other key national training organisations will migrate into the new Sector Skills Council, with its remit to set standards and manage workforce development.

The Institute for Learning (IfL) describes itself as the emerging professional body for PCET practitioners. Its aims are to promote and support the development of teachers and trainers across the sector. The DfES has identified a significant role for the Institute:

- Designing the professional development record
- Registering those enrolled on the passport to teaching and those who complete it as holding a threshold licence to practise
- Registering those who enrol on the full course and awarding QTLS as the full licence to practise to teachers who complete the qualification
- Continuing to register those who take appropriate CPD
- Modelling good practice for teacher trainers across the sector
- Liaising with the GTC and the HE Academy to encourage coherence in development across the teaching profession as a whole

The benefits from the integration of the emerging bodies could be significant. 'Joined-up' thinking and working across sectors may be the positive outcome.

How does existing training relate to 14–19?

There is already a well-established tradition of training across the 14–19 age range but the current organisation naturally reflects existing cross-phase assumptions, divisions and educational structures. As a result, the existing initial training arrangements are very separate and prevent any radical cross-phase development in this area.

Many Secondary PGCE programmes always provided training from 11–18/19 and only the current political constraints led to some shifting their focus to 11–16. Even so, there is overlap with the post-compulsory sector training where both in-service and pre-service routes have always trained for 16-plus with no ceiling. The fact that there is considerable shared ground guarantees neither great similarity nor agreement on principle. Those involved tend to make significant play of the differences that have evolved over time in the training approaches but in fact there are many similarities and professionals transfer across the sectors quite frequently.

Training programmes such as the PGCE post-compulsory have seen increasing numbers of newly qualified PCET teachers, especially in shortage areas like mathematics, sciences and ICT, make immediate transfers into school posts. The routes for facilitating such transfers can be somewhat confusing. In some cases mentoring over a period is deemed sufficient and the issues surrounding qualified teacher status are passed over. GTTR is a way forward but there is all the frustration of repetition and lack of recognition of the professional development achieved. These problematic areas relating to the equivalence and compatibility of the different qualifications are quite serious and have therefore been the focus of considerable discussion and consultation.

As usual the post-compulsory sector has seen many changes in recent years. Since 2001 it has been a statutory requirement for all new entrants to teaching to train formally and achieve a professional teaching qualification that is FENTO endorsed. For the English system, this is currently governed by the Further Education Teachers' Qualifications (England) Regulations 2001. The key difference between many of these trainees and their counterparts in the school sector is the issue of graduate status since this is not a prerequisite in non-PGCE post-compulsory training. Students for this training come from a diverse range of backgrounds and bring wide experience and qualifications from the service, commercial and industrial sectors.

It follows that there are deficiencies and difficulties in training to appropriate levels through generic courses and this has led to a very individualised set of training programmes whose relevance beyond the post-compulsory context has been underestimated. At the same time the subject or vocational area specialisms do exist and receive support within the sector to varying degrees.

Initial teacher education

Initial teacher education and training must be seen in the context of all teacher training and development. This attitude is increasing as real benefits in terms of school and college improvement are shown to accrue from a continuous and planned institutional approach to individual staff development.

Pre-service, initial teacher training is very well established and in both secondary and post-compulsory versions has developed good quality one-year PGCE training across this age phase. New proposals and initiatives have raised many questions for training and the PCET situation in particular has been occupying minds in the main fora of debate.

What are the requirements of the teaching qualifications framework for PCET?

For those outside the post-compulsory system the current requirements of the teaching qualifications framework may need some explanation. The Department for Education and Skills publication 'Success for All' laid out the government's approach to reform in the post-compulsory sector and raised the bar for teaching and training standards. Once again the agenda combines economic growth and social inclusion.

The requirements demand:

- Teachers must be competent in the subject they will teach possessing either a level 4 qualification (PGCE or Cert. Ed.) or substantial occupational experience along with other qualifications.
- Teachers are expected to have or be working towards an approved teaching qualification – either an endorsed level 4 teacher-training qualification or a schools teaching qualification with QTS.
- The detail behind this specifies that for those who have been in post continuously since 1 September 2001 and already possess this qualification there may be a requirement to participate in some professional development in order to ensure familiarity with current standards.
- For the areas of literacy, numeracy and ESOL, there is a requirement to have or be working towards an LLUK/FENTO endorsed level 4 subject specialist award.

We can see here the emergence of a new externally imposed rigour on a previously flexible and self-managed sector. The most striking feature of this and a concern for many is the subject-qualification emphasis. This suggests much greater future convergence with schools.

How are NQTs who work across the phase to receive appropriate support and guidance?

The DfES Standards Unit is currently focusing considerable attention on Initial Teacher Education in the Learning and Skills sector. The aim is to ensure that trainee teachers are given adequate support and mentoring to work with the younger, 14–16 learners. Along with FENTO (SVUK) and LLUK the Standards Unit is developing more appropriate guidelines for provision.

Standards and requirements for QTS cover the 14–19 agenda as it applies to schools. It will, of course, be the responsibility of Ofsted to monitor the performance of ITT providers and trainees.

All new training provision for this phase must be coherent and build on the national strategies for primary and Key Stage 3. The aim is to ensure that NQTs who enter schools:

- Are aware of arrangements for progression through the 14–19 phase in school, college and work-based settings
- Are familiar with Key Skills as specified by the QCA and the National Qualifications Framework
- Know the progression within and from their own subject and the range of qualifications to which their subject contributes
- Understand how courses are combined in students' curricula

Clearly, there are positive central moves affecting both sectors – schools, and learning and skills – but the historic separations still leave a great deal of work to be done to provide more coherent and flexible initial training. These do not go nearly far enough.

For all the difficulties inherent in the dual qualification and phase specific training, and these are indeed being encountered and overcome at present, there are huge advantages in developing training that takes place in relevant contexts and with teams of people working in partnership across the phase. Trainees should not just be learning the theory and practice of existing arrangements, but be exposed to innovative and constructive ways of working with learners in this phase to engage and inspire them.

GTTR

In schools the GTTR scheme established as a work-based route into the profession has proved very successful. Those schools who have bought into this training approach have, on the whole, been satisfied and the progression rates have been good. There are some immediate apparent advantages which explain the perhaps surprising success of this route. In terms of efficiency the school gains a new member of staff who learns on the job, absorbing the school culture and becoming a member of teams without having to lose the time that would be spent at the HEI on a more traditional education faculty-based course. The attraction for students is the direct entry into work with salary and, often, the opportunity for a more permanent post. The training bursaries cannot compete and both school and student appear to be drawn to the control and access provided by this arrangement.

CPD

Continuing Professional Development (CPD) is a very wide term used to mean almost any activity that supports and improves the effectiveness, knowledge and understanding of teachers and lecturers.

CPD for post-compulsory

These issues are not exclusive to the 14–19 phase and there is increasing awareness of the more general need to progress continuing professional development in a more open way. Increasing numbers of teachers who have entered the field in one subject or phase find themselves extending their expertise and moving to work in other learning contexts. Learning support staff of all kinds now benefit from opportunities to build on their technical or other skills and to enter education environments as teachers. This is particularly relevant to the vocational areas where the desirable expertise cannot always be found in existing subject specialist teachers. Increasingly, the development of an ability to work flexibly across a range of contexts is required by professionals

CPD for schools

The elements currently established and operating to high standards in secondary schools include probationary periods, development customised for the NQT, higher-level qualifications, meeting specific school and sector development needs, and career development and progression. The best way to illustrate the role of CPD in 14–19 in the current climate is through the experiences of individual schools. Some have used their partnership links and the expertise of college and work-based training providers to support and develop existing staff, and on a reciprocal basis experienced school teachers have been sharing advice and expertise with colleagues in colleges. All those involved in the examples visited felt very strongly that the process had been positive but too limited and too reactive. This should not be a troubleshooting exercise but a planned and formally accredited process with the expertise and evidence gained being disseminated as widely as possible. The hope is that new modules for the phase will reflect and utilise best practice and that time and credit will be attached to the work of those who participate.

Clearly, the demand for staff development in a rapidly changing field is only partially met at present. Between 'off the peg packages' from the UK and internationally, private trainers, government agency and school, FE and HE home-grown provision there is no broad, joined-up framework. The construction of something more coherent from the existing piecemeal network is an obvious priority.

The funding for this area was provided through ring-fenced DfES grants and specific programmes but will now be made available as part of the local government finance system.

How will the quality and value of training be raised in the Learning and Skills sector?

Institutions have always been able to support staff development and to make some individual decisions but these are often subject to quite rapidly shifting business and policy agendas. As part of the drive to build on the best practice, the government is developing the Institute for Learning as a professional body for the Lifelong Learning sector.

What changes are planned for England?

The Learning and Skills sector Initial Teacher Training plans

Plans for the reform of initial teacher training can be found in the DfES document 'Equipping our Teachers for the Future' (DfES 2004). Publication of this document followed a short period of consultation from November 2003 to February 2004 and it forms the basis for future strategy in this area.

This sector provides learning for about six million people every year. One of the more interesting aspects of the document is the reference to the vision of new partnerships:

> The reforms set out in this document will raise the standard of teacher training across the whole sector. Over time they will result in greater public esteem for teachers, their institutions and their sector; they will help achieve joint working with schools, leading to parity of status and professionalism.
>
> (DfES 2004b)

There is specific reference to the fact that lecturers will be trained and qualified in 'the skills and the subjects they teach at the levels appropriate to their teaching'. This focus on both skills and subject expertise continues to be emphasised in the references to CPD. There is also a real acknowledgement made of the changing work context of the future.

The new LSC sector teacher training embraces all tutors in work-based and community learning and from public- and large private-sector industry teaching and training contexts. The definition of the teacher is being extended to include those involved in increasingly blurred educational contexts.

The key demands and concerns of those involved in delivering learning within the sector have been considered in the production of the proposals but there are also significant pressures from government and industry quarters.

The strategic proposals regarding reform for ITT under LLUK are at this stage simply proposals: 'there are as yet no specific sector changes to report upon' (www.lifelonglearninguk.org). The main changes include:

- Revision of teaching standards by LLUK – spring 2006
- Mentor pilot 2004–2007 with subject-teaching focus
- New legislation in 2007
- New funding to become available for development from April 2005 and for delivery from September 2007
- Full HEI and awarding body courses leading to QTLS (Qualified Teacher Learning and Skills) to be delivered from September 2007
- Systems to register trainee and qualified teachers and to award QTLS to be set up by the Institute for Learning in time for first trainees to register on the passport course in 2007. (DfES 2004b)

How will a new teacher train in the PCET sector?

QTLS

In colleges of FE the situation is very different as the LLUK agenda for change approaches the early phases of implementation. The number of non-graduates currently teaching in the learning and skills sector is very high. In addition to the introduction of the passport award there will be changes to allow newly qualified school teachers to complete their induction year in further-education colleges which meet the required standards.

LLUK has the central role in ITT and, through dialogue with others and as part of the Children's workforce network, will clarify the skills and knowledge to meet the needs of employers in other sectors.

What is the picture across the other three UK countries?

Just as England attempts to increase flexibility, so the other countries in the UK are working in similar directions. They are less committed to the Tomlinson process but are watching with interest as they pursue their own parallel yet independent routes. In Scotland there are primary, secondary and FE teaching qualifications, and all standards are currently the subject of an interim report with a new unit reviewing standards. The intention is to develop closer alignment between school and college provision and to move more 14–16 work into college settings. In Wales, the position is fairly advanced. The approach there has long been that the qualifications of teachers and the response of the education system should reflect real needs within the educational institutions.

This diagram demonstrates the qualification process for all teachers in the learning and skills secto

- all are given initial assessment leading to an individual learning plan
- subject-specific and generic mentors and coaches are provided
- all have to achieve the passport to teaching, except visiting speakers
- those with only a limited teaching role may exit at this stage
- part-time, full-time and fractional teachers, and anyone who wishes to, then starts the full qualification
- teachers exit this stage with a full qualification, Qualified Teacher Learning and Skills, licenc to practise...with a commitment to fulfil annual continuing professional development requirements
- continuing professional development carries on throughout career

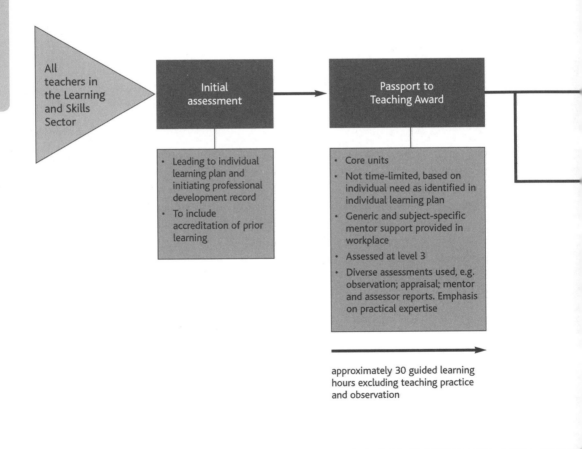

Figure 3.1 Qualification process for all teachers in learning and skills sector

- Core-units
- Level 4
- Qualification delivered in-house or externally; pre-service or in-service; via awarding body or higher education institute
- Contextualised to learning and skills sub-sector, age ranges, etc.
- Large element of practical skills, e.g. observation and other varied assessments

Awarded by Institute for Learning

Full qualification for part-time, full-time and fractional teachers

Qualified teacher learning and skills awarded – full licence to practise

Continuing professional development phase – varied delivery options, annual requirement for all teachers

Exit point for those with limited teaching role

When award is achieved – registered as professionally competent if not required to achieve full qualification. Licensed to practise within specific context.

- Based on option/additional units
- Part of requirement to maintain licence to practise
- Allows contextualisation to:
  - Sub-sectors (further education, work-based learning, adult and community learning)
  - Sub-contexts, e.g. prisons, specific learning difficulties and disabilities, etc. to meet changing requirements
  - Subject-specific aspects, e.g. specialist updating and progression
  - Age ranges, e.g. 14-16
  - Skills for life and other initiatives as they roll out
  - Other, e.g. health and safety, first aid, behaviour management, counselling, etc.

Qualified Teacher Learning and Skills full qualification can be achieved via this route by those who exited following the Passport to Teaching Award.

Ongoing throughout career, reviewed annually by Institute for Learning, based on continuing professional development requirements

ITE case studies

Post-compulsory PGCE student

An increasingly common situation for those working with 14–19 students can be illustrated by the case of the Post-Compulsory PGCE trainee who entered initial teacher training with a BSc and over ten years of industrial experience. His early sense of having a vocation to teach had always been challenged by a lack of confidence and knowledge of the area. He had become involved with training, induction and informal mentoring of adults in his workplace and had taken some courses linked to a college. This influenced his choice of teaching sector and he adapted well to the post-compulsory environment and completed successfully.

During the programme this student was given the opportunity to experience other contexts through a complementary experience, and with raised confidence, increased knowledge and practical skills he was able to undertake work with disaffected young learners 14–16. This encouraged the individual to explore school employment routes and he ended up taking a post in a secondary school with developing links to alternative provision for 14–19-year-olds.

This particular trainee felt that it was the different approaches, attitudes and options he had acquired that provided him with an advantage in such work and he also believed that without the opening in his ITT year to experience school-level working that he would not have be able to straddle the sectors in this way. He would also be very confident to continue to teach in either context and is currently working towards QTS in school.

PGCE 14–19 student

This student teacher entered training on the unique dual-qualification programme leading to the achievement of qualified teacher status in both sectors. The programme enabled the trainee to experience placements in school and FE and to establish contacts in both. Some trainees had an early preference for one context but this individual enjoyed the challenges of both. Initially this student found the programme demanding but, like many others entering teaching with considerable experience of working, was soon rewarded with good responses from professionals, pupils and students. The student completed successfully and progressed by choice to a combination of part-time employment across sectors, including education work outside the school and college context in museum/gallery settings. This enables an artistic career strand to be maintained. The advantages for the individual who wished to keep these elements in their life are apparent but it should also be clear that learners in the 14–19 phase can gain considerable benefit from contact with a teacher who is involved with many relevant areas. This applies to other vocational subjects and is a feature of the special nature of the transition phase.

What happens to the Further Education National Training Organisation (FENTO) and the endorsement of post-compulsory standards?

There will be continuity, and evolution, in this area. LLUK is establishing a wholly owned subsidiary called Standards Verification UK tasked to continue the endorsement and approval work previously done by FENTO. Even as FENTO is absorbed into LLUK it is necessary to consider its impact on the present and future of training for this sector. Its standards for teaching and supporting learning in further education in England and Wales were developed following widespread consultation with managers, staff developers and teachers, and college-based trials in FE. As such they are very specific to their context.

These standards are exclusive to the post-compulsory sector and are very different from the more widely used and understood teaching standards. They were specifically created for the purpose of endorsing training providers' programmes and are not standards to be applied directly to the trainee in the same sense as the teaching standards. When a programme has been endorsed, its programme as a whole, including its own assessment strategy, will have been deemed to satisfy FENTO requirements. The responsibility for trainee achievement lies with the programme.

A further key difference is the nature of the standards themselves. Their purpose is expressed as follows:

- To provide an agreed set of standards that can be used to inform the design of accredited awards for FE teachers, validated within the national framework or by higher-education institutions or other awarding bodies. It is likely that there will be different qualifications to meet a range of possible needs.
- To provide standards that can be used to inform professional development activity within FE.
- To assist institution based activities such as recruitment, appraisal and the identification of training needs.

The chief caveat is as follows: 'It is not the purpose of the standards to prescribe the detailed nature of qualifications for teachers…where standards exist and teachers require accreditation there will need to be an appropriate assessment strategy' (FENTO 2001). The awards are the responsibility of awarding institutions and the standards support and inform this design process. Once again it is worth noting that in Northern Ireland and Scotland separate standards for FE have been developed.

Should teacher education be based on generic skills rather than learning how to teach a specialism?

Among numerous issues and questions raised by the possibility of more integrated training structures is the highly significant area of difference relating to subject focus. It has recently received a great deal of attention yet, in order to consider the real difficulties, it is necessary to deal with some fundamental misconceptions. Teachers in the post-compulsory sector tend not to be broad generalists. The majority actually do possess what could be deemed specialist subjects. The fact that there are many practising teachers in FE colleges and other training contexts who do not have degrees tends to reinforce the belief that specialisms and in-depth subject knowledge are not so prevalent. In fact there are large numbers of very specialised lecturers whose qualifications and industry experience give them equivalent levels of expertise in craft and vocational areas. For some crafts and trades there is no direct route for comparison in spite of the work done on the National Qualifications Framework.

The lecturers who should be part of the solution can in fact be a part of the problem. Questioning the level and suitability of the qualifications and background of individual teachers is a symptom of the move towards greater uniformity and standardisation in the search for what we call professional status. In order to achieve respect and external recognition and in order for one phase to recognise the ability and suitability of another to take responsibility for their learners, proofs are increasingly demanded. So teachers and specifically head teachers are loath to give 14–16-year-olds into the care of lecturers, however interesting and effective the programmes, without a sense of trust in their professional training and codes of practice. These concerns are even more pronounced in situations where the school is the principal provider and is establishing teams to deliver vocational courses.

Generic skills are learned through teaching a specialism. The notion of teaching how to learn is often placed in opposition to that of teaching something. Content and process are opposed, as are: knowledge and skills. Yet in practice teacher education has become increasingly focused over recent years on teaching students and pupils how to learn. Respect for the profession is based on skilful application of knowledge, its provision of appropriate and relevant situations for student growth and development, and its ability to respond to many different types of people and challenging situations.

Diagnostic skills and the experience to plan for learning, which is able to integrate different sets of knowledge and skills so that they make transferable sense, are vital. All these professional elements feature in discussion with experienced and training practitioners. No single dimension approach will ever be a serious option.

Did the Tomlinson proposals point to a need for a single teaching qualification for 14–19?

For many the answer is as complex as the state of provision across the area. They favour some kind of new core and options post-compulsory model, which allows for 14–16 training modules. To ensure that this is practical, compatibility between the training standards and programmes becomes a priority. At present these programmes operate to a very tight time-frame. Time in HEI-based work is limited, as is the placement, and the additional pressure of supplying a range of contexts to provide the necessary variety of experience will only exacerbate this situation. Do we just continue to add more to this one-year full-time course? Do we move towards an extended practice-based model with additional HEI input in subsequent years?

At present both phases are providing established teacher-training routes. Planned reforms will affect both without drawing them together. In terms of review and possible revision of standards, there may well be alignment to allow for a coherent shared set with specialist elements. This approach would be most welcome since it would enable teachers to speak the same standards language. In the meantime, pilot programmes are beginning to deliver cross-phase vocational PGCEs to fulfil the needs generated by 14–19 initiatives and even dual qualification to QTS and FENTO/LLUK standard (see Canterbury Christ Church Dual Qualification and other case studies below). What is required is not necessarily greater prescription but increased flexibility so that given the appropriate experience in a relevant context and an integrated set of courses, learning opportunities and supporting the trainee can develop in any phase whether initially or at a later stage in their career.

Should differences in age affect the inspection of education and care 0–19?

Between 10 February and 8 April 2004 Ofsted sought views on the proposals to change the approach to inspection of education and childcare, as set out in 'The Future of Inspection Consultation Paper'. The majority of responses favoured the changes, with an average of 77 per cent supporting and 9 per cent opposing. Groups approached included parents, teachers, head teachers, pupils/students, LEAs and national organisations. Modification will result from the consultation and pilot inspections will continue this evaluative process. The question relating to consistency across all age ranges produced a supportive response of 97 per cent. The majority of respondents wanted assurance that a consistent inspection model would not be rigorously applied without taking account of the substantive differences in education and care for different age groups. The new short, sharp inspection with a faster reporting regime seemed to be welcomed, as did the frequent light-touch approach designed to run alongside internal self-evaluation and planning.

How is quality assured across the new phase?

Government commitment to a coherent 14–19 phase can be clearly seen in the design of the 14–19 area inspections. These were introduced as early as October 1999 and originally covered 16–19 learning in phases 1 and 2 of Excellence in Cities areas. In March 2003 Area Inspections were extended to cover 14–19 learning and were rolled out to other areas in England. They cover collaboration, strategic planning, quality, coverage and cost-effectiveness of learning and training, and identify the action needed in order to improve learner opportunity and success.

How is 14–19 area provision inspected?

The Learning and Skills Act 2000 set out the statutory basis for the inspection of all provision of non-higher education and training made by LEAs, local LSCs and their partners in each area. Ofsted, as the lead body, and the Adult Learning Inspectorate (ALI) under the Common Inspection Framework, carry out these inspections under section 65 of the Act. An Area Inspection is an assessment of the quality of provision for education and training for 14–19-year-olds in an area, normally within the boundaries of a single local LSC. Some inspections may cross boundaries to take account of geographical and economic factors affecting provision. By the end of 2006 inspections will be completed in at least a part of each local LSC area.

The following factors are used to make the area choices:

- Whether a local LSC area is a 14–19 pathfinder
- Whether an LEA area is an Excellence in Cities phase 3 area
- Whether there are weaknesses in provision as identified by other inspections, including those of institutions and training provision

In order to 'join up' inspection information more effectively and to minimise the impact on area providers, there will be careful co-ordination in the planning process to take account of other inspections (LEA, college, Connexions Partnerships and thematic surveys).

Inspection takes the following form:

- An analysis of all recent inspection reports and documents and the Self Evaluation Report submitted jointly by the LEA and local LSC.
- Preparation meeting between Inspection Team leaders and the appropriate Authority and Council representatives.
- Inspection week with sampling of schools, college, pupil referral units, training providers and providers of voluntary provision. While there is not normally any direct observation of teaching and learning, there are meetings with learners, teachers, principals and heads, and managers are consulted, as well as other stakeholders from employment, families, the local authority and the community.

The final published report includes judgements and grades against each of the headings or aspects identified in the evaluation schedule of the framework:

- Strategy for education and training 14–19 in the area
- Achievement
- Access to and participation in education and training
- Guidance and support
- Leadership and management

Reporting is on the basis of how effective and efficient the provision is across the area in meeting the needs of learners, employers and the community. Re-inspection will result if the provision is judged to be unsatisfactory (three-year-period).

What are the broad findings emerging from early quality inspection?

The findings should support and inform local and national strategy by providing objective consideration of current arrangements for the full 14–19 phase. There have been 52 16–19 Area Inspections and 15 14–19 Area Inspections completed and published. Of the latter, four were graded unsatisfactory and will be re-inspected and one graded weak will also be re-inspected. This total represents 31 LSC areas, just under half of LEA areas.

What weaknesses and strengths are being identified to date?

Common weaknesses included:

- Lack of clear 14–19 strategy
- Weak work-based learning
- Insufficient level 1 and 2 provision
- Some instances of weak sixth-form curriculum offer and cost effectiveness

Strengths included:

- Increased joint planning between LLSC and LEAs
- Positive impact of IFP and some effective local collaboration

In general the new framework is overwhelmingly supported, with all stakeholders who have undergone Area Inspection being in favour of the process. One concern was the link between Strategic Area Review and Area Inspection and therefore the potential for duplication inherent in the twin approach.

The LSC National Office draws together key findings in an annual report and has found that while, on the whole, action plans were being effectively implemented, there had been far too little progress made on Work-based Learning, VfM issues, post-16 provision at levels 1 and 2 and in reducing the not-in-education or training (NEET) figures. The current 14–19 Area Inspection programme will continue separately until December 2005, when joint area reviews are due to be introduced as a result of the Green Paper 'Every Child Matters'. As guidance, the DfES has published the document 'DfES Advice on Post Area Inspection Action Planning' to support local stakeholders. In addition there is the LSC National Office 'Advice and Guidance for Area Inspections' and the Ofsted 'Area Inspection Framework'.

What is the Ofsted view of vocational education?

In their reporting on Vocational GCSE and A levels Ofsted (2004c), identified a number of weaknesses in the areas of delivery and standards. Some aspects of these were attributed to staffing. It was judged that not enough teachers, especially in schools, had recent and relevant 'industrial experience'. This means that methods, teaching and learning strategies, and structures for providing real work experience and for applying learning to a range of relevant contexts cannot be of an acceptable quality.

They found that many teachers were unsure about the assessment arrangements on vocational courses and lacked confidence in their judgements against the criteria set by the awarding bodies. They reported that key skills were not well integrated in many cases and, perhaps most serious, that vocational courses were often used for lower-attaining pupils, particularly in relation to applied GCSE.

Staffing was a real issue in some subject areas though not in others and there were, as expected, differences between colleges and schools. Where there is already an academic base for a subject within schools, then the staff tend to be adequately qualified and experienced, and the transfer to new courses and modes of working was often seen by school teachers as productive and exciting. Among the examples of this are art and design, science and ICT, though the staff in the last subject often lack up-to-date business or industry experience and knowledge.

In FE colleges, where staff are established in vocational subjects, they are usually adequately qualified and experienced, though the need for updating was an issue in some cases. There were significant weaknesses identified in terms of staff ability to teach their vocational subject to younger 14–19 learners. 'Teaching staff in FE colleges and training providers, in the main, need training to help them improve their capability to engage pupils in the 14–16 age range' (Ofsted 2005: 40). Health and social care, and leisure and tourism were both subject areas where the majority of school staff had little or no specific vocational experience or background and qualification in relevant areas. Neither had professional development time been allowed in the planning. This means that, in spite of enthusiasm and plenty of hard work on the part of many staff, students embarking on these programmes will not experience the best quality provision.

Ofsted has made its own recommendations for teacher training:

- Providing sufficient teachers with appropriate vocational qualifications and experience to teach these courses by:
  - Defining minimum standards of competence for the teaching of each course
  - Training new teachers who are qualified and experienced in vocational subjects
  - Providing resources for existing teachers to update their knowledge, including through work placements as appropriate

These present further questions and issues already raised elsewhere. How do minimum standards relate to QTS standards? What are the implications of training new teachers for recruitment and selection?

What are the inspection implications of this for ITT programmes?

The following questions are high on inspection agendas in the current climate:

- For vocational courses how do they relate to other provision?
- How is the target audience for recruitment to vocational courses determined? (Issues related to recruitment – trainee qualifications and experience)
- Will trainees have opportunities to teach across the full age and ability range, including high ability students/pupils?
- Teaching and learning – will trainees have opportunities to develop an appropriate range of teaching and learning strategies? Will they be able to learn from good practice in schools/colleges?
- How does a provider ensure good coherence between components of the course and contexts where learning takes place?
- Does training provide opportunities for trainees to meet all of the standards?

The above questions give some idea of the focus of inspection. The 14–19 area with its vocational emphasis, is currently being treated to an innovations category-inspection approach. This means that evidence from the inspection of vocational subjects will not contribute to the overall management and Quality Assurance judgements for the provider. The first reports will be unpublished and issued to the provider and the TTA at the end of the inspection.

The emerging role of CPD

It is possible to achieve a great deal within one year but only if this is seen as the basis for subsequent continuing development. As things stand, there is CPD but it lacks a national structure and consistency. Some schools, colleges and staff participate enthusiastically in development at both individual and institutional level, gaining Master's-level qualifications and benefiting from excellent contacts nationally and internationally. Others approach post-qualification development in a piecemeal way and even mentoring for newly qualified or employed teachers and lecturers can be poor.

How should the vocational element be introduced into the training?

In general, FE seems to be the most appropriate location for the majority of vocational education and therefore the natural home for the training in these contexts.

It must be remembered that sharing learners does not guarantee true co-operation in the curriculum. Those involved need to engage in real dialogue and planning in order for vocational learning to be fully integrated for all students.

Without increased trust and communication, both vocational education and teacher training and development will not flourish. A proportion of schools have concerns about the quality of educational experience available in colleges and hesitate to enter long-term or extensive partnerships. Within colleges there is a view that only the weakest students or those with behaviour issues will be sent for vocational options, often as an alternative to exclusion.

There are aspects of the culture in colleges that hold and facilitate learners who have previously been less engaged. These do not have to be the most disaffected of students, nor those who have failed to achieve. They can just be students who have never found reason to become enthusiastic. At 14, the introduction of a vocational area can be the stimulus for renewed active learning and the FE context can contain more school-type pastoral and disciplinary structures than is commonly assumed.

What support is there for the challenges of dealing with work-related learning and the links with careers education and guidance?

A set of recommended learning outcomes for work-related learning has been developed by the QCA. These have been mapped against the learning outcomes in the CEG framework and this has demonstrated the overlap between the two.

The Careers Education Support Programme (a DfES initiative producing web-based learning resources) is developing materials to help improve the coherence of delivery in these curriculum areas and some schools are well down the road of increased integration.

Funding has also been provided to support Advanced Skills Teacher posts and thus the development of other teachers. It is already the case that all teachers have, as an element of their terms and conditions of employment, a responsibility to provide advice and guidance on educational and social matters and on their further education and future careers. The DfES has developed a reference guide for school-based staff to help 14–19-year-olds make good choices.

So who could be recruited to teach in this phase?

Recruitment and selection is a key element and, as always, the success of the trainee and the programme as a whole depends upon the initial advice and guidance and the preliminary stages. Selection of good candidates for the teaching profession who have reached an appropriate stage of experience and commitment and are prepared for the challenges of training in a rewarding yet very demanding environment is crucial to the future of education. But just as adequate resources are vital for the success of this endeavour so they are equally necessary to support those professionals working or wishing to work in the area who are seeking to increase their own knowledge and skills relating to the phase and its evolution.

The consensus of opinion is that vocational teaching, within the phase as much as beyond, requires specialised qualifications and appropriate commercial and industrial experience. Of course this presents immediate and rather obvious problems: the very shortages driving the new initiatives have an impact on high-quality recruitment.

This issue needs to be addressed as a matter of urgency. Potential teachers are currently attracted to the profession through fairly traditional routes boosted by marketing that emphasises conventional subjects and makes no reference to teachers' backgrounds. ITT institutions cannot remedy the dearth of effective marketing and general lack of awareness of the need for specialists in vocational subjects. By working with the local LSC, LSDA and other partners, the HEIs, schools and colleges can begin to address shortages and to match appropriately for individuals, local needs and with resources and partner strengths in mind.

There are many potential recruits who would not conventionally be identified as teacher-training material. The vocational 14–19 teacher may not have considered teaching as a career on the grounds that their degree-subject area or lack of a degree disqualifies them from training to teach this age group. Now that new opportunities are emerging, the strategies to access suitable individuals are also different. Promising sources for non-traditional recruits include business and industry publications, internal marketing within HEIs with a focus on mature students where experience is necessary, and the use of employment and careers channels.

Subject specialism and the 14–19 phase

In this area the training issues become more complex. Some graduates in the vocational subjects will have confidence and the background for the specific qualifications. However, they will not necessarily possess the appropriate skills and expertise in sufficient relevant areas of the school curriculum to contribute across a broad-enough spectrum. There are both Key Stage and subject implications involved here. In order to provide vocational qualifications new to their context, some schools have to deploy staff outside their specialisms or to require some breadth of delivery from the trainee. The Leisure and Tourism area is a particular case in point.

Some teachers in FE are less formally qualified in the subjects they are called upon to teach than their counterparts in schools or higher education. The history, economics and structures of the system have led to this situation. The very issues which the Tomlinson working party is attempting to address have led to this situation. Craft and trade lecturers in many fields can be disadvantaged by the low status of their qualifications and by the lack of value attached to their industry experience by the education sector.

The LLUK's revision of standards due in spring 2006 will involve in 2004 a mentoring pilot with an evaluation completion target of March 2007. This will be followed by national mentoring arrangements. For the 14–19 phase there are some important implications. The aim is to equip teachers with the skills of teaching their own subjects in addition to the skills acquired during the generic training programme.

This will in theory address some of the issues relating to training differences in the school and PCET routes. With a new focus on improving subject expertise the quality deficits identified in some areas would receive attention. It would also move the phases closer in terms of establishing requirements for greater subject-based skills and knowledge. There are, however, many prepared to voice criticism of such attempts. Their objections are based on the definition of subject, the very nature of different kinds of knowledge and skills, and the diversity of teaching contexts encountered by some professionals.

The contention is that teachers in PCET need not be confined within narrow subject disciplines but may teach across a wide range of programmes using flexible skills. Examples of this often focus on those who are engaged in key skills and support areas of the curriculum or whose teaching timetables involve the provision of input into many different areas. However, there is a case to be made for the specialist knowledge required in all these situations in the cause of quality improvement. The literacy, numeracy and ESOL qualifications for teachers are a good example of the movement towards greater subject training as these contain subject elements not present in generic training.

Subject expertise is also seen as increasingly significant in terms of quality improvement on vocational-course delivery. For example, Business Studies specialists with appropriate qualifications at level 4 and above are sought as ideal team members on a wide range of programmes. This does not mean that their subject knowledge is valued over the industry experience of other team members with specific Tourism and Leisure, Media Production or Performing Arts experience. Clearly these trained individuals will have valuable industry-specific and/or degree background more relevant in many ways but the appropriately integrated specialist can contribute to specific units and aspects of a programme. Vocational qualifications are usually designed and delivered by teams, and the concept of a leader and a group being responsible for learning is not at odds with the development of the specialist. In many ways such models support and encourage specialisation through team working.

How can the broader context experience required be achieved?

Ideally the experience would be gained in existing school/college partnerships and be mentored by established and experienced 14–19 professionals. In reality, the training providers are involved with developing placements and supporting the trainee in institutions still in the early stages of partnerships. In some cases the schools and colleges are providing very separate and contrasting experiences, and the HEI acts as the bridge to integrate the professional learning.

How can the necessary standards be gained within the same time-frame?

Existing frameworks for training are very prescriptive and in the early stages of evolving new programmes there is less opportunity for really radical solutions without the risk of compromising the training quality and employment prospects of the trainees involved. High-quality professional training can be achieved within the time, through identification of areas of commonality between the standards and through careful tutoring, mentoring and support. The disadvantages and pressures of working in a less than ideal assessment environment are balanced by the opportunities for learning and enrichment available in the cross-phase contexts.

Mentoring

Always a vital component in teacher training, mentoring has been given more attention and become the focus of more research in recent years.

The roles have evolved rather differently in school and FE. Responsibilities and expectations vary and the range of practice can be quite wide. The guidelines are designed and interpreted with more latitude in some institutions and, in spite of the increasing constraints on practice and the quality-assurance mechanisms, this area is still perceived to be ripe for improvement.

In FE there are specific national issues relating to mentor quality. These are rooted in the conditions prevailing in the sector and in the wider political and economic climate. The specific references to mentoring in 'Equipping our Teachers for the Future' are particularly significant. The aim is to improve teaching quality in both subject and professional terms through high-quality support. Provision of sufficient good mentors cannot be assumed, though with appropriate accreditation and professional reward for mentoring development it should become a key element in an institution's planning for CPD among staff. As in the best training schools, this requires senior management leadership and the provision of adequate resources locally and centrally.

Training models

In advance of the final policy decisions there are several programmes designed to deal more specifically with the initiatives. In particular the vocational GCSEs have produced a strong response from some schools and HEIs in terms of dedicated training courses. The Teacher Training Agency provided considerable support for these and there is useful information emerging from the early pilots.

Canterbury Christ Church programme

The training programme, now in its second year, being piloted and monitored at Canterbury Christ Church provides dual certification. Current movement in the development of common standards should enable trainees to work within a more coherent system. Until new solutions emerge, compromises are inevitable, but the achievements and quality of trainees have led to very promising results.

Working within different contexts is a crucial element of the training. Not only do trainees have to perform within the highly structured school contexts and the constantly changing FE environments but also in conjunction with work-placement providers and as initiators of new partnerships. Every aspect of these situations requires management and those trusted with the responsibility are increasingly accountable. Newly employed trainees have found themselves running innovative new projects and introducing the vocational area programmes. Such a state of affairs is hardly surprising in an employment environment that is currently so driven by supply and demand.

This innovative development is aligned with the principles for future training and teaching approaches espoused in many policy statements. The new, more multi-agency, cross-sector approaches in both child and adult services and the connections between them require professionals prepared for effective working in these environments. Just as the needs of children may be met through working with parents, so the needs of young people in work and life will be met through linked and long-term strategies. Good quality initial training will recognise this through values-based development in a range of relevant contexts.

Evaluation issues

The inspection of the new programmes falls into an innovations category designed to ensure supervision of quality yet to allow reasonable latitude for the developmental stage. Feedback from the TTA is also provided and there is considerable networking as the sectors involved build new partnerships and capitalise on existing strong contacts.

How do we train?

With such a plethora of routes into teaching, another phase seems to some to be an unnecessary complication. New directions in initial and continuing teacher education and development are emphasising the need for greater adaptability, as the training is aimed at producing and enabling new flexible professionals.

But what does this mean in practice for teacher educators? Central to the process is an emphasis on CPD and in particular a form of professional development more structured than a continuation of reflective practice. Proactive networking, continuation of industry contacts, building and continuing to develop vocational skills are all desirable features in promoting adaptability in professionals. The sense that quality training should be about far more than the achievement of minimum levels of competence and the survival of a probationary period is at the heart of the best programmes.

Is full-time training a better option?

The concentration and intensity of the full-time programmes is particularly challenging both for learners and for ITT programme designers. Additional specialisms and rapid change only serve to increase the quantity of material and the difficulties encountered in this field. This type of programme does provide the opportunity to place learners in a range of contexts and this pattern occurs more frequently especially now that particular vocational programmes are being sought for practice purposes. Where there are shortages, the needs of trainees for real experience can perhaps only be met through a mixed placement experience.

While the significant shift from one context to another can and does present serious challenges to some trainees, there are also great advantages in terms of learning perspectives and opportunities. Learners from a great variety of backgrounds and experiences can be observed and encountered in a range of contexts, and the value of the comparative practice in terms of trainee skills development, insight and learning can be great.

Part-time training

The same challenges facing the new teacher or lecturer exist in the sector for numerous working professionals. Those involved in 14–19 work will recognise the usual mixture of interest and suspicion displayed when the subject of crossing the compulsory line first arises. Opinions expressed by the professionals working in this field usually emphasise the need for greater support in terms of staff development and consultation. If qualifying to teach children was made more accessible within PCET contexts, through the growing partnership arrangements, then continuing professional development could potentially meet these needs. Compatibility of existing QTS with QTLS and flexible additional training would improve the lot of many practising teachers and recognise the efforts of participating individuals with appropriate accreditation. As the situation stands at present, both greater breadth and depth are missing from the short intensive training programmes and the existing structure inhibits rather than supports cross-phase teacher development.

Funding for Initial Teacher Education and Training

What are 'golden hello' payments?

These are one-off payments of up to £4,000 available to new teachers in both the school and FE sectors who fulfil the following conditions:

- Must be employed in FE, or HE delivering FE, or non-independent sector specialist college
- Must have minimum of 50 per cent teaching contact time in a shortage subject – mathematics, science, ICT, engineering, construction, English, modern languages, design and technology, literacy, numeracy or ESOL
- Should be qualified in line with attending a course leading to an approved teaching qualification
- Should be in the second year of teaching, having successfully completed the first year
- Must have a permanent or fixed-term contract for at least one term in the second year

The scheme excludes those who are employed by a private teaching agency and this has implications in some areas where these are used extensively. Also excluded are the following institutions: work-based learning providers; adult and community provision; prison education outside the FE sector; dance and drama schools; and University for Industry hubs. The mainstream is receiving the support and the drive is towards establishing a more structured teaching career path for subsequent development. Returners to teaching are also excluded, though part-time and fractional staff can apply.

At the moment this scheme, administered by the local LSCs, is open-ended and provides a means of responding to current shortages.

What is the £6,000 Training Bursary?

From April 2004 the bursary pilot, already extended to the post-compulsory sector, was confirmed until 2005–6. It is available to those on full-time Initial Teacher Training programmes leading to PGCE/Cert. Ed. (FE/PCET) within the pilot scheme administered through 31 teacher-training institutions.

Table 3.1 List of teacher-training institutions implementing the bursary pilot

Birmingham, University of Central England	London University – Institute of Education
Blackpool and Fylde College	Manchester Metropolitan University
Bolton Institute of Higher Education	Northbrook College, Sussex
Brighton University	Norwich City College
Burton College	Nottingham Trent University
Canterbury Christ Church University College	University of Nottingham
Carlisle College	University of Oxford Brookes
University of Central Lancashire	University of Plymouth
Derby University	University of Portsmouth
East Lancashire Institute of Higher Education	Reading College
University of East London	Sheffield Hallam University
University of Exeter	Suffolk College
University of Greenwich	University of Sunderland
University of Huddersfield	University of West of England
Hull College	Wigan and Leigh
	University of Wolverhampton

The scheme is designed to provide an incentive for high-calibre individuals to bring their skills, knowledge and experience into the Lifelong Learning sector. The hope is that this will balance the draw of other work sectors and even of the schools sector, which have to some extent denuded this area of key specialist teachers. In view of the desire to build constructive cross-phase and cross-sector partnerships, such initiatives can only be positive.

What is the RTL scheme?

A further incentive in the shortage area is the Repayment of Teachers' Loans scheme. Newly qualified teachers and lecturers in shortage subjects can be eligible for repayment of student loans. This repayment applies both to first-degree loans and to the period of teacher training, providing these are still outstanding upon first appointment. To qualify, applicants must:

- Take up an appropriate appointment between 1 July 2002 and 30 June 2005
- Be employed to teach a shortage subject for at least 50 per cent of the normal teaching week
- Work full time and be employed within an eligible teaching post for ten years if they are on income contingent loans and five to seven years on mortgage-style loans. (For those working part time, loans are written off pro-rata to the FTE hours taught.)

The shortage subject list is the same as that for the 'golden hello' payment with the addition of Welsh. Once again the move extending this kind of scheme across the school and FE sectors increases parity and helps to create conditions of greater parity in which partnerships are more likely to flourish. This kind of new incentive is additional to existing tuition-fee remission for ITE through LEAs and to student loans.

Where can you teach with the different qualifications?

A teacher with full QTS can obviously teach in schools but what is less understood is that they can transfer this to an FE or post-compulsory setting. A teacher who has gained teaching qualifications specifically within FE is not qualified to teach in school, though, on a small scale, the Graduate Training Programme is quite routinely used as a means of bridging the different sectors. (For exceptions see the Statutory Instrument 2001, No. 2896, section 10a.) In such cases there is a very individual approach taken to existing skills and prior learning and experience. These are accredited through prior-learning assessment, which may be a substantial proportion, portfolio building or continuing professional development. The flexibility of this process has allowed individual schools to fill their shortages more rapidly. However, because the process is flexible and not that widely understood there are often questions and areas of misunderstanding. Not surprisingly, one such area is that of the relationship between the standards applying to each sector.

Designing a 14–19 ITT/CPD programme

Before embarking on the design and development of a training programme or choosing a programme to attend, there are some quality indicators to take into account.

- Awareness of key government policies and initiatives – a detailed understanding of the agenda is vital to ensure a good understanding of the issues and programmes

- Team building to provide an appropriate blend of qualified and experienced staff, mentors and support staff to deliver in a complex range of settings with multiple partners

- Partnership building for learners – ideally the teacher-training partnerships will contain all the stakeholders involved including: schools, colleges, the HEI (including cross-phase collaboration within its structure), LSC representation, employers, other PCET partners and training providers, and careers and guidance representatives

- Facilities and resources for research and evaluation – this can be supported and facilitated by internal HEI structures and externally through the main agencies and bodies (TTA, Standards Unit, LSDA)

- Lead time and resources for planning

- Partnership building among providers and appropriate government agencies – the collaborations between new providers, from the Vocational ITT working group (TTA) to the support and consultation available through UCET and between HEIs, are an invaluable source of advice and constructive criticism

- Identification of good-practice institutions for the provision of high-quality placements for trainees

- Significant investment in mentor training and development is a vital component in assuring quality provision

Conclusion

With the changes introduced through the government's five-year strategy for children and learners and the implications of the skills agenda there are clear signs of a move to locally organised but centrally controlled structures for lifelong learning. Reviews are taking place over 2005–6 which will have an impact on standards, training and approaches to delivery for the 14–19 phase. The sectors are being given new freedom from restrictions in some respects but are subject to closer scrutiny and there is a 'joining up' as the direction is set for the next decade. The teaching profession and the wider workforce require high-quality professional programmes offered in a range of modes and contexts but linked within a coherent framework of standards and founded on the best available research.

New learners and new contexts

This White Paper introduces new opportunities for young people to enjoy new styles of learning and to learn in a different setting. There will be more opportunities for practical, applied learning. There will be more opportunities to learn in a different, often more adult, environment including the potential for a significant experience of the workplace. Equally, there will be a continued focus on improving teaching and learning through the Secondary National Strategy and through the improvements in post-16 teaching supported by the DfES Standards Unit as part of Success for All.

(DfES 2005a)

It seems that the new agenda for this phase brings with it new definitions of the 14–19 learner and learning environment. Certainly, there are those who would wish to see these established. However, for most of the professionals involved there is an acceptance of the same group, same problems but different sets of solutions.

Student selection has always existed in the UK and has principally been a matter of overt state-sponsored elitism. In other parts of the world, it is more tacit and purports to be contest based while remaining effectively class and income driven. Early opportunities often effectively set a person's life chances and, in this respect, the years 11–19 are arguably the most influential of all.

In schools, FE, workplaces and with other training providers there is a new emphasis on innovative curriculum choices and different styles of teaching and learning. In part this is a negative reaction to perceived failures and concerns for the disaffected and disengaged, and for the government's fears for society and the economy, but in part there is a positive agenda promoting high-status vocational education, scholarship, success and 'stretch' for all and new, responsible citizens. Whatever camp you find yourself in, there is work to be done and in terms of party political standpoints there will be funding mechanism distinctions but few major strategy differences.

Profiling the 14–19 learner

For any young person, 16 is a crucial transition point between the compulsory education of their childhood and a more adult world of training, work or being a student preparing for higher education or the world of work. The interesting thing for those who work with learners in this category is that the judgements made at this stage are informed as much by peers, media and other external influences as by the more conventional or formal guidance structures, teachers and parents. Where teachers do figure strongly there is often a sense of real empathy and connection in the relationship with the young person. An inspirational teacher who provides the confidence for a first-generation step into degree study, or an adviser who pursues aspirations with a young person and supplies access to real experience and examples, are the significant factors in personal choice within the system. Without such significant engagement, choices are more usually driven by preconceptions, fears and unquestioned assumptions.

Engaging all young people – how will this be done?

The policies designed to prepare all young people for skilled employment or higher education by the age of 19 are quite ambitious and will alter educational approaches across this phase. The development of these policies is a response to employment-sector needs but also to address the perceived needs and previous failures of the group concerned. Financial problems and the lack of reliable packages are a real problem for many young people. Having identified some of the issues affecting achievement among the 14–19 learners, there are some very practical solutions proposed.

There is a strong message in the policies being developed that we are succeeding in many areas but failing certain vulnerable groups. If new social and economic initiatives are to work as planned they must take account of minorities for whom all previous programmes proved ineffective. The range of curriculum choices and approaches to teaching and learning is now being adapted to meet the perceived needs of twenty-first-century society.

This more supportive agenda is focusing attention on the drive to include and make productive those previously left out of education and successful career paths. The inclusion agenda is apparent in the titles of all the key papers, for example 'Success for All' and 'Every Child Matters'.

For those young people who have been excluded or are in danger of missing opportunities and becoming a burden on society, new initiatives in supported learning and carefully designed programmes are being championed. Foundation and entry-level qualifications meet these learners on their own ground with additional support and guidance in place. Targets have been set to bring all young people into education and training at higher levels over the next ten years.

Before trying to solve the problems of individuals, the groups in question have to be recognised and their needs examined. According to the White Paper (DfES 2005a: 63) there are three main categories:

- students who drop out at least partly because the curriculum, qualifications or learning styles available do not motivate them;

- students whose low achievement may be due to personal problems which have nothing to do with the curriculum or qualifications on offer; and
- students with learning difficulties.

The reform of qualifications cannot be called radical but there are still some significant shifts in approach. Instead of structuring qualifications with assessment of content in mind, there is now far more awareness of the needs of all stakeholders, from learners trying to work their way up a progression ladder to employers trying to make sense of the information it generates.

'Supporting Young People to Achieve: Towards a New Deal for Skills', is a report from the DfES setting out the intentions and the more detailed plans for the implementation of appropriate incentives and support for learners 16–19. The main steps include:

- In order to provide the same level of support for learners in work-based training as those in full-time education, Child Benefit, Income Support and Child Tax Credit will be extended to cover parents and carers of unwaged trainees (those on work-based training who receive the Minimum Training Allowance and do not receive a wage)
- Guidance and information to assist students in navigating their financial entitlements
- There would be additional support to enable those who are 19 to complete courses they have already begun.
- From October 2004 a national minimum wage of £3 per hour will be introduced for 16- and 17-year-olds

The intention is that these measures help the families and individuals concerned but also signal increased commitment to the prospects of these learners. There are students who make considerable sacrifices for their educational achievements and many whose attitudes are poor and whose expectations are low. For all these individuals the extension of financial support and the message relating to their improved status are welcome changes.

While professionals have clearer profiles of many of the learners in question, there are significant groups in the 14–16 age range who may share or be developing the same sets of issues and attitudes in relation to education and training as their near contemporaries. These students require more than the straightforward provision of additional funding and wider community and family strategies, and regeneration projects are intended to target the broad context as well as just the individual's needs.

What exactly is a NEET?

As usual, new initiatives have produced new acronyms and NEET is very popular with politicians. To refer to those 'not in education, employment or training' may appear to provide clarification but the definition and a real grasp of the nature of this group is a little more complex. After all, measures designed to re-engage a learner with social and emotional difficulties would be wholly inappropriate if applied to a person choosing to take a gap year. High-quality information and research is, as always, not easy to find but the effort put into establishing a reliable evidence base before taking action in these areas would be an efficient use of resources.

To some extent there seems to be reasonable data on certain important aspects of this group. One rather cynical explanation for the interest they generate and the information that has been gathered could be deduced from the cost to the taxpayer of the NEETs. The economic and social costs are highlighted in the White Paper but, of course, many professionals will be very aware of the personal costs in the lives of individuals who fail. Many teachers in FE see work with those who have suffered from their membership of this category as a key element in their motivation or vocation as educators. The statistics tell us that in 2003, this label could be applied to approximately 9 per cent of 16–18-year-olds. Only a very small percentage (1 per cent) remain in the cohort long term, i.e. for the full three years, and it is a very diverse group, emphasising the need for careful profiling.

The problems leading to underachievement are being researched and the following risk factors have been identified for the most vulnerable. They are more likely to be in the NEET group if they:

- have low attainment at GCSE
- are from lower socio-economic groups
- were persistent truants in year 11
- are teenage mothers

One of the answers to the complex problems of these young people is early intervention. This preferred approach is reflected in the preventative and proactive emphasis of the policies. Key Stage 3 has received much attention in order to capture the hearts and minds of learners at an earlier stage, to address the skills deficits and to build constructive learning behaviour. Even earlier there is work being done in early years and with families in order to lay better foundations, Sure Start provides an example of some positive practice of this kind.

'Every Child Matters' sets out a range of proposals for promoting the welfare of children and young people. These include the teenage-pregnancy strategy, drug and alcohol abuse reduction programmes and behaviour-support interventions. These should have a considerable impact over time on the 14–19 age group. The strategies being implemented do not only address learning in schools and colleges but outside in the community and their reach is equally wide, addressing as it does issues of wider social import relating to the criminal justice system, youth services and employment. As the work on qualifications has shown, the attention being paid to basics, especially the functional skills so vital both for their own value to the individual and for their impact on the wider ability of the young person to learn.

Advising the 14–19 learner

All the emphasis on choice presupposes learners prepared to make appropriate choices. Even when professionals and others who support learners are adequately trained and informed to give timely and relevant advice and guidance, parents need to be engaged and informed sufficiently to participate fully in the process. The 14–19 age range is a time of upheaval and rapid change for the person. In every significant respect, there are particular social and spiritual issues, emotions and physical changes to endure and enjoy. Unlike the earlier phases of life, pupils and students themselves understand that this last Key Stage will set their course possibly for life, but certainly with the inherent risk that it could make or break a very special, transitional time. Whether they seem to focus or appear disengaged there is little doubt that young people are aware of this as a crucial stage.

Careers education as a specialist area is taking a more central role and the new emphasis on breadth of choice and on the potential early vocational choice only serves to increase its importance. The need for enhanced advice and support has led the DfES to extend the duty on schools to deliver careers education to the younger pupils in years 7 and 8. The result of this should be to produce a set of learners who are better prepared to make informed choices at the critical year 9, Key Stage 4 options point. The new national framework for careers education will cover the 11–19 age range and extends into the post-compulsory sector to continue the consistent and coherent focus on real career management. Existing requirements for a planned programme of careers education throughout the year 9–11 curriculum are designed to enable learners to manage the key decisions. This recognises the need to develop the young person's career-management skills at an earlier stage to ensure their readiness for entering the Key Stage 4 options in a constructive way.

At this stage for years 9–11 the learners should be enabled to:

- Explore the available learning and career opportunities
- Make informed choices about learning and careers options
- Understand how these choices affect their aspirations and long-term plans
- Manage key transition points

New measures to recognise the key role of qualified advisers include:

- Increases in the numbers of careers co-ordinators and teachers gaining recognised careers qualifications
- A national support programme (www.cegnet.co.uk) designed to provide and develop innovative classroom materials for careers education practitioners

Between March and June 2004, the DfES carried out an end-to-end review of careers education and guidance focused on the support provided to 11–19-year-olds to assist with the choices for the new 14–19 phase of education. The review covered the careers education and advice:

- In schools, particularly in Key Stage 3, leading to decisions about learning routes in Key Stage 4 and in Key Stage 4 on post-16 choices
- In both schools and colleges, on post-16 learning and subsequent progression to work, higher education and professional training
- By the Connexions service

The results of this are available in the Youth Green Paper (July 2005).

The Enhancing Learner Choice project is designed in parallel to the restructuring and training programmes as a means to improve the quality of information available to young people. The project was initiated to explore replacement possibilities for the recently revoked Section 50 returns. Many of the 14–19 Area Inspections are highlighting the need for improved information for learners and the latest AoC survey notes that a third of learners felt that the information they had received was not adequate.

The Progress File is a set of interactive materials that has been produced to assist young people in the process of making informed decisions in a more independent way. The file is intended to support transitions through specific skills development in the following areas: recognising and evaluating evidence of achievements; setting goals/targets and planning ways to achieve these; reflecting on progress; and recording and presenting achievement. A Progress File kit has been produced consisting of:

- A working file – hard or e-copy for organising Individual Learning Plans, evidence of learning and development
- A presenter – slim folder for presenting and celebrating achievements
- Five guides – containing information, exercises and examples to support learners of different ages

The demise of Connexions

Having completed its national roll-out and been made available for 13–19-year-olds, Connexions was destined to become a precursor of the new focus on employment in this phase. The independent status of the service made its role even more vital and it was intended to play a key role in supporting the more vulnerable learners at risk of missing opportunities and facing greater barriers to their progress. The Connexions card was available to post-16 learners as an incentive to continuous participation and attainment.

The Connexions Partnerships also provided advice on curriculum design and development to schools, colleges and work-based training providers. This included specialist INSET support to the staff, and while the presence of an impartial and informed adviser was welcomed by many, there were always difficulties in ensuring that this system worked consistently across all contexts. Connexions did support a wide range of young people, including those who had dropped out and those struggling with various disadvantages in their lives. It was conceived in 2001 with a dual remit to provide universal advice to all 13–19-year-olds and to support the progression of those at greatest risk.

The multi-agency approach, successful in some contexts, involving 17 of the youth welfare, counselling and careers-advice providers, was large scale and, by nature, problematic. Yet it has been successful in many respects. For example, by February 2005 there was a cut of 14 per cent in the number of NEETs and much evidence to demonstrate that improvements in specific areas were exceeding this and that young people were gaining speedier access to better-quality impartial advice across the board. The new national database was capable of tracking the progress of 93 per cent of 16–18-year-olds.

In spite of the efforts of large numbers of committed individuals who created, developed and sustained effective working partnerships, the service is being radically altered. The decision appears to have been based on the perception that schools and colleges can deliver better, given the £450 million budget. In the system overhaul connexions will go 'local' and integrate with a range of other support services.

Targets for reducing NEETs may have been exceeded but at the expense of the universal advice services. The National Audit Office reported that there was a shortfall of 50 per cent in the total number of advisers, mainly due to underfunding. Under anticipated new arrangements, 60 per cent of existing Connexions funding will go to new Children's Trusts and 40 per cent directly to schools. However, there will be no new funding and many redundancies, so the picture remains unclear. Professionals hope that the new structures will take prior account of the views and experiences of those involved in what transpired to be this huge experiment.

There is consensus that whatever shape the redesigned service may take it should recognise the pivotal role of key professionals. Trained and well-resourced people who can relate to the individuals, their families and teachers are a vital link in the guidance process. Growing European awareness of the importance of careers services is reflected in high-level statements within the UK but the translation of policy into practice may fall short of the ideal. The president of the Institute of Careers Guidance expressed some of the concerns of professionals awaiting the Green Paper:

> What is the Government's position now on this ministerial resolution that every citizen of an EU member state has a clear entitlement to career guidance? With children's trusts in development and policy on youth support the subject of future consultation, now is not the time to destabilise or destroy existing young people's services.

> (www.tes.co.uk, 25 March 2005)

The learner's voice

The new agendas claim that they will incorporate many opinions and attempt to meet the needs of diverse stakeholders. We need to take care, in all the transformation of systems, to avoid overlooking the learner. New qualifications and frameworks, the relationships between partners and the external requirements for assuring quality, could all conspire to push the learner's independence and control into the background. This would be counter to the stated aims of the new proposals and to ensure against such an outcome it may be wise to apply certain safeguards.

Students should complete and document the individual planning processes in a supported situation where trained guidance is available. Well-meaning and occasional general chats with a career teacher for whom the responsibility is marginal are inadequate to the more complex task of supporting students in this shifting environment.

In spite of the retention of the familiar academic qualifications there is no doubt that the options for pupils at Key Stage 4 are broader. Choices made by 14-year-olds are intended to be preparation for a five-year programme of study and work for the young person. In advance of the planned changes in careers education, all schools are being encouraged to hold a review with each young person at the end of Key Stage 3. Significantly, this should involve the young person's parent or carer and result in an individual learning plan for the 14–19 phase.

All schools are now encouraged to hold reviews with each pupil at the end of Key Stage 3. This should involve the parent/carer and lead to the development of a personal learning plan. This plan in turn enables the professionals, the individual and the family to monitor and review progress in a comprehensive way throughout the 14–19 phase. It should:

- Record progress made during KS3
- Help inform specific choices about the subjects/learning programme they will study during KS4
- Establish broad learning and career goals for the whole 14–19 phase, including identifying wider development activities that the young person might participate in
- Provide the basis for continued monitoring and review of progress during the 14–19 phase

The approach is designed to target learners who had not previously considered further or higher education and whose families had no history of participation in these sectors. The whole individual review and planning approach is supported by the 14–19 Pathfinder's initiative.

How are barriers to wider learning options to be overcome?

This collaboration with parents and others reflects the new wider partnership approach. The aim is to use more specialists across wider areas of both teaching and guidance in order to raise quality. There is also a recognition in this of the need to draw parents and carers into the decision-making and to raise general awareness of available routes into careers and higher education.

The Connexions personal advisers are a key element in the individualised approach. As well as supporting INSET training in provider institutions, they can be called in to assist learners who may not be making adequate progress or who need help to keep on track. The breadth of knowledge introduced by the specialist advisers should extend the choices of learners, especially in relation to out-of-school opportunities. The Connexions service has been relatively successful at retaining and returning learners to education in this age range.

For those most at risk of social exclusion and committing crime, the DfES has created the Positive Activities for Young People programme (PAYP). This aims to divert and develop this group away from anti-social activities and into structured training and work opportunities. Specialist advice is at the heart of this scheme to overcome barriers for disadvantaged students. Further support is being made available through the Neighbourhood Support Fund (NSF). This initiative follows a successful three-year pilot in 40 of the most deprived areas in England. It addresses the problems of those in danger of dropping out or those who have dropped out of mainstream education.

Personal problems

There is no doubt that personal problems are the barrier for many young people. These involve a very wide range of issues and problems.

- Some 10,000 over 16s are classed as 'looked after', as are more than 25,000 10–15-year-olds.
- 17,000 16–19-year-olds are subject to supervision orders, of whom 5,000 are NEET.
- 2,500 are in custodial institutions.
- Teenage pregnancy. Three-quarters of 18-year-old mothers are NEET.
- Research suggests that a significant proportion of the 'long-term' NEET have become disaffected with society and marginalised. This is frequently associated with dysfunctional family relationships, emotional or behavioural difficulties, homelessness, drug or alcohol abuse or criminal activity.

What is Education Maintenance Allowance (EMA) and is it the only financial support?

This allowance of £30 per week, for young people who stay on in education after the statutory leaving age, was made available in England from September 2004.

Students can also achieve bonus payments of £100 if they stay on their course and reach good levels of achievement. In order to qualify for the allowance (paid at three levels: £10, £20 and £30), household income is taken into account. The APB or national assessment and payment body runs the scheme.

There are some disadvantages emerging as professionals working with the allowance system begin to experience difficulties in putting it into practice. Institutions are finding that while attendance might be increased, the motivation of students is not necessarily improved. Some colleges claim that the supervision and administration of the scheme has added to existing workload burdens. The school sector has been slower to profit from the scheme on behalf of their learners.

The EMA is not the only strand of support available for those facing financial constraints to learning. The package includes the EMA, Learner Support Funds, fee remission and the Connexions card. Learner Support Funds contain four funding strands: transport, childcare, residential and general funding. The first two are universal and the last are specialist and discretionary in nature to allow local learning institutions the ability to target the help to meet specific needs. Evaluation of the early pilots has shown they increased participation by 6 per cent and reduced the number of 16-year-olds joining the NEET group by almost 3 per cent.

What will be done in the phase for learners with special educational needs?

The new developments are designed to meet the needs of all young people. This includes those with special educational needs at all levels of ability. These learners are, not surprisingly, among those most at risk of dropping out of education. They are twice as likely to fall into the NEET category as others and 12.5 per cent of the group not in education, employment or training have learning difficulties or disabilities. Many of the 14–19 pathfinders include special schools and these are examining the new opportunities for their young people that may be found within the 14–19 strategy. Work placements with arrangements to support particular learning difficulties are of particular interest.

In this area of work learners can already be disapplied from all or part of the National Curriculum to support a more personalised approach to learning that will meet their needs. Schools are required to work with Connexions and to draw up a plan from year 9 onwards for the transition to post-school life. The SEN Code of Practice and Section 10 of the SEN toolkit give details of this Transition Planning process (http://www.teachernet.gov.uk/). There is a DfES strategy relating to SEN learners entitled 'Removing Barriers to Achievement'. This is aligned to the general strategy for the phase and describes the links expected between the two aspects of learner development in this age phase.

More fundamentally, the qualifications offer has been designed with all categories of learner in mind. The new level 1 Diploma allows for those who can only achieve in this range initially but provides clear progression and support opportunities through the structures common to all Diplomas. In addition, the identification of a clearly defined functional core for KS4 will ensure that fewer young people slip through the basic skills net. Students who do not achieve level 2 are entitled to continue to study functional English and mathematics post-16.

Entry-level qualifications and the development of a framework of provision below level 2 for inclusion in the new Framework for Achievement will contribute to a more coherent qualifications ladder for these students. 'Bite-sized' qualification units will allow for customised programmes in an SEN context and support inclusion.

A great deal of work is being done to promote and support improved transition by many bodies, including the Strategy Unit and the Learning Disability Partnership Boards. The LSC is also very active in the area as it seeks to improve the life skills and achievements of this group. They have undertaken a strategic review of planning and funding post-16 provision for learners with learning difficulties which aims to improve quality, availability and cost effectiveness. The Learning Disability Task Force is currently reporting their recommendations for the creation of employment opportunities.

Aim higher

This is a national unified outreach programme merged (since August 2004) with the HEFC/LSC-funded Partnerships for Progression to provide an intensive support focus in the most disadvantaged areas. The programme has been central to progressing the government target of 50 per cent participation of 18–30-year-olds in HE by 2010. It lays foundations among younger learners to encourage raised aspirations and awareness of sources of information and advice to fulfil potential as they progress through the reformed system. Schools, colleges and universities are all involved in activities such as summer schools, visits and mentoring schemes.

Youth services

New learners will be seen in a broader sense and communication with them should be far more integrated. They will be accessed in both formal and informal contexts to improve the contact with them. This means that both the statutory-sector LEA provision for youth and the range of voluntary organisations are being involved.

The priority group is 13–19 though youth services can also target the 11–13 and the 19–25 groups. The obvious venues for support include clubs and centres, and youth workers operate in a range of settings in order to engage the socially excluded and the vulnerable in this population. The support in this area has always been aimed at increasing independence, informing choice and reducing the risks by a range of strategies. Additional funding to the tune of £83 million has been made available to the partners in this work for the period 2002–6. It is vital to see the wider perspectives informing new policy and the integration of services is key to this. The breadth of vision is important because learning in formal settings is only a part of the age-phase reforms. The wider agenda involves drawing in other contexts for learning and other professionals in the 14–19 phase.

The 'Transforming Youth Work: Resourcing Excellent Youth Services' (2002) document sets out the expectations for the reformed and integrated service, and emphasis is placed on partnership. Specific funding has been provided from the Transforming Youth Work Development Fund, for the local authority youth services work to meet their responsibilities under the Special Educational Needs Disability Act (SENDA) 2001.

In addition, there has been support for the National Voluntary Youth Organisations and the more widely known links with the Connexions Partnerships, though with the demise of the latter the whole structure will shift. The division between school-based and external support will return and there will be a loss of overt impartiality since the external guidance will not be available to all. There could also be a threat to the more inclusive 'one-stop-shop' practice where all learners were seen to access the same guidance provision.

What is work-related learning for 14–19 learners?

Work-related learning is a term bandied about a great deal in this vocationally driven period. This concept is not restricted to the learners in specific vocational areas but is a broader perspective informing all learning contexts. It covers any planned activity that employs work as a context for learning. In its widest sense this can include skills for employment, learning about work, citizenship and economic awareness, and the applications of the National Curriculum and other subjects to the world of work.

Programmes which could be titled work-related would contain significant proportions of work experience or placement of some kind, careers-related activities and opportunities to build relevant skills, knowledge and attitudes to support them in future working contexts. As the term suggests, the learning does not have to take place within work itself but could, instead, include elements like mini-enterprise and other projects and links to the world of work.

Vocational courses actually promote an area of work and develop a student's ability to enter the industry or sector with an acceptable range of skills, specialist knowledge and understanding and, ideally, some contact with the world of work it represents.

What do new 14–16-year-old learners gain from work-related and work-based learning?

Students' learning experiences vary and the proportion of work-related learning depends on the learner and the context. There are few fixed restrictions about where the learning is achieved and it could take place right across the curriculum. Some students have the WRL built into their subject learning, PSHE and citizenship with careers education and some additional work experience. This could mean extensive time spent in an FE college or with a training provider or employer.

Learners should gain a range of learning benefits from contact with personnel in different roles to the practice and development of skills in a variety of contexts. These include:

- Enterprise skills
- Employer expectations regarding skills and attributes
- Career opportunities
- Real experience of the workplace, e.g. demands, rewards, team working
- Knowledge regarding wider business function and contexts
- Responsibility and increased maturity to prepare the individual for work roles

Is it welcomed by teachers?

The above is the kind of wish list usually attached to work-related learning. It covers the skills, attributes and opportunities mentioned repeatedly in consultations and discussions surrounding proposed reform. It is welcomed as a means to motivate all learners and, specifically, to re-engage the disaffected. The approach most teachers favour is that more immediate opportunities to apply skills and knowledge and the contact with role models and real-world examples of the relevance of their education will be very powerful.

While few teachers argue that the acquisition of these work-related learning benefits is negative, there are those who believe that to focus so exclusively on work-related and enterprise learning and on its contexts will be detrimental to young learners in the long term. The 'common sense' and relevance to work agenda so apparent in the aims and objectives of this new learning is criticised for what it excludes rather than what it includes.

What problems will new learners and providers encounter in real workplaces?

One of the major challenges presented by the new definitions in the 14–19 phase is the need to address the concerns of professionals and employers about the nature and robustness of the arrangements governing learners in new contexts. In the broadest sense these problems, raised by teachers, employers and parents fall into a number of categories:

- Staff training
- Supervision
- Health and safety
- Parental consent and involvement
- The danger of exploitation of young people working
- Tensions between learner interests and employer interests

One very significant issue which questions the very principles driving the strategy relates to the suitability of the workplace for the immature individual. Those who disagree with the whole approach claim that although learning does take place at work it is only a safe and appropriate environment for those already prepared and more mature. The interest and engagement gained must, according to this view, be offset against the disadvantages and dangers of too early an exposure to real workplaces.

The bottom line in the workplace is inevitably different from that in a school or college and conflict of some kind will be inevitable. Where educational institutions prioritise the learner at all times, the workplace will put other things first: profit, delivery to deadline, product quality, line-management discipline, to name a few. Early exposure to this environment may well have some positive effects but failure within it could be very damaging and even those who extol the virtues of work-based learning most enthusiastically are aware of the potential pitfalls.

Not all these issues have been systematically addressed and they continue to exercise the minds of those currently involved and those who will find themselves in similar situations as the reforms expand. Poor matching of students to placements, weak preparation and planning, and inadequate support will destroy not only individual learner chances but the benefit and reputation of the wider programmes.

How will we cope with new young learners in work-related contexts?

For those involved in the teaching of this phase there are many concerns, especially those relating to legal and work-related context issues. While health, safety, legal and other matters all have potentially serious implications for learners across the phases, the 14–16 learners present new challenges for educators. The requirement to ensure that accurate and current information is fed to parents and guardians at all times is paramount. This includes the need for written consents in advance covering any arrangements made on a child's behalf regarding programme activities.

The 'Increased Flexibility for 14–16-year-olds' programme has emphasised new routes and innovative approaches relevant to work. The DfES found that this triggered concerns from practitioners already committed in the field and those anticipating involvement. In order to address these they have produced a document providing advice for practitioners on legal and other matters. 'Work-related Learning at Key Stage 4' (DfES 2004d) goes some way to answering common questions. However, this is never going to be a simple area of operation and the Department for Education and Skills does refrain from providing absolute guarantees. The document explains that the legal background:

> Is not an authoritative legal interpretation of the provisions of the relevant Acts of Parliament or other regulations: that is exclusively a matter for the Courts. While we have endeavoured to give definitive answers to questions, the answer will often vary according to the circumstances.
>
> (DfES 2004d)

It may be true (see Chapters 5 and 6) that schools or colleges have established experience in handling their traditional learners and learning contexts but the combination of the 'child' and the workplace is distinctly novel and intimidating, even unwelcome, for large numbers of both FE and school professionals. The document is quite detailed and helpful in what is a complicated area. Questions of supervision are uppermost in the minds of those involved in teaching this age group.

'Do pupils of compulsory school age have to be supervised at all times when on college premises and in extended work placements?'

The answer given to this refers to the duty of care responsibilities of the school and to the use of a formal risk-assessment process. It is for the school to negotiate levels of supervision with the provider. The key element in off-school site attendance for the staff involved seems to be one of training. It is interesting to note the impact such a 'requirement' will have on the future training of professionals to teach and supervise in the phase: 'Assessing any risk to the health, safety of all pupils is not a complicated procedure, but does require training' (DfES 2004d).

The guidance goes on to provide a list of factors to be taken into account when making judgements about the appropriate level of supervision. These include maturity of the student, parents' wishes, age, likely behaviour, presence of potentially unsuitable role models having access, inherent risks within the proposed activity and environment, the advantages of independence, and of increasing confidence and motivation through improving self-esteem. 'Where pupils are "in-filled" in FE programmes with pupils over the age of 18, they should be supervised by an "approved adult", in other words, a lecturer or trainer who has been police checked' (DfES 2004d).

Clearly the initial sense that there might be secure guidelines and responses to all concerns is unrealistic. What is provided is rather a distillation of common sense, good procedures, careful communication and professional judgement. Some professionals will be satisfied with this and be prepared to enter or remain in these work-related learning contexts in spite of their risks and because of their advantages. For others, such a qualified and provisional guidance structure will always be insufficient. Perhaps the majority will ask for further elaboration and a more developed set of examples before they are prepared to consolidate links into serious working partnerships. Apart from general supervision and suitability issues there are the specific questions from teachers, parents and others.

What about lunch times and 'non-contact' times when in a college or workplace the trained staff may not be present and others leave the site?

It is easy enough to say that:

> Case law has held that the need for supervision over the lunch period at schools is obvious and accords with standard practice. Any movement away from this standard of supervision, when pupils are studying off-site, would depend on the result of a risk assessment for a particular pupil, or a generic risk-assessment for a number of pupils who fall into the same category.
>
> (DfES 2004d)

An example is given of arranging for a more 'vulnerable pupil' to have lunch provided near a staff area and to remain on site with clear instructions on how to summon help if they feel intimidated.

Reactions from some professionals to this kind of advice are that it is inadequate to the circumstances. If application of the guidelines is too individual then it fails to provide the reassurance and security many require before they will participate in such work. Real take-up and acceptance of new practices and contexts may well depend on the development and deployment of an extended workforce of trained staff and the growth of more fixed codes of practice for the phase.

The emphasis is placed on the highest-quality communication between schools, colleges and other partners. Pupils are the responsibility of their school in the first instance, as they must vouch for the satisfactory assessment of risks. Parental or equivalent permission for off-site lunch or for different lengths of day and for travelling arrangements is always required and especially where the level of supervision is likely to be lower than usually provided in school. This permission and any delegated responsibilities must all be adequately communicated around the partnership.

The levels of organisation and liaison needed to run partnership programmes to a high standard with minimal risks are, in fact, much higher than those involved in more conventional situations.

The following response to a question provides an interesting example of the questioning approach suggested. In the case of alternative start and finish times to the day:

> Q. One college ran a programme from 11am–1pm and 2–4pm. Whose responsibility were the pupils between 9am and 11am?
>
> …irrespective of the context, it is important to ensure that parents and pupils are aware of the difference between the provider 'shifts' and those of the school. Do these pose any significant increase in risk (for example, travel in the dark)? Do all parties agree that all reasonable steps have been taken to reduce or eliminate any risk? Have pupils and parents had the opportunity to suggest a safer alternative? The college has a responsibility for the health and safety of anyone on the college premises, so it will be responsible for a pupil on the premises between 9 and 11am even if they are not in a lecture or involved in an activity
>
> In the end it would be for the courts to decide liability in the event of an accident, but proof of efficient risk-management by the placing school would be valuable as a piece of evidence.
>
> (DfES 2004d)

Is it the responsibility of the college, school or Education Business Partnership (where they are the college placement broker) to ensure that the curriculum offered is within the law?

In the first instance it is the responsibility of the school to ensure that the young person is following a curriculum that meets the Key Stage 4 requirements and, secondly, that the programme attended leads to an external qualification approved for use pre-16. Where this is not the case or it is not on the DfES Section 96 list it should not be started. Sometimes courses are offered that award internal certificates or none at all and, while this is not a barrier, the long-term interests of the learner may not be best served by such a course. EPB brokering should be carefully handled, the head teacher is responsible for approving the 'curriculum' and the EPB should ensure that the school is satisfied that there is compliance in any arrangements they make with a provider. Approved qualifications can be found listed at www.dfes.gov.uk/section /96. The approval categories are:

- Approved for learners aged under 16 and 16–18-year-olds
- Approved for 16–18-year-olds only
- Approved for 18-year-olds only

Normally only qualifications in the NQF are approved and, as described elsewhere, the proposed reforms will be having a significant effect on this situation in future.

Who is generally responsible for health and safety on work placements?

Children on work placements are designated employees for the purpose of health and safety. Either the LEA or the school governing body and the FE college governing body or the employer provider will have responsibility for the health and safety of a pupil on placement and for risk assessment. All those involved must discuss these issues so there is no room for doubt and all agree the arrangements. The bottom line is that responsibility cannot be transferred from the home institution and that there is a great deal of work involved in the checking processes. Institutions and employers should all do whatever they can to control any risk. Employers must inform parents/guardians of pupils of school age of the findings of relevant risk assessments and the control measures to minimise or eliminate any that are significant (Management of Health and Safety at Work Regulations, 1999). This is better provided in writing in case of dispute should an accident or incident occur.

Are there any occupational areas from which pupils are banned for the purposes of work experience?

Yes, not only areas and sites but specific tools, and shift patterns and working hours regulations apply. Some activities would be lawful but inadvisable and it is the responsibility of the placement organiser to make a considered judgement based on available advice. This would include making use of the industry-specific knowledge of the provider. As stated before, the only safe approach is to ensure training for the person approving placements, which would include health and safety training, as well as mentoring by an experienced person, and access to specialist advice. (More details can be found on specific issues in Chapters 5 and 6 on school and PCET.)

Can a student fulfil the requirement with their part-time job?

Part-time work does not fully cover the requirement since the range of experience would not be wide enough, though it can contribute to the overall amount. Good advice for the learner should enable them to put any part-time work to use in their programme.

What is the difference between the school year 10 work experience and the work-related learning?

For most young people their work experience in school consists of a one- or two-week period and is not sufficient, in itself, to fulfil the WRL requirement. The concentrated experience of the world of work is essential to this entitlement. It is intended to be flexible so that it can be adjusted to suit the individual and could include activities such as work shadowing or an extended placement.

Advice and guidance

Clearly, the levels of career guidance, skills and transition-to-work support required as a result of the new phase planning are high. They underline the key importance of these learners to the government's aims for the future. There may be difficulties ahead. In the area of qualifications and training, the commitment to an employment agenda and the signs of enduring ambitions in the realms of social justice are still very evident. One of the strong recommendations of the Working Group was that real reform and choice in learning must be supported by the best possible advice and guidance. This should be impartial and expert advice with access to current information. This particular area of the Working Group's recommendations has been fully accepted and incorporated into policy.

The rationalisation of qualifications will assist in the process of providing clear information. The overall life chances of young learners are being improved through the establishment of a national entitlement to programmes, financial support and advice and guidance at key points to be specified in future plans. The following improvements will support the 14–19 phase:

- Better information about options – through entitlement, qualifications rationalisation, and national and local websites
- Better information from employers about career routes – defining the key elements vital for progression in specific careers
- A better integrated curriculum – containing real connections between subjects and linking the curriculum more closely to the working world
- Early intervention – extending serious advice and guidance work to the start of secondary education in response to the reality that poor choices can be set very early and are then difficult to shift

The whole advice and guidance agenda will rely on wide links with all parties concerned. This includes both parents and young people, and considers the wider 14–19 peer group itself as a source and channel of information. One suggestion is that the new learners in KS4 will share their understanding with the KS3 group.

Teachers should also have access to the best advice and training to enable them to guide well and to liaise appropriately with others.

What kind of skills do new learners need in new contexts?

The role of the individual learner in developing their own personal and learning skills is constantly emphasised and as the skills framework is extended these are being defined and fleshed out. As the QCA completes consultation and brings these into the qualifications framework learners will be able to provide credentials in areas of life and interaction previously outside the formal system. Of course, there have always been personal, character and employment skills references but these are inevitably limited to some extent, and young people with less stable and more volatile education trajectories may be more disadvantaged as formalisation of this area increases. The reach of the skills is extensive and debates surrounding both integration within the curriculum and the impact on learners are bound to continue.

Thinking and learning skills

- Enquiry, includes: asking relevant questions, planning and testing conclusions
- Creative thinking, includes: suggesting hypotheses, imaginatively challenging ideas
- Information processing, includes: locating and classifying information
- Reasoning, includes: explaining opinions, actions and decisions, using deduction
- Evaluation, includes: assessing evidence, judging against criteria and values

Personal skills

- Communication and personal presentation for a range of audiences
- Diligence, reliability and capability to improve, includes: organisation, initiative and willingness to learn
- Working with others, includes: negotiating, awareness of others' needs, leadership
- Moral and ethical awareness, includes: understanding right and wrong, responsibilities to family and community and their own potential

Where does the 14–19 phase begin and end?

Skills for Life links core skills for adults and young people and is designed to address the causes of the skills deficits in a more permanent way. The strengthening of 14–19 education and training should have a great impact on those above and below these age boundaries. The issue of where to draw such lines has naturally been a matter for debate and in the end if the issue is resolved it will be in new flexible approaches as the learners themselves colonise the extended learning environments. The focus on the 14–19 phase will be most creative and successful if it acknowledges existing circumstances, like the significance of part-time working and wider social activities.

What is the effect of the White Paper on thinking and planning in the new phase?

Learners do not have the basics – what is being done?

Doing what interests you and being allowed to develop interests through coming into contact with a wider range of experiences gives new importance to policies for the 14–19 learner of the future. It does not, however, take priority over the achievement of high standards in the basics of functional English and maths, and ultimately other key skills.

The basic skills agenda for all age phases is not just about functional maths and English for survival in life or in employment but for progression in learning. The continued development of the learner from level to level within the education system rests on their grasp of certain fundamentals. Of course it can, and will, be argued that those identified are narrow and too applied. For some, the maths is too focused on the real world of transactions, measurement and problem-solving and too little directed at the principles which may trigger deeper insights in the future or lay the foundations for harder, longer-term explorations.

There is some acknowledgement of these arguments in terms of new requirements setting only the minimum achievement levels to add value and credibility to all qualifications and to enable progress. Few would disagree about the basics as long as the promised flexibility is forthcoming for those whose pace of learning is different. The bone of contention is that by moving the focus to 14 and increasing the pressure to achieve functional skills targets there may be unspecified losses in other areas.

To help with the industrial and commercial needs identified by other areas of government, science and technology are being worked into the new priorities. The addition of science as a compulsory subject at National Curriculum Key Stage 4 is being enhanced by efforts to increase participation post-16. Other subjects, not compulsory, are now entitlements and these include humanities, arts, design and technology, and modern languages. How this will actually unfold in practice, especially if learners are emancipated and enthused to demand real choice and stimulating combinations of options, remains to be seen but the structures are being put in place.

The skills deficit is recognised as a fundamental problem and a part of the DfES strategy involves a multi-agency approach and a long-term focus on training. They are collaborating with the QCA, LSC and SSDA on the drive to improve key skills teaching, assessment and funding. There is already a support programme for teachers and trainers in schools, colleges and among work-based providers that provides training consultancy and materials. Achievement rates have been increasing over the past three years by well over a third.

Key skills, unlike many other qualifications, are available across all post-16 routes in England, Wales and Northern Ireland at levels 1–4. Wider key skills are also available and became accredited qualifications from September 2004. The former (Communication, Application of Number and IT) are assessed through portfolio and external tests and the latter (Working with Others, Improving Own Learning and Performance or Problem Solving) through the portfolio component alone.

The key skills do attract UCAS points and the importance of this kind of functional core for students can be seen throughout the strategies for 14–19. One of the reasons why not all universities recognise the key skills is because they are not available to all and this underlines the need for a more coherent and consistent framework for the phase. Planning for skills acquisition at all levels is designed to equalise and improve opportunity for all.

As early as 1996 the Dearing Review recommended that key skills should be available across both work-based and academic routes and the White Paper (DfES 2005a) seems to be lining up the structures to fulfil this ideal. There are now very specific targets relating to Key Stages 3 and 4, with provision for catch-up and in-built functional skills all aimed at a minimum of level 2 A* to C equivalents in the three core areas as a solid basis for the 16-year-old.

Where does active citizenship fit in all these changes?

It is a subject and yet more than just a subject, and this is evidenced by the cross-disciplinary range of professionals involving themselves in its delivery. It has a high profile in the media and there are naturally exciting ways in which this subject can be portrayed or be seen to be effective, though the potential is a little more controversial. It returns us to more fundamental debate regarding the purpose of education. In the White Paper, this emerges as the following:

> Beyond these subjects, we need to be confident that everyone leaving education is equipped to be an informed, responsible, active citizen. In an ever more complex, interdependent world, where an engaged population is crucial to the health of our society, we continue to put citizenship at its heart too. And we need real confidence that our schools and colleges really do give young people the skills they need for employability for a young person who is not employable has few opportunities in life and for further learning.
>
> (DfES 2005a: 23)

How can there be real difference for the 14–16-year-old group if GCSEs are retained?

This has been identified by some as a real stumbling block in the reforms. The problems and disruption of introducing a completely new set of qualifications may have been avoided but the retention of GCSEs calls into question the claim that the fixed point at 16 will shift. There has always been a certain amount of flexibility in this, with good schools being responsive to early and late developing students' needs, but there are practical issues, so the type and level of the exam and the nature of the course preparation will dictate the end point. Schools have to organise and direct the learning of quite large groups of students and consider all of their needs and offering new choices within older structures may well strain the existing system and present a real challenge.

How will the re-engagement of 'drop-outs' be achieved?

The proportion of NEETs currently produced by the system is still far too high. Nine per cent of the 16–19 age group fall into this category and there is a pressing need to address this for the benefit of both individuals and of society. The longer-term approach involving work with young children and parents is a part of the strategy. Learners are supposed to enjoy their learning and to have a greater sense of ownership and control. The newly configured system is being designed to deliver more choice, more variety and, most importantly, more relevance. However, what really exists will not change rapidly but incrementally and the pressures of accountability can be counter-productive.

According to the plan, the system will be made more accessible, responsive and attractive to young learners through the growth of local consultation and collaboration. All institutions will be expected to participate in the process of implementing reform in a creative and locally appropriate way. In order to ensure that the improvements are executed and reach all the learners in the group to provide a better-quality, consistent educational experience, the inspectorate and funding bodies will be key agents. Schools and colleges will face robust and determined new regimes which will hold them to account on new fronts. These will include the provision of working partnerships and evidence to demonstrate that they are meeting the needs of the new phase as defined in the broadest sense.

The contexts will not just be physical but rather learning contexts judged on the experience of the individual 14–19-year-old in terms of accessing advice, experiencing a workplace environment and being supported in gaining opportunities to stretch their skills and knowledge in an area of talent and interest. It is a tall order and teachers and lecturers are naturally concerned about being held to account for results and satisfactory experiences before they have had sufficient chance to develop the frameworks, staffing and expertise to deliver. Many new strategies are being developed and implemented for supporting those with difficulties and disabilities; for redesigning qualifications so that they are more accessible and comprehensible; for adjusting teaching, learning and all assessment to re-engage learners; and for directing attention to the needs of the individual rather than the requirements of the system.

What is E2E and how does it affect these new learners?

The idea of E2E (Entry to Employment) is that it provides contact with young people who would not be working, training or learning otherwise. It has always been aimed at attracting 16–19-year-olds with lower attainment in education and a higher risk of dropping out. The approaches are specifically designed to remotivate and to appeal to this group in terms of relevance both to the individual's own context and to real employment opportunities.

At present there is no 14–19 element in this, though the need for an equivalent has obviously been recognised. The younger half of this age phase is both more vulnerable and more susceptible to the positive effect of good-quality guidance and examples, so more specific work in this area is long overdue. The main difficulty faced by those involved with these links is that of building and maintaining relationships with employers in spite of the challenges presented by the learners themselves. These young people do not have the necessary skills and their poor behaviour, personal presentation and communication will often be very detrimental not only to their own chances within a scheme but to the scheme as a whole. It takes great dedication from all the partners and robust structures and systems to preserve and develop successful initiatives of this kind.

The lessons learned through E2E will be carried over into a new work-focused programme for those facing serious barriers to re-engagement. (See Chapter 9 for more detail.)

Are these concerns about accountability for new demands in new contexts unfounded?

It is always hard to unite policy and practice, and the current situation is no exception. Much has been promised, including the following assurances:

> The degree of change implied by this agenda is significant. It will be neither a simple nor a short-term task. A key measure of our success will be that we do not, in any way damage public confidence in the education and exam system as we make the changes. It will be equally important that the teachers and others who will be crucial to making the changes work have the support that they need to do so and are not overloaded with change, so that they can continue to offer their best to the young people in their care.
>
> (DfES 2005a)

This sounds very supportive and realistic but to gain real reassurance we will have to wait for implementation.

Conclusion

A new phase label does not deliver new learners but exposure to new contexts and forms of learning will have an effect on those involved. The question remains one of cause and effect. Is it true that the learners have changed and that their expectations and the demands of their future and of society require radical changes to the learning contexts? Or are we attempting to re-engineer society once again, and is this possible?

14–19 in school

According to the recent White Paper 14–19 Education and Skills (DfES 2005a), there is a clear steer for all educational institutions involved with this age phase towards what is termed responsiveness. What this means is accountability for new flexible provision. The proposals in this White Paper, together with the forthcoming Skills White Paper, address our aim of equipping young people and adults with the skills they need to be employable and to achieve success later in life. The two White Papers offer employers the opportunity to contribute to the long-term transformation of vocational education in support of a high-productivity, flexible economy:

> In setting out our long-term course, we send a clear signal that our intention is that the system should be fashioned around the needs of the learner and be responsive to the needs of employers. The job of educational institutions is to ensure, locality by locality, that the full range of programmes is made available to young people.
>
> (DfES 2005a: 11)

The responsibility to provide the range of choices to learners in this age phase could be a heavy one. If development work has not been undertaken and the local relationships are immature then the 14–19 students attending school and college in such an area would be disadvantaged.

The concept of a coherent new 14–19 phase emerged from the school sector's own issues as much as from the demands of employers, higher education and the wider community. The need to address the disaffection of learners who currently drop out and underachieve, combined with the need to interest and engage students of all levels in study and experiences that are relevant to their lives and aspirations, is central to government policy-making in this phase. The White Paper 'Schools – Achieving Success' was built on these components and on the need to develop more vocational opportunities linked to employment and higher education.

Since September 2004, the DfES have been developing what they termed 'a new relationship with schools' designed to build capacity for school improvement by reducing bureaucracy and enabling schools to access support more efficiently without duplicative bidding, planning and accountability systems. The trials involve six secondary schools and will be used to inform emerging policy. Schools have implemented and managed many major policy initiatives over past decades. Recent changes will certainly continue this relentless process as the education system bears the burden for the future economic health of the nation.

What does the government mean by the term 'educated 14-year-old'?

This is a key question for schools as the onus is inescapably placed upon school professionals to produce this individual. The changes demanded from 11–14 are intended to level the playing field for more learners without reducing the prospects of the most able. Strong foundations, the basics and a notion of 'getting everyone to the starting line of the 14–19 phase' are the prerequisites of the reformed system. The following description of the educated 14-year-old is furnished in the White Paper:

> Our vision of educated 14-year-olds is simply expressed. First and foremost, we want them to have achieved high standards in the basics, because without these, we know that young people do not flourish in education, employment or life. Second, we want them to have a broad range of knowledge across a rich curriculum. Third, we want to be confident that every young person has experienced a range of learning opportunities within and outside school. As a result, we want young people to be enthusiastic and expert learners and to continue learning and developing their skills throughout their adult lives.

> (DfES 2005a: 26)

What recognition is there of the successes within the school system?

Significant improvements in the literacy and numeracy results for primary schools provide evidence of a steady rise in standards. International survey evidence for English, maths and science demonstrate good progress and high positions in the trend tables across all three areas. Building on the primary achievements, there have been very positive moves in the secondary system since 1997. From a position where only 45 per cent of young people achieved five or more GCSEs at grade C (or equivalent) or above, the figure is now 53 per cent and rising. Just as important are improvements in test results for 14-year-olds. Key Stage 3 strategy as delivered by schools has proved successful in many respects and this has led to the wider development of strategies to improve skills and to open up the curriculum further in Key Stage 4 to enable individual learners to be more fully engaged.

How will learners be stretched and challenged in Key Stage 3?

All the discussion surrounding the extension of opportunities for the 14–19 phase emphasises the need to work on pace and progression issues. The view is that though

GCSEs are being retained there should be far more flexibility to take these exams early, to skip some or to sit some post-16 in light of individual ability and aptitude. The Key Stage 3 strategy broadened the context for the 14–19 work. It involved motivating, stretching and supporting young people to study and develop at a pace related to abilities later in the 14–19 phase. This 11-19 perspective is widely perceived to be a vital starting point for success in the reform of the phase.

Existing good practice is often quoted and there are a number of initiatives for assessment, special educational needs, and the gifted and talented in place and being developed to support the changes. The Key Stage 3 curriculum is being asked to deliver a number of important policy elements:

- grounding in the basics
- stretch, relevance and interest
- reduction in prescription in the curriculum
- increased breadth
- support for learners who fall behind
- improved coherence in subjects with identified problems
- ensuring that more pupils achieve National Curriculum level 5 in English, maths, science and ICT

Schools will be accountable for all the targets related to this and with the general responsibility for establishing the strong foundations so central to the whole 14–19 reform.

If appropriate choices are to be made in an informed way at 14 years of age, the groundwork has to be put in place years before. This work does not just involve teaching, learning and assessment of basics but a far wider push to enthuse and engage the young learners and provide them with the motivation to continue with their own individual development up to and beyond 19. The target for the age group is that at least 85 per cent of 14-year-olds achieve a minimum of level 5 in English, maths and ICT and 80 per cent in science by 2007. By 2008 the target is for 50 per cent of pupils in all schools to achieve this minimum.

What exactly is meant by the National Curriculum level 5 English and maths achievement?

For English

Pupils should be able to talk and listen confidently in a wide range of contexts, including some that are of a formal nature. Pupils should show understanding of a range of texts, identifying key features, themes, information and characters. Pupils' writing should be varied and interesting, conveying meaning clearly in a range of forms for different readers, using a more formal style where appropriate.

For maths

In order to carry through tasks and solve mathematical problems, pupils should be able to identify and obtain necessary information. They should check their results, considering whether these are sensible. Pupils must add, subtract, multiply and divide with decimals to two places and can calculate fractional or percentage parts of quantities. Pupils must multiply and divide any three-digit number by any two-digit number without a calculator. They must know the rough metric equivalents of imperial units still in daily use. They must make sensible estimates of a range of measures in relation to everyday situations. Detailed descriptions of standards requirements in all subjects can be found on the website www.nc.uk.net.

As a result of the Key Stage 3 National Strategy, Ofsted has reported improvements in teaching and learning. With additional funding this will now become the Secondary National Strategy and provide support for Key Stage 4. The new online test in ICT is scheduled for introduction in 2008 following trials, and inclusion in league tables alongside pupils' maths, English and science results.

What impact will the emphasis on wider skills have on the teaching of individual subjects?

In spite of the importance of the basics the focus is much wider and there is an emphasis on learning and social skills in both Key Stages. The idea behind this is to prepare learners for the demands of learning and working more independently in a range of different situations. There is a perceived need to equip more learners for degree-level study and to furnish all students, as potential employees, with realistic expectations of the workplace and the skills to adapt and flourish there.

The teaching of these wider skills is intended to be an integrated affair; they should be tackled in the context of other curriculum subjects. The richness of the existing curriculum is emphasised in the policy and the claim is that this breadth and subject strength will not be threatened. It is quite difficult for some staff in schools to accept this when they already feel that their subject has insufficient time and suffers from an overly prescriptive approach. Music is one example of an area where, along with other performing arts, the teachers feel that curriculum time is too limited and that real quality is only achieved through extensive work and effort outside the formal curriculum. The enthusiasm and commitment is often given but there is also a sense that there is insufficient remuneration and allowance within the established system.

Where creativity agendas are being publicised it is often the more obvious, media-friendly areas like art and music that receive attention. Once this is switched off, the reality is often less sexy and exciting, and more a very pedestrian struggle to produce results with low levels of resource and time in quite a pressured school environment.

Sport in schools frequently enters the spotlight whenever the nation's health, children's weight, selling off school land or other related items are in the news. On a day-to-day basis the profile of PE in schools is often less healthy and relies, once again, on the dedication and enterprise of energetic staff and parents. These teams and individuals gain sponsorship, put in volunteer time, raise funds themselves and maintain programmes of extra-curricular sporting activity and fixtures. Where the strong infrastructures are missing and schools, homes and communities are less able to compensate, learners simply have fewer opportunities and perform less well.

One of the common elements in these situations is the inflexibility felt in schools. When there are multiple external pressures and demands and a heavy schedule of testing, examinations, inspection and reporting there is a tendency to avoid additional burdens and experimental projects. For some schools this means that art, sports, languages or other subject trips and events are shelved so that they will not impact on other more pressing school business. Sadly this can mean that the stretch, creativity and high-level achievements that such efforts can produce become the exclusive province of the specialist school. These are hard-headed decisions and not lightly taken but they do have an effect on the teaching and learning in the school as a whole and their benefits cannot be simply restored with an entitlement directive.

The PE and School Sport Strategy gives children two hours of sport each week and better access to local sports clubs but it is not welcomed as a strong boost to the subject. It is too little, too late for many. The fact that links to clubs and other external activities are being encouraged is not a guarantee of improvement and will not ensure consistency or support the schools in the areas with greatest challenges.

Subject key concepts and underpinning knowledge are not always well established with learners and the new strategy will address this as part of its objectives. This includes all subjects not just those which are compulsory. RE, Citizenship and PSHE are increasingly seen as instrumental in producing the well-rounded individual or, in this case, the 'educated 14-year-old'.

What is the place of enrichment in future?

Enrichment is an existing element in a complex curriculum and it seems as if there is a trend for today's enrichment to become tomorrow's entitlement. Just as some schools and local areas have been in advance of others with their use of contracts, collaborations and enterprise projects, there are clear signs that the enrichment agenda will see the same kind of evolving effect from informal and voluntary to embedded and compulsory. This can be beneficial and exciting where resources and encouragement support the schools less able to participate, never mind pioneer, but failing this, the cycle of demoralisation can adversely affect those who cannot keep up.

This is not to criticise the excellent endeavours of the high-flying schools, some of which are in severely disadvantaged areas and relying on the extraordinary efforts of staff, pupils and friends in the community to achieve their special results. It is said rather to point out the barriers to wider implementation well known to staff on the ground who understand how local and institutional barriers to the replication of best practice are not always obvious or surmountable in the short term.

The London Pledge is a classic example of voluntary good practice likely to be adopted as obligatory. Through its network of collaborating schools and other partners the capital is able to provide opportunities to learn in the following areas:

- contributing views on London issues;
- recognition of students' early success;
- taking part in a display seen by an audience (sports, music, dance or visual arts);
- experience involving the spoken word;
- residential experience;
- experience of volunteering;
- experience of attending an arts or sports event as part of the audience;
- experience of other languages and cultures;
- experience of seeing a practical project through from beginning to end; and
- experience of cutting-edge science and technology.

So is there a new Key Stage 3?

In spite of the improvements achieved through the National Strategy, especially the Leading in Learning programme, there are weaknesses to be addressed as the new Secondary Strategy takes over. One of the key areas for action is, unsurprisingly, that of curriculum design. The pressures on this cannot be overstated and there is unlikely to be any easing of this situation in a future where the education sector carries responsibility for so many ambitious plans. This means that efficiency and effectiveness, already familiar terms in the marketised world of twenty-first-century education, are being promoted more enthusiastically than before. Across subjects, the attention and criticism of those assuring quality may fall wherever they find unnecessary repetition or an opportunity for application of knowledge that has not been adequately exploited.

One key area is that of additional support, and robust diagnostic testing is vital in the early stages so that appropriate assistance to develop skills and acquire knowledge can be given before a pupil falls too far behind peers. If this kind of serious slippage occurs in pupil progress or needs go unidentified then the support necessary can prove far more costly or ineffective and the school is increasingly accountable.

The Key Stage 3 strategy has been renamed the Secondary National Strategy as some of its work is extended to KS4. In addition to the ICT online test and the Pupil Profile, there are changes to science in response to review. QCA will continue reviewing the KS3 curriculum to explore the quantity and quality issues. Following the Key Stage 4 innovations, the approach to science at Key Stage 3 will also be changed to make it more exciting, conceptual and challenging, and less of a difficult, tedious, fact-learning experience. The removal of the present emphasis on facts and the reliance on highly specified tasks is an objective placed on other subjects apart from science. The idea is not to reduce the time allocated to these subjects but to lessen the burden of content acquisition and the time-consuming elements of assessment in order to free up space for more crossover curricular activities. The justification for the removal of these elements in order to replace what is termed a curriculum that 'sets out a long shopping list of facts to be learnt' with something more relevant is far more controversial. It assumes an increasingly prevalent but not uncontested view of the world in which facts and knowledge are less relevant than skills and experiences.

It is acknowledged that the kinds of changes required to produce this more coherent curriculum will be quite significant. The intention set out in the policy documents is that the outcomes will repay the effort by increasing achievements against targets in the 11–14 group and thus lay an adequate foundation for 14–19. Of many possible models for innovative approaches to curriculum change which have been piloted, one involves the compression of KS3 down to just two years, allowing increased latitude for individual approaches and support from the time released. The question will be whether the elements discarded as duplication or unnecessary padding are genuinely inessential or not. The intention through these and additional pilots is to build on an evidence base and link this with the QCA review as part of the change programme. Weaknesses in assessment were identified by Ofsted. In particular the use of assessment to support the individual needs of learners was considered to be lacking in too many Key Stage 3 learning environments.

How has Key Stage 4 changed?

At the beginning of KS4 there will now be a new set of performance data available in the Pupil Profile for the learner and those responsible for delivery and support to take as a starting point for planning progress. The importance of Key Stage 4 is rightly emphasised and a great deal of work has gone into restructuring the curriculum at this stage to allow for new flexibility. One of the main changes has been the reduction in the number of compulsory subjects, a reform with as many critics as supporters. English, Mathematics, Science and ICT remain compulsory, with the GCSE as the target qualification for each. Careers, Religious and Sex Education are compulsory for all 14–19 students along with Physical Education, and these areas of learning must be integrated to support non-statutory wider personal, social and health education (PSHE) and development of the student. This reduction in the curriculum is designed to create space for the wider options like vocational qualifications and for more personalised learning programmes.

The central focus on the achievement of basics continues beyond 14 as all learners move towards the achievement of a GCSE at grade C or higher (level 2 in the National Qualifications Framework). Learners who have not reached the expected level at 14 will obviously be at some disadvantage and they will be given additional support to catch up and ultimately reach the level 2 target. Mastering functional maths and English means demonstrating the ability to apply them in a range of everyday contexts and where just this element is achieved the young person will have this recognised separately. Where a learner cannot gain the full GCSE, they will be provided with alternatives to be studied alongside KS4, but the ultimate learning goal should be the GCSE (level 2).

ICT

Competence in ICT has a statutory programme of study in the KS4 National Curriculum and this has increased the take-up of GCSE ICT. Many professionals believe that ICT should really be taught within all subjects across the curriculum and this kind of approach will be encouraged within a more flexibly organised curriculum. For the future, a functional skills unit approach similar to that in English and maths will be identified, which builds on the ICT Skills for Life standards and ICT Key Skills qualification. This unit would then be available in its own right and be supported by the KS4 programme.

Entitlements were introduced to ensure that good-quality choices are made available to students. Otherwise the fear was that the so-called 'new flexibility' may become a mere theoretical model with few real options for the majority of students and many practical barriers. These entitlement areas included Arts, Humanities, Design and Technology, and Modern Foreign Languages. The entitlement element requires that a minimum of one course in each area with an approved qualification must be made available. Each learner should be able to access all four areas.

Changes to KS4 Science will be achieved by September 2006 as a result of consultation with the science community. This priority has led to the introduction of a statutory entitlement to science study with an expectation that at least 80 per cent of students will continue to take at least two science GCSEs. The revised science programme has a core of scientific literacy extended with options and links to other subjects. Study of the existing range of academic subjects described above remains in place. The focus on social knowledge and skills is strengthened through increased relevance in the way these are taught, and through citizenship and guidance in the development of personal, thinking and learning skills throughout the curriculum.

Delivering the Diplomas – how can the entitlement requirements be met by schools?

The detail on the new qualification and how it has been designed to interlock with apprenticeships and existing academic and vocational qualifications is dealt with in Chapter 8. Issues of funding and partnership are also very important but there does seem to be realistic acknowledgement of the practical issues raised by requirements for schools to offer wide choice as an entitlement. Specialist schools, FE colleges and other training providers will all be involved and the following statement is a good indication of the practical approach:

This does not, of course, mean that we expect every school and college to offer all of these lines. That would be unrealistic and undeliverable. However, we do expect that each young person will have access to each of the lines within a reasonable distance of home. In every area, providers will ensure that between them they are making a full offer to young people.

(DfES 2005a: 55)

This still leaves questions of definition to be resolved, most glaringly, what is a reasonable distance? The actual operation of tailored timetables, supervision, tracking, liaison over assessment and support provision, transport and costs, procedures when programmes collapse and numerous other issues will require real dedication, staff development and significant government and local support to enable constructive, practical solutions to emerge.

Is there anything new in the Preparation for Society agenda?

For the committed and forward-looking school this section of the new agenda will present no surprises. The definition of the 14-year-old as a pre-adult justifies a focus for education in this phase based on the provision of knowledge and skills considered crucial to living, learning and working in modern society. Some of these are practical and business enterprise focused:

- Financial capability with the use and management of money in adult and working life (ideally integrated with business studies, maths, PSHE, citizenship and careers education, and central to the new functional maths within the maths curriculum)
- Enterprise capability and economic and business understanding (through the Enterprise Education Initiative)

Others are personal or related to citizenship and other aspects of social education:

- Thinking and learning skills, including how to learn independently and adapt to a range of circumstances
- Skills giving the ability to manage self and to develop effective social and working relationships and to deal with real-world problems

Work is currently being done on RE, PE, PSHE, sex education and citizenship to increase the co-ordination of teaching in these subjects. This builds on existing guidance and many schools have very integrated approaches already, so further changes are to be expected. The difficulty may arise from the use of links to reduce subject-specific teaching time in order to create the curriculum space required for other purposes.

How do schools timetable for 14–19?

The question may seem like an oversimplification but it is frequently asked by those tasked with the challenge, and they answer, 'only with difficulty'. Organising to deliver the curriculum is often problematic and always becomes a series of compromises but the new vocational options and soon extensive entitlements for all learners in this age range are already proving very testing. The main experience of the area for most schools to date is with vocational GCSE, GNVQ and AVCE, with perhaps some BTEC work. Inspection feedback on the vocational GCSE work gives a good reflection on the practical issues faced by schools introducing more vocational teaching and learning.

It is most important to focus on the allocation of teaching time as adequate provision of time was identified by inspectors as 'a crucial factor in the success of introduction'. A course like a double award GCSE would normally be taught in 20 per cent of the timetable in school and this does reduce the range of options available. They found that in practice some of the applied subjects really were given this amount of time, for example engineering, manufacturing and applied art and design, and these tended to work better. Where they were timetabled, in a few cases, as single awards additional experience was plugged in with lunch and twilight sessions and a block of time in FE. 'Such provision allows courses to flourish.'

Where subjects are perhaps viewed as less practical and vocational in a different sense there is a tendency to allocate less time (10 per cent being common). The areas that suffered from this were ICT, applied business studies, and leisure and tourism. Of course this reduces the breadth, depth and effectiveness of the courses and can actually eradicate many of the advantages they might have in engaging and stretching learners. The elements dropped from any vocational course when the time is tight will inevitably be visits, longer projects, contact with employment, learner-directed work, and other enrichments and applications. The focus narrows down and preparation for assessment and formal sessions of content input take priority.

The creation of larger blocks of time, half and full days and in some cases full weeks for long projects and perhaps visits abroad (very effective for leisure and tourism and art and design) is difficult for timetablers whose framework has not been adjusted for this kind of provision. The way in which work experience and enterprise activities are organised separately from the new courses in most schools means that the two are not sufficiently linked and the full benefits are lost. For the school the re-organisation of the curriculum across the Key Stages concerned is a challenging operation but a worthwhile long-term investment. The necessary collaboration with FE, work and training centres relies upon careful planning of blocks of time and a certain amount of in-built flexibility, since arrangements with so many individuals and institutions are liable to shift over time. In schools which did not allow for these larger blocks the full range of teaching and learning experience has been affected. Inspectors suggested a sensible review of timetabling structures.

The contact with FE and industry for larger amounts of time is not just about efficient sessions with vocationally experienced teachers or access to specialised work environments or plant and machinery; it is also about the opportunities to become fully immersed in their own and others' activities. Learning can involve shadowing an apprentice so that the school pupil gets the feel of what their own experience might be a couple of years down the line. Equally it may be experiencing the independence of costing, planning and running a trip rather than sitting in a geography room. The timetabler is a key member of staff in the provision of this experience. Unsurprisingly, those with longer-term experience were among the most successful and those schools more committed to this area of work and involved in a wider range of courses and external relationships found that organisation became easier over time.

The networks of relationships and established practices should begin to provide solutions to the many problems.

What assessment issues emerge from new 14–19 work?

Many schools are not in long-term, structured collaborative relationships with training companies, CoVEs and colleges. This means that a single teacher may have to work extremely hard producing materials, organising assessment and struggling with all the requirements of an unfamiliar specification. Even where this is well done, the individual's hard-earned expertise is lost to others in colleges and schools who would certainly have benefited. Where schools have had the advantage of strong and supportive links it has been the assessment that improves and the processes that move students through learning and assessment in a positive and more seamless way which grow and develop.

Specifications are often quite complex and the creation of effective teaching units from these can be a real challenge. One weakness identified by inspectors relating to vocational GCSE was the failure effectively to link the active elements of such courses to the assessment:

> Work experience and enterprise activities can provide an excellent vocational experience related to the GCSE course, but rarely do these contribute to GCSE coursework. In part this is because teachers' interpretations of the course specifications and assessment procedures lead them to believe that it is inappropriate to build such activities into their teaching and assessing of the new courses.
>
> (Ofsted 2005)

The level of readiness among school pupils is also a real issue in the sense that much previous learning and assessment has not prepared them for the forms and processes in place in vocational courses. As the new flexibility is extended, and assuming that we really do get more students mixing options in a creative and individual way, these problems will become even more acute. Students will be taking more responsibility for their learning but they will be facing assessment in very different forms and against diverse types of criteria. There will certainly be a greater need for awareness and responsiveness among teachers.

Colleges help in terms of employer links and, very practically, with writing and sharing vocationally applied assessments, including the professional development of individuals as assessors through the opportunities for comparison that collaboration presents. Naturally enough, schools with longer experience in applied GCSE, GNVQ and those with some real vocational links found the whole process easier, though experienced assistance certainly raises confidence and the quality of practice.

The training courses run by awarding bodies support teachers quite well, perhaps more because of the contacts they provide than for their immediate efficacy. The specialist staff employed by these bodies are often a good source of advice and can refer individuals to others for help. These bodies have also responded to teachers' need for guidance by issuing samples of assessed assignments in courses, by providing some feedback on draft assessments and laying on specific training courses. As time passes, teachers' familiarity with new requirements, external and internal, does naturally improve but there is still an understandable uncertainty regarding aspects like marking criteria and standardisation at each level. There is a tendency among staff new to any course and less secure and experienced in their assessment to read and interpret criteria more literally, and it is only through contact with others in assessment-related activity that the support and development necessary can be achieved.

Quite rightly, teaching and learning are fundamental to the whole process. There are particular issues with course, project and practical assessed-work elements. Issues range from over-generous marking and inappropriate support and intervention to very poor and delayed marking by staff too unsure to feedback in a robust way at an early stage in the course. According to inspectors commenting on the 14–16-year-olds studying for vocational GCSE: 'Some teachers are shelving serious problems [with assessment] for later on in year 11. Unless this is rectified, it is likely that the generally good achievement of many pupils will not be properly realised in their coursework.'

One further serious issue that many schools will need to address is the development of assessment of key functional skills across programmes. If the curriculum is to be more effectively organised, then integration and the reduction of duplication especially through missed assessment opportunities is vital. Assessment and the learner's experience of this aspect of learning as positive, relevant and non-intrusive is an essential component in the re-engagement effort.

What are the challenges for leadership and management in schools?

Most schools have not yet had the opportunity, resources or the need to build and implement a fully coherent, high-quality strategy for partnership, extended learning options and specialised staff development in the new areas. Those who are further down the line in matters relating to the 14–19 phase have often appointed a person with vocational and work related responsibility at a senior level to ensure that change management is effective.

This effectiveness includes taking action on curriculum organisation; timetabling staff, students and all development and learning experiences, including the essential guidance components; communication with all parties involved – parents, staff and pupils; and network building beyond the school not only with local authority, LSC, community links, training providers and employers but with the national support now available. It is very important that there is recognition of the investment in time, effort and expertise required to implement the new policies effectively in schools; in particular, the administrative time needed to support the individualised programmes and to track the students in varied contexts as well as to service the developing external links.

Senior management are well aware of the feelings of staff in relation to the status of vocational work in particular. It is at this level, where individuals have reported feeling coerced and unsupported, left with the low-achieving pupils and expected to work miracles with little extra time or facilities, that the cracks are exposed. Teams are an essential requirement of this kind of innovation and senior-level backing and, perhaps more significantly, interest is often the factor that makes or breaks the new introduction of such programmes. The balance between allowing staff autonomy and space in a new endeavour and remaining in touch with both practical and professional support is tricky yet vital.

Finally, the key role of the leaders and managers of schools will be to push forward the partnerships and configure the system around learners. This might mean that heads and deputies are spending considerable amounts of time outside their own schools but since the idea is to take learning beyond institutions the pressures to work in this way look set to increase. The levers built into the new accountability framework are designed to move all institutions into joined-up and cost-effective operation; insularity will not be rewarded.

What about insurance and responsibility issues for pupils in colleges and on work placement?

A number of these are covered elsewhere (Chapters 4 and 6) but the key principles are fairly clear. Although others must assume levels of responsibility themselves, for example 'in loco parentis' duty for care, the school, in placing a pupil elsewhere, must be sure they have done everything in their power to safeguard the individual and to continue to monitor that this is the case. There are many contexts, situations, persons and even equipment out of bounds in law to those under 18 and the checking is always the school's responsibility, as is the provision of a suitably trained person making placement arrangements.

In terms of insurance cover, schools must check that this is in place. They may wish to take out additional higher-level cover for those studying off site. It is advisable to take advice from an LEA legal adviser and the college or provider should be involved in assessing the situation. Claims on insurance are not that frequent, though it must be remembered that these situations will grow.

Main risks include:

- Injury to the pupil themselves or to others on or off the premises
- Damage to or loss of college or placement property

These risks are higher if:

- Customers are involved
- The pupil is in transit between sites or out on an organised visit
- The pupil is participating in extra-curricular activities at a college.

Some school/college agreements allow for Associate Student status allowing access to college services and facilities. The supervising teacher or person in charge should remain in constant contact and for some this means a pager is used. The area of working is full of potential dangers as well as rewards and to work well, as it often does, careful planning and forethought is required.

(For more advice on disclosure, see Chapter 6.)

How will schools be supported through these changes?

What are being called new flexibilities are an essential preparation for successful 14–19 phase policy implementation. In order to help with the process of introducing change, the following measures are being put in place:

- supporting schools through the National Strategy, so that teachers have the materials they need and the professional development to help them deliver the new curriculum effectively;
- incentivising schools to get more young people to level 5 by 14, through the New Relationship with Schools, through continued publication of performance tables, including value-added information and through the Key Stage 3 targets; and
- incentivising stretch for the most able, both through the New Relationship with Schools and the measures it will introduce to hold schools more fully to account for stretching all young people, and through the work of the National Academy for Gifted and Talented Youth, helping schools to meet the teaching challenges of gifted pupils.

The Secondary National Strategy has a particular focus on support for curriculum organisation in order to help create space for the additional support and enrichment, and to assist schools in adapting current teaching to deliver in a more integrated way. Some schools, both in pilot schemes and outside, are currently experimenting with alternative materials, lesson structures and new rich curriculum approaches designed to improve the teaching of basics, personal and social development, and learning skills.

SIPs (School Improvement Partners) will provide part of the new support for schools to assist in raising achievement and improving progression in specific groups. These may include the highest or lowest 20 per cent or other underperforming pupils identified as being at risk. The National Centre for Excellence in Mathematics Teaching will provide additional school support. All the maths changes will take place in the context of the 'Making Mathematics Count' report (Smith 2004).

Is there support for the new, more personalised learning?

Staff are having to become more skilled in managing a wide variety of programmes and pathways for pupils and in ensuring that learners have relevant and up-to-date careers and study advice for their extended 14–19 choices. From 2005–6, every school will receive guidance covering research evidence and best practice on effective CPD activity. This will provide advice on how to organise in school to deliver the highest-quality personalised learning. It will also advise on the effective use of the Performance Management process to help identify and address the strengths and the training and management needs of teachers.

What is the existing accountability programme?

Key components of the existing accountability framework	
Tests	At 14: External tests in English, maths, science and, from 2008, ICT. From 16–19: External qualifications in most subjects studied.
Tables	The School and College Achievement and Attainment Tables report **At age 14:** ■ the percentage of pupils achieving level 5 in English, maths, science, and, from 2008, ICT; and ■ value added from Key Stage 2 or 3. **At age 16:** ■ the percentage of learners achieving level 2, i.e. 5 or more A*–C GCSE or equivalent; ■ the percentage of learners achieving level 1, i.e. 5 or more A*–G GCSE or equivalent; ■ the percentage of learners achieving at least one entry level qualification; and ■ value added from Key Stage 2 to 4 and from Key Stage 3 to 4. **At age 18:** ■ average A level (or equivalent) point score per student; ■ average point score per examination; and ■ from 2006, value added at level 3.

	We separately publish learner outcomes in FE colleges and work-based learning, including a measure of the number of young people achieving level 2 and level 3 by age 19. Detailed benchmarking data on Success, Retention and Achievement Rates in FE Colleges is published by the LSC.
Targets and plans	Schools set targets for: ■ achievement at Key Stage 3 (statutory target); and ■ achievement at age 16 (statutory target). Schools will produce their Development Plans with the support and challenge of a School Improvement Partner – an experienced education professional. They will identify priority areas for improvement and set targets to do so. FE colleges must set improvement targets in their three-year development plans and agree them with the LSC. A proportion of their funding is conditional on setting and meeting those targets. FE colleges and training providers must set targets for learner success rates. They must meet national floor targets by 2006. Colleges must also set improvement targets for the level of employer engagement in their provision. National PSA targets to increase the proportion of young people achieving level 2 and level 3 define the goals for each part of the education system. We have set targets to: ■ increase the proportion of 19-year-olds who achieve at least level 2 by 3 percentage points between 2004 and 2006; ■ increase that number by a further 2 percentage points between 2006 and 2008; and ■ increase the proportion of young people who achieve level 3.
Inspection	New inspection arrangements are being introduced in schools and colleges from September 2005. These will focus more on evidence from self-evaluation and the robustness of the institution's management. The overall burden of inspection will be cut, and notice periods for schools shortened. However, inspections will be more frequent in weak institutions.

Figure 5.1 Key components of the existing accountability framework

Source: DfES 2005a

In what ways are schools now accountable?

Without taking too negative a view, the issue of accountability is central and contains significant new elements that will inevitably increase the pressure on schools. In the long term we may believe that improvements in learner engagement and achievement, school funding, workforce training and support, and wider social and behavioural benefits will result in a more positive and less pressured role for school professionals, but over the next few years there are new responsibilities and accountabilities to be undertaken.

The White Paper uses the term 'sharp' in the chapter title to describe this accountability framework. This may be pointing more towards a highly focused and fair system rather than a punitive and unforgiving approach, and the language of support, encouragement and incentives used in the following text does perhaps uphold the former interpretation. Schools can only hope that there will indeed be clear information and a great deal of support since so much is being asked of the sector.

It may be true to say that new partnerships are a central element in realising the ambitious vision for learners over the next ten years, but there should perhaps be more emphasis on the school's role in this. This is particularly important in terms of the accountability framework since each learner will be based in an institution with a planned programme and a system of goal setting, monitoring, liaison and tracking, and the reins and therefore the accountability must rest there. While components of a programme may prove successful or unsuccessful and day to day as well as long-term problems will certainly be expected, it will be the actual outcomes and the overall management of this process that must finally submit to scrutiny. The partnership vision is clearly present in the aim expressed that 'the accountability framework and the informed choices of learners should together mobilise and motivate institutions to deliver that vision' (DfES 2005a).

Working together with other institutions will generate advances but will, inevitably, be the source of difficulties. The public accountability will provide transparency and therefore information for parents and students and will draw local authorities, the LSC and the inspectorate into more informed discussions with providers but the process will need to be handled with some sensitivity. The government is reassuring institutions that the changes to the accountability framework relating to the 14–19 phase are not major and will be thoughtfully implemented. There are significant areas of accountability to ensure that:

■ schools make sure that 14-year-olds have secure functional skills and are ready for a range of options

■ functional skills are prioritised throughout the 14–19 phase

■ institutions encourage young people to progress as soon as they are able

■ institutions encourage a culture of staying on and achieving worthwhile qualifications until 19

■ the achievements of all young people are recognised, promoting equality of opportunity, regardless of background

■ all institutions, including 11–16 schools, work towards these goals

In order to gauge the sensitivity of this framework we can examine the published range of levers designed to incentivise those concerned to achieve the desired outcomes. Most of these are familiar and there are no real surprises. The test will be in the interpretation of this set of measures:

- Tests measure the attainment of young people at a specific moment in their learning, usually at the end of a particular phase of learning.

- Achievement and Attainment Tables and school profiles aggregate the test results of a year-group of learners to give a measure of the success of the institutions teaching them.

- Targets are set for individual learners, institutions, groups of institutions and bodies like local authorities and local LSCs.

- Inspection provides a detailed and expert appraisal of how well a provider is meeting the needs of its learners, or the performance of institutions across a whole geographic area.

- Performance management allows teachers and tutors to agree objectives, including for professional development, aligned with the priorities of their institution.

The whole point of the accountability levers as described is to push forward the collaboration of institutions and so extend the choice and quality of provision for learners.

Functional skills are central for all 14–19 learners and the accountability system for schools makes this very clear. This relates to achievement in functional skills and knowledge in English, maths, science and ICT at 14, and to learner access to the full opportunities provided by the 14–19 phase. The School and College Achievement and Attainment Tables report these achievements already and the introduction of Key Stage 3 ICT testing in 2008 will add this information to the existing spread of data. The Pupil Profile from KS3 will be given to the young person and their parents or carers, continuing the whole drive towards increased transparency. In this document the results of the individual will be set in the wider context of local school and national results to provide a full picture for all concerned. This means that schools should include their KS3 results in these profiles which will be available online as a means of demonstrating how the school prepares learners for the 14–19 phase. The results from national tests for English, maths, science and ICT (from 2008) will be available as schools are expected to report on pupil progress from teacher assessment of KS3.

National Curriculum level 5 functional skills will now be considered essential for entry to the 14–19 phase and level 2 (C and above at GCSE in the National Qualifications Framework) as the minimum achievement for the majority at 16. In terms of accountability, the numbers of students achieving this level and the 5 A*–C grades in GCSE (or equivalent qualifications) are measured. This will be changed to extract the number of students achieving Diploma standard, i.e. 5 A*–C grades (or equivalent), including English and maths. The intention is, clearly, to prioritise the functional skills in this 14–16 group.

Schools will be responsible for improving the performance of any underachieving individuals and groups and the value added and other data will provide a tool to assist in this process. The New Relationship with Schools is intended to provide support in this process of improvement as does the support from School

Improvement Partners (SIPs). Schools will be expected to identify the action they are taking to improve the standards of specified groups when they construct their school profile. Tables already contain information on the achievement of learners in approved qualifications and new material will be added as it is developed. Proper recognition will be given to the Diploma and it is interesting to note that the DfES have referred to this as follows: 'We will ensure that the Tables give proper recognition to the achievement of a full Diploma, attaching more weight to that than achieving a mix of unrelated vocational qualifications' (DfES 2005a). It certainly sounds as though, at least within the Tables, there will be additional credit for the work involved in achieving a new Diploma. The Tables also recognise the achievements of 16-year-old learners at level 1 and entry level, and these will soon be extended by the addition of post-16 progression measures. From September 2005 Joint Area Reviews will be introduced to analyse the quality of learning opportunities and the reliability of information, guidance and support on offer.

What happens if a young person achieves GCSEs or AS levels before they are 16?

In such cases their results are 'banked' and counted as part of their year group statistics in the school or colleges tables. The majority of these learners will be on a school roll even if they are attending a substantial number of hours per week in a college or with another training provider. The good news is that by entering early results an institution does not lose out in the Tables. A pilot last year established the practice that, from 2005, the Tables will report learner performance from the end of KS4 rather than from the end of compulsory education. Just as post-16 results are currently reported after two years of advanced study whether the student is 17, 18 or 19, so the KS3 results will be reported after the last of the three tests in maths, English and science, and the KS4 results on completion, regardless of the age of the student.

The current position allows the institution to count the achievements of a young person gaining AS levels by 16 and this is valued at more than A* at GCSE in the overall institution results, so encouraging all concerned to stretch the brightest. Young learners who fall into this category should also be able to progress to HE modules under new arrangements and this may soon be recognised in the post-16 tables.

The development of progression measures based on qualifications and achievement data for the 11–19 group, wherever they are subsequently based, will provide information on the impact of individual schools on the final destinations and achievements of students from their roll. This is a significant development in the accountability stakes, with the usual threats and opportunities attached. It will provide information allowing a subsequent analysis to point the finger at the importance of the earlier educational experience upon later achievements and progression. Obviously such data may be very valuable though it should be subject to careful interpretation.

How will performance tables change?

The School and College Achievement and Attainment Tables were never intended to hinder a 14–19 strategy and are meant to support and incentivise both sectors in the drive to raise standards. Their use for assessing the core will be maintained and, in addition to the knowledge and skills in English, maths and science assessed at 14 through external tests, an equivalent ICT test is being developed. This will take the form of an online assessment with e-marking. The ICT test will be introduced with others from 2008 and is currently being piloted. Schools can already access sample tests in order to help plan and prepare for the additional external assessment. The results will be published along with the others in the Achievement and Attainment Tables.

There are natural concerns about the competitive tendencies encouraged by institution-based performance tables but these remain an essential component in the accountability processes. However, with collaboration in mind concern has been expressed and consultation has taken place about the detrimental effect such reporting might have on the willingness of institutions to share investment and efforts. The issues of removing the barriers within the tables as they are currently structured are being explored further.

What are the new entitlements?

Work-related learning

Work-related learning is now a requirement, though schools can interpret this and determine the exact nature of provision. This means that, unlike a conventional subject, it can be taught across the curriculum in different contexts and environments and delivery can be adapted to suit the needs of the school and the learners. From 2005–6 it will include the funded provision of the Enterprise Education Entitlement to five days of enterprise experience for all Key Stage 4 learners.

The definitions of work-related terms are quite important and there is a whole new vocabulary for the area. In the glossary provided by the DfES the key definitions are as follows:

> Work-related learning is any planned activity that uses work as the context for learning. It can involve learning 'through' work context, 'about' work and working practices, or 'for' work by developing personal attributes and employability skills. The term describes a broad range of activities for learners of all ages and includes awareness of the local and broader economy, applications to work of national curriculum and other subjects, and careers education. It connects learners' understanding of the role of the active citizen with awareness of the economy.
>
> (DfES 2003e)

The science component is reduced and has been updated for implementation from September 2006 when it will become a statutory subject. The more limited core will apply to all students and lead to a range of qualifications including a new single-award GCSE, though the expectation is that most students will study a considerable amount of science and work towards the equivalent of a double-award GCSE.

In addition to these developments, an Enterprise Education Entitlement has made the provision of the equivalent of five days of enterprise experience compulsory from September 2005. As part of the government drive to encourage enterprise culture, schools will be allocated £60 million for enterprise entitlement. This investment follows Howard Davies's review of enterprise and the economy, (http://www.dfes.gov.uk/ebnet), and its aims will focus on the development of enterprise capabilities, including risk management and taking, innovation, creativity, and financial and business understanding. Enterprise Advisers are a key element of the initiative and £16 million has been provided by the LSC to fund this support. Those head teachers using the advisers in up to 1,000 schools will receive help to deliver enterprise education and improve enterprise practice, especially in disadvantaged areas. There is a clearly visible social and economic agenda in this part of the enterprise work with strong links to the pathfinders' work and into other lifelong learning initiatives.

Arts for the 14–19 phase covers media arts, performing arts and the broad art and design area. Design and Technology spans a huge range of courses from engineering and electronics, through hospitality, catering and food technology, to product design and manufacturing. The Humanities entitlement would be met by providing one of the existing National Curriculum subjects of History and Geography. Finally, one course in an official working language of the EU leading to an approved qualification would meet the Modern Foreign Languages entitlement.

In order to guide young learners through the 14–19 phase, the individual learning plans are being developed with a supporting structure of specifically designed information and trained advisers and teaching staff (see Chapter 4). Schools are strongly encouraged to embrace personalised assessment and the development of personal learning. Ofsted report that currently 40 per cent of schools have taken up Assessment for Learning. The goal is for this to be raised to 100 per cent (www.qca.org.uk).

What does this mean for Modern Foreign Languages?

Now that the compulsory subjects at Key Stage 4 have been reduced, there are some concerns about the effect on young people who might have been encouraged to study one or more of the modern foreign languages. As explained, there is still an entitlement to this study for a 14–16-year-old. The National Languages Strategy (December 2002) sets out the DfES commitment to languages in terms of national aims to improve competence in this area. The strategies for teaching languages are shifting so that almost half of all primary schools now offer language learning, and lifelong approaches are also being implemented.

The Centre for Information on Language Teaching (Cilt Language Trends 2004) found that two thirds of children were no longer required to study a language at Key

Stage 4 (since September 2004) as a result of the drop from 57 per cent of state schools where languages were compulsory to only 30 per cent. The survey was based on findings from 800 state and 180 independent schools. The latter remained far more committed to language teaching and learning and 97 per cent made it compulsory to 16 years old.

There is a wide recognition of the poor teaching and learning record in modern languages and a published strategy to address the problems identified. The solution is not necessarily seen to lie in the compulsory study of MFL for all 14–16 learners. The focus has shifted to encouraging the development of interest in learning languages at an earlier age and to provide opportunities to maintain and build on this start. The entitlement will be introduced at Key Stage 2 and continue it through Stage 3 and beyond in the form of increased flexible approaches.

'Languages for All: Languages for Life – A Strategy for England' (December 2002) began the process of moving languages out of the traditional teaching model. Modern foreign languages still retains a position in the curriculum as described but languages for children and for those in post-compulsory education, both areas where the provision has been weak, will be significantly increased.

New recognition scheme

This new voluntary national recognition scheme will allow learners to have their achievements recognised at all stages. Launched in September 2005, it complements the existing national qualification framework and the Common European Framework.

What is the situation with disapplication?

Where delivering the full National Curriculum is not the most appropriate route, disapplication can be considered. Obviously, the new entitlement areas remove the need for disapplication arrangements for Modern Foreign Languages (see Disapplication of the National Curriculum).

E-learning

From Key Stage 4 onwards learners in school are under increasing pressure to extend their ICT learning into a range of situations and applications. The rationale for this progression demonstrates the ambitious nature of expectations. ICT and e-learning:

- Offer the potential for more flexibility in the way the curriculum can be broken down and delivered to match individual needs
- Can open up more flexible progression routes
- Can transform how teaching and learning is delivered 'in the classroom' – livening it up and improving retention and achievement through use of tools like video conferencing and electronic whiteboards

- Can allow distance learning – at the time and place to suit individuals – helping to widen access
- Can strengthen school/college 'management information' (e.g. tracking and sharing of student attainment/assessment/progress reporting)

What is the position of the school sixth form?

Learning 14–19 is not governed by a fixed plan, but underpinned by five key principles:

- High quality
- Distinct 16–19 provision
- Diversity to ensure curriculum breadth
- Learner choice
- Value for money and affordability

With the needs of the learner given central place, institutional demands should be shaped to make allowance for this. The Learning Skills Council is taking the lead in planning all post-16 provision. It works in collaboration with local partners and in wide consultation with stakeholders. The LSC has powers to establish, close or alter sixth-form provision in schools. It is able to propose changes to school sixth forms following an Area Inspection or, and this is an interesting addition, where they can demonstrate they have improved participation, raised standards of provision or broadened the range of opportunities from re-organisation. The Secretary of State retains responsibility for the final decisions.

The small sixth form with a strong local support should not be under any pressure to close. However, in line with the 14–19 strategy they should be considering collaboration with other providers to fulfil requirements to offer choice. Ensuring the diversity of provision for learners and the raising of standards is the role of the school. The relevant documents detailing the LSC procedures relating to proposals in this area are the 'School Organisation Proposals by the Learning and Skills Council Regulations 2003' and 'School Reorganisation Proposals by the Learning and Skills Council Guidance'.

The process relating to schools is as follows;

- LSC publishes a needs analysis
- Publication of preliminary notice – two-month consultation period
- Approval by Young People's Learning Committee
- Publication of Formal Notice – two-month objection period

Since June 2003 successful secondary schools have also been able to make proposals to add a sixth form in addition to LEAs and other stakeholders, and decisions are made by the School Organisation Committee (SOC). Where there are conflicting proposals the Secretary of State will have the final say.

What about under-performing sixth forms?

These will not be closed automatically. There is a central recognition of local problems and specific conditions. Under-performing or weak 16–19 providers will be supported and encouraged to improve. Arrangements exist to inspect and monitor any institutions where quality is weak, which includes school sixth forms, colleges and work-based training providers. If, however, sufficient improvements are not achieved following support and adequate time being allowed, then the LSC will take action and close the provision in the interests of the learners.

Small sixth forms in areas where the population and resources are low should not be disadvantaged by the new arrangements. The rural school sixth form is a prime example of the real advantages of new collaborations. The high-quality but limited range of options on offer could be greatly enhanced for learners if included in a well-managed partnership across a local area.

How will new proposals affect the operation of School Organisation Committees (SOCs)?

SOCs will retain their existing powers regarding inadequate sixth-form proposals on the part of schools. In addition they will have the right to comment on LSC proposals introduced under the 2002 Act. The scope and determination of LSC proposals is very wide and plans must be considered across FE colleges and training providers, as well as schools. This places the work outside the expertise or remit of the SOCs.

How will funding work in the future?

There are some clearer messages emerging on funding:

- For 14–16-year-olds the school is responsible for purchasing provision from others – colleges and training providers
- Along with colleges, schools are obliged to provide the full new entitlements to all the learners on their roll

The 14–19 system is currently supported by two main funding streams with local authorities funding the 14–16 group in schools and the Learning Skills Council funding 16–19-year-olds. The consultation document published recently by the DfES proposes simplifications to the system from 2006 in order to improve stability and address problems recently experienced. Further proposals are in the pipeline as the LSC reviews ways to push more resources into the 14–19 developments at this crucial point.

Further detail on funding for both school and PCET sectors can be found in Chapter 7.

What is 'Building Schools for the Future'?

For schools there is also significant capital investment through the 'Building Schools for the Future' programme. This is a new programme being introduced from 2005–6. It will furnish £2 billion for first-year projects and is designed to improve standards by rebuilding and renewing all secondary schools within 10–15 years from 2005–6. This promise is qualified (as it would be prior to an election) with the words subject to future spending decisions, though the sum has not been affected by the budget. The focus for all this spending is area by area improvement through concentrating resources.

What are the Academies?

Academies are intended to be a new kind of school and can be defined as publicly funded independent schools. Academies are supposed to lead through innovative practice in areas of greatest need in order to promote excellence and address underachievement. The external sponsorship factor and the generous funding have set the academies apart and are intended to signal and to effect real commitment to troubled and failing areas in the sector.

They are not selective schools but may, like maintained schools with a specialism, opt to admit up to 10 per cent of their pupils each year on the basis of their aptitude for this area. The School Standards and Framework Act 1998 allows the following specialisms: design and technology, modern foreign languages, performing and visual arts, and sport. In terms of curriculum there is a wide range of specialisms and combinations which can be used to focus the curriculum, including business and enterprise, engineering, computing and science, as well as those already mentioned. The schools are not bound by the National Curriculum and are free to adopt innovative approaches, though they must carry out Key Stage 4 assessments and offer qualifications within the national framework and submit to inspection by Ofsted. Clearly the ends rather than the means are being prioritised.

The Academies programme locates these all-ability schools in areas of disadvantage where they may replace one or more existing schools or fill a need for a new institution. Strategically, LEAs should be considering their own local need for high-quality provision and proposing new arrangements where appropriate. The key quality measures require that the academies deliver teaching and learning comparable with the best within the maintained sector. They offer a broad and balanced curriculum with a special focus on one or more subject areas, and eventually the expertise should become a key resource for other schools and the wider community.

Individuals, organisations or a group in consortium form can all be sponsors. Some sponsors are businesses, some are faith groups and there is no requirement for the sponsor to have any previous experience of running a school. The sponsor has considerable control over all aspects of the academy from the design of the buildings to the design of the curriculum. They make decisions about the vision, ethos and even the structures for governing and managing the school. This area of operation is one of the most contentious since the sponsor/s appoint the majority of members of the governing body which will run the Academy.

How are they funded?

They are set up as companies limited by guarantee with charitable status. Academies receive three types of funding:

- Initial grants to fund feasibility and establishment costs
- Capital grants for building
- Funding for running costs

The implementation costs cover all the project management, consultancy and set-up costs from partnership announcement to the opening day.

The capital grants require the sponsor to contribute £2 million towards building costs, with the government finding the full remaining balance within the agreed budget. Building may be new build or refurbishment and the decisions relating to this take account of the views of sponsors.

The final funding area, that of running costs, takes the form of a General Annual Grant from the Secretary of State on the basis of the funding formula of the LEA in which it is situated, with an additional allowance for the money which LEAs hold back from maintained schools. This also includes a per pupil allowance in relation to the Academy specialism in the same way as maintained schools. The fact that Academies receive the majority of their funding directly from the government gives them more autonomy over a higher proportion of their budget and this is designed to encourage them to innovate and excel in their area. Academies are also eligible for Standards Fund grant and Leadership Incentive Grant.

Why are City Academies being criticised?

Third-term plans include the establishment of a whole network of these new City Academies across the country as a means of addressing the issues raised by failing schools, poor localised standards and parental disillusionment. These are hugely controversial and have attracted a great deal of criticism from unions and other influential bodies. For just a small investment, business people, religious groups, corporations and others can buy into the education system. The heaviest criticism is reserved for a system which allows massive privileges to the relatively small investor. For example, an Academy may cost hundreds of millions to build and commission and perhaps £45 million per annum to run, yet none of this is paid for by the powerful sponsor. The investor gets to dictate the curriculum, the intake, and the strategy and direction of the school, as well as benefiting from the marketing opportunities provided, but carries none of the ongoing burden of cost and very little of the original capital bill. They may buy in for less than £1 million and even this can be on very easy terms.

The City Academies have been labelled elitist and divisive. Are they just the privatisation of comprehensives resulting in the introduction of a two-tier system which further disadvantages the most vulnerable learners? The Academies were introduced to raise standards and expectations but the results to date have not delivered. Some improvements have occurred but on the whole there are no real gains and some losses, though in view of the extent of the original problems it is perhaps rather early to be too critical. Academies have been subjected to considerable criticism not only on the grounds of early rather disappointing results but also in terms of their financial arrangements.

What are the Specialist Schools?

More than 75 per cent of the secondary schools in England now have Specialist School status. While these maintained English secondary schools teach the full National Curriculum, they give particular attention to a selected specialist subject. On the whole, these schools are wide-ability comprehensive schools specialising in one of the following: arts, business and enterprise, engineering, languages, science, mathematics, computing, sport, technology or humanities.

They have to commit to developing more coherent pathways and collaborations for the 14–19 phase and this includes involvement with industry and local business. They must raise £50,000 of private-sector sponsorship, demonstrate how they will raise overall standards, show how they will increase achievement in specialist standards and work with at least six partner schools to raise standards. For these efforts they receive a one-off grant of £100,000 from the DfES and £129 per pupil in annual recurrent funding, one third of which must be spent helping partner schools. The Specialist School status only lasts for four years, after which new bids must be submitted. At this point, schools which are performing well can bid for a second specialism and receive additional funding of £60 per pupil per year.

Will the role of Specialist Schools alter?

Since all schools will be required to provide increasing amounts of extended vocational provision, the Specialist Schools will be expected to provide vital support in the form of facilities and expertise. As well as being the local centres of expertise, the best of the Specialist Schools will be able to become leading schools with a remit to 'drive forward change' in the school system and to increase vocational provision across an area. They are absolutely crucial to the strategy devised for 14–19. Funding of an additional £30,000 in addition to the £60 per pupil for a second specialism would be paid.

The Specialist Schools will have a key role to play in the improvements to science teaching following the consultations with the science community. The scientific literacy core is emphasised but also the links with other subjects, and this should impact on curriculum re-organisation. Engineering, technology, maths and computing Specialist Schools will be expected to support other schools in raising standards and developing staff.

How can schools fulfil their responsibilities to provide 14–19 learners with their entitlement?

Individual institutions, with support, will be accountable for quality and the extended choices for learners in this phase. Without the capacity to deliver a wide range of the vocational education options or the links with employment-based training, many schools would find this impossible. Support with capacity-building issues and long time-frames have been put in place to recognise the situation. The practical approach from a school point of view may be to offer some vocational and many academic options as part of a new locally organised consortium or federation. Specialist schools and colleges of FE will play a more pivotal role in supporting schools and organising work-related entitlement but they would take advantage of particular strengths in individual schools which match the interests and talents of some of their own learners.

School learners would still be based in school but may spend up to two days per week in another context. The school would purchase provision for vocational routes but also develop its own within the local support structures discussed elsewhere.

Checklist

What should schools be doing in relation to 14–19?

- Auditing and where necessary improving Key Stage 3 to ensure a strong foundation
- Developing the new Key Stage 4 in conjunction with partners rather than in isolation
- Updating to deliver the Secondary National Strategy
- Developing and extending community and business links
- Formalising partnership arrangements with LSC, LEA, colleges and other schools and providers
- Working with partners on high-quality provision of student entitlement in new relevant contexts
- Preparing to become a Specialist School within the five-year planned limit
- Developing the life skills of students in a more integrated way through existing subject teaching
- Building the work-related learning opportunities
- Considering existing and future provision of student enrichment

- Ensuring that support is in place for all learners with clear access arrangements to additional support for those facing more barriers to learning
- Establishing wide, expert advice across the whole range of routes into employment and HE
- Exploring curriculum design to support the efficient incorporation of new demands with existing strengths and learner needs
- Including their KS3 results in the Pupil Profiles and online
- Preparing for all the national test results to be included automatically
- Reporting on the progress from teacher assessment of Key Stage 3
- Being aware of the new accountability for functional skills reflected in the changes to reporting which will in future extract the number of students achieving Diploma standard, i.e. 5 A*–C grades (or equivalent), including English and maths

Is 14 the new 16?

This is a legitimate question, which arises directly because of the emphasis now placed on entry to the 14–19 phase as a significant transition point to final pre-adult training and preparation. Instead of being viewed as a period of freedom for development, testing, errors and study for its own sake, there is a real shift to a more directed approach with clear focus and a programmed set of targets. In order to make a supported transition from KS3 to 4, a pupil will have all their achievements in every subject recorded in a Pupil Profile.

This transition point is indeed being emphasised and the Pupil Profile, intended for parents and pupils, is also an announcement of this. It will highlight strengths and areas for work. As for school or college needs, the Profile will provide information on the all-important foundations for learning. If these are in place then the Profile will testify to the fact and if there are deficits in the basics then the areas for 'catch-up' will be identified in the same way. In addition to the external testing of core subjects, including the introduction of ICT e-assessment, the assessment of foundation subjects is increasing in importance.

The White Paper (DfES 2005a: 33) makes reference to the latest report of the Chief Inspector of Schools and his finding that: 'the use of assessment in meeting individual pupils' needs remains a weakness generally and is unsatisfactory in over a tenth of schools'. Strategies are being sought with which to address this area, including training, development, external moderation and new materials to support the process. The Pupil Profile is a document for the beginning of the new phase which will provide information for providers from schools, colleges, advice and guidance bodies, and training providers so that they can collaborate in the education of the learner.

What are the key issues for schools?

Although a radical reform of education 14–19 would have involved significant work for schools in implementing the changes, there was widespread support for Tomlinson's proposed diploma system and the retention of existing exams has been a real disappointment. City Academies are not generally welcomed and there are fears that they will drain funds and staff from schools and have a detrimental effect on existing state schools. Diversity and greater choice are being promised but the costs may be too high. Tomlinson and others have pointed out that inclusion can suffer when some schools and parents can take advantage of a system based on wider choices but others cannot.

Schools are concerned about the use of unqualified staff and the means by which teachers' workloads might be reduced. They remain concerned about the impact on teachers of potential increases in teacher assessment. The management of pupils in multiple contexts is a serious concern for many staff, especially if the vocational options are mainly used by the lower-achieving students.

Conclusion

Finally, while the delegation of powers and local management have been significantly increased, the level of centralisation in the education system is still high. The control of government departments over teacher and wider workforce training, quality, the curriculum standards and targets of all kinds is greater than ever. For some the lack of influence on the curriculum is unacceptable. As the Key Stage 3 Strategy develops into a Secondary Strategy covering the whole of the 11–16 stage, so the 14–19 phase moves the focus for learners and teachers out into the wider environments of FE/HE and work. With investment, time and support, schools can be central to the process but much depends on the manner in which change is implemented. Schools are accustomed to responding effectively and efficiently to change but consultation, support to develop and sufficient levels of resources are vital to success.

14–19 in post-compulsory education and training

Post-compulsory education and training is an unwieldy label for a complex and diverse sector of education. The only real defining factor was the post-compulsory nature of provision and, as those who work within this shifting world are already well aware, even this has not been an accurate descriptor for some time. Fourteen- and fifteen-year-olds have attended colleges for years in both formal and informal capacities. Often these customers for education have been low achievers, the excluded or unwanted refugees from the school rolls. Yet this is not invariably the case. A minority of younger students has always been enrolled in subjects unavailable in schools and for this reason has used both full- and part-time academic courses.

It has not been uncommon in further and adult education in the past to find occasional 14-year-olds taking evening classes alongside pensioners, or 15-year-olds looking for curriculum flexibility to take law or philosophy or participating in special project groups specifically designed for them. The sector has always contained more latitude to permit special cases and exceptions. The relative success of such groups and individuals has never been comprehensively researched though the increased profile for the phase will certainly lead to more detailed investigation of this area.

Compared to other similar countries, our levels of participation in post-compulsory education are very low and vocational education has considerably less impact on skills levels in this country than it does elsewhere. In spite of rising achievements up to the age of 13, there seems to be a resistance post-16 to retention in any kind of study or training: 'Tackling disengagement, truancy and poor behaviour at school are essential; providing motivating routes to success a necessity' (DfES 2005a: 15).

Although it may seem to some as though there is a poorly behaved minority in schools who could be farmed out to colleges this would be a gross distortion of reality and would exacerbate the problems. In fact, many learners, parents, HE and school professionals, and employers are unfamiliar with PCET options. They do not understand the overlapping plethora of vocational qualifications and progression routes. There are, indeed, weaknesses in the PCET system and it has, on occasion, been used as a 'dumping ground' for young people not well matched to under-resourced courses, resulting in a bad internal and external reputation for those involved. In a similar way, some schools have failed certain pupils when, for whatever reason, they have been unable or unwilling to provide an appropriate motivating and structured approach to learning. From both sides there are important contributions to be made but the strengths and weaknesses of the other context must be understood or the 'motivating routes' referred to above will not materialise.

What is post-compulsory education and training?

The broadest post-compulsory label is, as we know, already out of date since younger students have participated in PCET for many years. In spite of its size and importance, and yet perhaps because of this scope and the flexible nature of areas of provision, there is no fixed definition of the sector. Just a brief overview of the area demonstrates its complexity and we find that for almost every rule there is an exception.

FE colleges are the main centres for post-compulsory education and training and, with the awarding and industry lead bodies, they have established and developed many of the vocational qualifications. The piecemeal evolution of vocational and occupational training has led to the disjointed and over-complex range of provision but within this are individual success stories and examples of high-quality qualifications accepted throughout the world. In spite of this, it must be admitted that vocational education in the UK does not command the kind of respect given to the sector in other countries. Employers and trainees are consumer or client groups and they, on the whole, do not express high levels of satisfaction. Recent consultations have aired the many misgivings of employers concerning the skills deficits within the population and the means of addressing these.

Contrary to popular belief, not all students in PCET have chosen to be there. Many students are required to complete courses by their employers and, increasingly, there are school students for whom the courses in FE are a part of their formal education. In a further category are students who may be less committed and motivated than the uninitiated would expect – persuaded by relatives, disillusioned by previous failures, still unsure about direction, challenged by special needs of all kinds, these students of all ages can feel as compelled or intimidated by their learning situations as any school child. Having said this, there are many very committed learners, including those who have overcome such barriers and progressed to more advanced courses.

The age range of students is vast with 14- and even 13-year-olds attending alongside students who are well past retirement age and returning to learning. Their modes of attendance are as varied. In PCET, day and block release, work-based learning, distance learning and many other options extend and complicate the more familiar full- and part-time distinctions. PCET may take place across an extended day and, increasingly, throughout the year. In addition to traditional evening classes, colleges and adult and community learning centres are usually open at weekends and in summer.

PCET is located in a huge number of places and there seem to be few limits. The vocational courses alone open up almost any workplace, from an old people's home to a holiday destination abroad and from a concert hall to a garage. Community-based learning can mean laptops in parish centre or even a pub, and the equestrian, horticulture, building and construction courses may be partly located on college property but the learners should not spend too much time in a traditional classroom. Issues of expectation and environments in schools and colleges are explored in more detail in Chapters 5 and 6.

All kinds of centres and institutions are involved in PCET, including FE colleges, tertiary and sixth-form colleges, adult-learning centres, specialist colleges (e.g. art, agriculture, dance and drama) and an increasing number of outreach centres in community locations. The myth that PCET is all about vocational education and training is common. For many parents, teachers and employers the FE college and the wider PCET sector is not an academic environment. The truth is that high-quality academic provision from A levels to Access to degree-level work is a key element of this sector and the standards are sometimes far better than those in comparable sixth forms. Neither are the vocational programmes without intellectual challenge and academic content. The student undertaking one of these routes often needs a wider general education background and a broad range of skills and knowledge to gain the full benefit of the learning programme. High-quality vocational training should not be a second-rate option.

In the past, there were youth-training programmes delivered on the cheap which earned a very poor reputation. Two decades later, with grand yet compromised designs for vocational training, the government needs to take care in this complex sector. They are using old labels, loaded with values and associations, for new concepts and are drawing together very disparate elements without a clear overarching new framework. It may be seen by some to be a safe option but it could prove to be the risky alternative.

How is the sector funded?

Funding is both private and public and providers of post-compulsory education and training rely on LSC/FEFC, HEFC, LEA/school and many sources of local funding and supported schemes. A wide range of regulatory/inspection bodies are inevitably involved as a result and this can increase both the weight of central systems and the pressures on individual sections and departments. These are often organised as cost or profit centres and may function along the lines of separate business units. In some ways, this can encourage enterprise and allow for speedy responses to needs and opportunities but this can lead to difficulties in terms of coherent responses across an institution to new strategic directions. The timing and quality of such developments very much depend on the effectiveness of an institution's senior-management team (see Chapter 7).

Courses in PCET may lead to formal academic and/or vocational qualifications, to college-based certificates or entry to programmes, or may just be attended for leisure/community activities, and so on. There has been a huge decline in the informal provision of learning as the business focus of PCET has developed. What might once have been an informal art class with students returning year after year will provide both qualification and progression.

The LSC is currently reviewing ways in which additional resources can be directed at the new and existing provision for the 14–19 phase. Capital investment in colleges has always been a more problematic area. Some colleges have been extremely successful in attracting funding from a wide range of sources while others lack the expertise or background to make a case. The LSC's capital investment programme will address this area in order to improve facilities for 14–19 reform.

What is the role of colleges in providing for 14–19 learners and is involvement a choice?

Colleges will find themselves responsible within local partnerships for the provision of significant amounts of vocational opportunities. In the early stages of the reforms, only Specialist Schools, CoVEs and colleges will have sufficient vocational experience and facilities to offer even the range of choices proposed. Planning for the future does bring the entitlement to occupational lines like construction in at a later stage, and this reflects the preparedness of the sectors, but there will nevertheless be difficulties even in the early stages with the provision required.

Colleges will have less choice than they might think concerning the nature and extent of their institutional involvement since the funding mechanisms and accountability frameworks are being brought into play as levers. The encouragement and incentives to build partnerships and participate in new developments are certainly present though the element of resistance to aspects of change should not be underestimated. This should be taken into account as institutions shift to accommodate the demands of the 14–19 and skills strategies.

As well as 14–16 learners, the colleges will continue to be major providers of level 3 vocational pathways with the prospect of increased numbers. They should co-operate with and help partner institutions to set up their own vocational provision in appropriate areas.

Networks of local provision will be supported by the new national Skills Academies. These will be focused on the needs of the post-16 sector and will be supported by the CoVEs.

What kinds of teaching and learning might a 14–19 student experience in PCET?

Before considering the changes on the horizon, it is worth looking at the current scene and exploring the teaching and learning within the sector as it exists. FE colleges have changed considerably over recent years, introducing far more common elements and entitlements for all students, key skills, tutorial and PSHE systems. In spite of this the experience can feel quite different to students. The literature, teachers and the students explain the special elements in great detail, laying general emphasis on the following:

- Student-learning autonomy
- Relevance to employment
- Informality – first names, dress codes relaxed or removed
- Related practical work – opportunities to apply learning
- Emphasis on learning by doing
- Expectations teachers had of students
- Group working
- An adult classroom atmosphere – teaching styles, levels of discussion
- Diverse mixture of ages among students
- Teacher as manager of learning

Of course, such features shift and can be particular to certain types of courses but those mentioned are regularly identified by students as primary differences.

What is the Increased Flexibility Programme?

This scheme, started in 2002 and extended to 2006, enables students to select from a range of vocational and academic learning opportunities in schools and colleges. Some partnerships have been long established with 14–16-year-olds accepted on college courses for many years before such schemes began. In such cases the prospect of students below the age of 16 in training contexts, workshops and workplaces is not feared. Experienced staff are in place, lessons have been learned and the systems are in place to support learners and enable all to profit from the situation. Some students are full time but the majority are part time and those on the programme attend for only one or two days per week. In order to avoid the behavioural issues often associated with such collaborations the more successful colleges tend to select and screen applicants with care.

What problems do PCET staff face and anticipate with younger learners?

The college lecturers' union, NATFHE, has highlighted the issues facing increasing numbers of staff required to deal with younger learners in adult environments. The real dangers are that colleges just become a place to 'dump' the most difficult and disaffected pupils from schools unable to cope. In cases where practice is very poor there is no specific training or support and little planning, preparation or prior consultation. Once students are in place they can be left unsupervised or allowed to slip in terms of attendance and the monitoring and tracking of progress. Dan

Taubman of NATFHE has claimed that there is considerable evidence from FE lecturers to demonstrate that some schools are exploiting the programme to push their problems onto colleges. 'Our members feel that kids are being dumped on them' (http://education.guardian.co.uk, 5 April 2005).

What approaches have been successful with 14–19 learners in colleges?

The work with young learners who are motivated, well supported by schools and who have sufficient skills and preparation to undertake college programmes is very rewarding. Their enthusiasm and commitment can be a real asset and their growing confidence in practical and work-related settings often inspires them to improve in their wider academic study and gives a greater sense of relevance to their core skills.

However, there are also the young students whose perception of college is that it will give them freedom to ignore structures and to disrespect others, to escape from study and manipulate those in authority. Staff working with students of this kind who challenge the system and who are very poorly matched to a college-learning context can become very stressed and this can exacerbate the situation. Ideally all learners should be carefully selected and prepared but in all cases the minimum requirements should be that support and good communication are in place to deal speedily with issues as they arise. Good schools do not 'dump' their pupils and are always willing to collaborate in their best interests, and good practice in the colleges working successfully in this area relies upon this strong co-operative foundation.

Trust is a key element in the relationship with younger learners who are placed in unfamiliar settings. They do test the boundaries so they must find them to be firm and consistent and learn from the earliest stage that with adult freedoms and autonomy of learning in college come corresponding responsibilities to be reliable and trustworthy. Once again a shared set of values expressed in all their learning contexts and modelled by all teachers and staff will be the strongest way to convey this message so that learner behaviour is affected.

Time is an absolutely vital component in successful shared-learning contexts. Unfortunately it is costly and the dedicated staff involved in 14–19 initiatives often give their time freely and in excess of their obligations. It is certainly true that students who have benefited from the best college provision will identify the time selflessly given by key lecturers, instructors and support staff as the factor that turned their learning careers around or extended an already positive school experience.

This kind of provision is not just a means to bring in additional funding for courses already established for post-16 learners. It requires design and planning with the needs of this cohort in mind. Students and staff should be given additional time for individual tutorial support, for advice and guidance, and for the acquisition of additional skills. Those involved in the organisation and delivery need resources for team-building and communication and these must be available for the long term.

The rewards of improved results from new provision for 14–19 learners take time and cannot be reaped immediately. Unrealistic targets and budgets that are too tightly constrained are the chief cause of failed initiatives. For staff to 'buy in' to these schemes, they too must have trust. Trust that the funding will not evaporate after a few years, that blame will not fall on them the moment errors are made and that they will not be expected to work miracles on just a few teaching contact hours per week. Patience and real commitment will be the keys to success in this as in any kind of worthwhile teaching activity.

Ofsted and FE colleges – what have the findings been?

Ofsted has identified good advice and support of young people as a strength in FE colleges. The structures and trained staff can provide excellent services for students which go beyond the giving of advice and the provision of materials. Counselling and follow-up sessions, group work and tutorials as well as the public inputs are all recognised. New inspection arrangements being considered following the 2005 budget will certainly extend Ofsted's remit as ALI is subsumed within a larger Ofsted.

What is QuILL?

QuILL is the new national quality improvement body for post-16 to be set up from April 2006. It is the Quality Improvement Agency for Lifelong Learning. The agency has been under development for more than a year and is to improve the achievements of learners in the sector and for employers, communities and the economy. It has been set up to support 14–19 provision:

- Building on the programme managed by the Standards Unit, the agency will commission support materials and services to help providers drive up quality and respond to employer and learner needs.
- It will oversee a network of advisers who will produce tailored packages of support to address the needs of providers. It will support School Improvement Partners to advise on improvement in schools with sixth forms or making vocational provision.
- It will co-ordinate and support effective transfer of good practice and innovation in vocational provision, working with Skills Academies, CoVEs and others.

FE divisions and debates

FE is not a fully integrated, coherent sector but one full of diverse practice and provision, tension and contradiction. There was a time when pay differentials and promotion prospects favoured those working in a newly incorporated sector. Initiatives were short term and relatively well funded and the research base associated with the evaluation of projects was weak. These limited advantages have long since been eroded and in recent years the sector has suffered from criticism, low status and under-funding.

The history of the sector has been complex and fraught with conflict and division. This has left significant fault-lines across potential partnerships and undermined relationships, particularly with schools. According to Taubman (2000), the workforce in FE has reached a very low point. Policies and management post-incorporation have left professionals in an embattled and cynical state. They are underpaid and all the evidence suggests that they are demoralised and suffering from the stresses and strains put on them in their roles.

In the light of such claims that the staff are suffering from a significant lack of support it seems ironic to some that the culture of support for students has reached new heights. While it is certainly possible to look back and criticise previous FE/technical college approaches which allowed an 'attend and work if you like' attitude in many places, this was not necessarily the full picture. The profile of students accessing colleges was very different and the systems may not have been formalised but one-on-one support was often highly effective, personal and considerable.

The personalised learning agenda with its claims to be effective in re-engaging learners falls into a hotly debated area. Some versions and approaches seem more like the post-school therapy that has been the subject of powerful criticism in recent years. There are critics warning of the loss of knowledge and real vocational skill and understanding to the placebo approach which promotes individual self-esteem over real learning (Hayes 2004). The development of the 14–19 phase, as much as adult learning, will be a real testing ground for such questions if the necessary research is undertaken and if minds remain open.

There is not the space here to explore this kind of background to the sector but its importance should not be underestimated. It affects all aspects of the collaborative working proposals for the 14–19 phase. One of the key problems for training and supporting teachers for the phase as well as young learners themselves is that of finding experienced and supportive staff in colleges and work-based training to participate in making the initiatives work. This requires individuals who are dedicated, enthusiastic, experienced and then rewarding them appropriately for their efforts.

What is the Entry to Employment (E2E) programme?

E2E was launched in August 2003. It is an entry to a level 1 work-based programme for young people (16–18 with discretion to admit 19–24-year-olds) not yet ready to enter an apprenticeship or other formal level 2 provision. Attendance varies from 16 up to 40 hours dependent on the individual's needs and capability and is not time bound. It is deliberately left open so that the programme can adjust to the learner. It is set to become a more important pre-apprenticeship route and a model for younger learner provision. The fact that a learner takes part in the programme does not necessarily fix them in an apprenticeship route but the work and study will provide them with skills and preparation to enable them to progress to other routes as well. The programme is a key part of the agenda to keep all young people in some kind of learning until 19 and to enable them at that point to have achieved at least level 2 qualifications. Alongside this is the aim to reduce the proportion of 16–18-year-old NEETs.

Each programme is flexible within a broad framework but all contain three core areas of learning, including core skills, vocational learning, and personal and social development. The programme meets a lot of current government aims, working as it does with the groups most at risk of disengagement through social and emotional problems and other disadvantages evidenced in offending behaviour, and so on. By January 2004 there were over 32,000 young people taking part in E2E and the LSC has now committed funds to the programme as an entitlement where this learning option is most appropriate. The new broad proposals for engaging young people and breaking down barriers to achievement are being based on the positive outcomes of the post-16 Entry to Employment programme.

What is a CoVE?

Among all the new initiatives in FE, CoVEs, or Centres of Vocational Excellence, have received high praise and strong criticism. On the one hand, certain colleges with this status have achieved their aims of raising their profile and improving achievements. CoVE status has allowed them to emphasise their strengths and to focus on success as they work to redress issues in areas of weakness. Essentially the centre concept acts as a form of branding that has provided a much needed and often rapid boost to colleges where the provision was excellent in some specific areas but weaker elsewhere. In other situations centres have not experienced the significant status gains nor the positive student experiences, employer links and local impact in such a dramatic way.

The role of the CoVE in wider educational provision is an important part of future planning for the phase. The sharing of expertise and connections through developing local networks will be central to the new modes of delivery. Schools will not only draw on the resources of the CoVE but will also build their own specialisms and ultimately share their knowledge, skills and facilities.

How can we deal with 14–16-year-olds in our work placements and with training providers?

Many of those in FE who have spent years establishing relationships with vocational placements are genuinely concerned about the pitfalls facing young learners, employers and colleges as the younger age group arrive on the scene. This does not necessarily reflect opposition to the principles of earlier vocational training. On the contrary, FE lecturers in the trade and craft areas most involved, for example motor vehicle, engineering, construction or hotel and catering, are often passionate advocates of early choice and training and many came through youthful apprenticeship routes themselves. The history of these vocational areas will include elements of exploitation and hardship but these are balanced by long and proud traditions of training and expertise. Many practitioners look back to the status of these skills and roles in our past and their present value elsewhere in the world with some regret and envy. They also see higher-profile, reformed qualifications as a means of addressing industry shortages and issues of safety, reputation and quality for the consumer, which have had a detrimental effect over recent years.

There may be support in these areas for a revival of interest and an improved image among the young through education with high-value qualifications, but there are still serious fears about the inherent dangers of training situations. If they are not confident that liability issues have been adequately addressed, that insurances are in place, that parents/guardians have been consulted, and schools are accountable and well informed, college senior management will support, train and actively champion the new initiatives, protecting and troubleshooting the interests of the developers and participants, then they will resist or refuse to become involved.

Is specific guidance and training being provided?

From 2005–6, colleges will receive a guidance pack with advice and information on providing for young learners, with sections covering developing a partnership with schools and/or other colleges, planning, implementation and sustaining provision. There are also modules being developed by the TTA, SVUK (FENTO) and other relevant bodies specifically for teachers in FE and trainers in work-based settings who are increasingly working with 14 19-year-olds.

What are the legal requirements relating to supervision where there are adults and under-18s in the same class?

If there are under-18-year-old pupils in a group with those over 18 the sessions must be under the supervision of an approved adult, in other words one who is has a current valid police check, and this person is responsible for ensuring that other adults do not have 'substantial unsupervised access to the child'. Since not all staff are police checked, pupils may well come into contact with lecturers, support staff and others who are not checked. The situation demands that any college staff with responsibility for pupils under the minimum school-leaving age must be police checked and anyone else involved in teaching or support must not have 'substantial' access. The definition of terms is important and staff training is a real priority in these situations. For some, a more robust set of procedures which removes discretion from FE lecturers and places it on the institution is preferable and some staff are refusing to accept the burden of care.

What about work placements outside the school and college?

The child protection legislation requires police checks on those who will be in sole charge of children under 18. The work-experience placement is not a straightforward situation but the welfare of the pupil is always the determinant in all child protection issues. The new legislation does not require checks to be made on all people who might have contact with children. The scope of checks depends on the role and scale of contact. On a short work placement of a couple of weeks a check is not currently required; however, it would be necessary for someone employed by a training provider to work with under-18s. The requirements apply to placements arranged by third parties like colleges.

At present the guidance from the DfES suggests that practitioners should have specialist training before they take responsibility for positively vetting a placement as suitable on health and safety grounds. This also includes an element of value judgement concerning the people in place who devise the programme and allocate supervisory duties. In fact, this exercise really demands a risk assessment. Some cases are obvious, e.g. a residential placement, and others are less clear, though many institutions and authorities play safe and avoid the situation where a pupil works exclusively or even mainly with one adult.

Should 14–16-year-olds be police checked if they work with children?

No, not if the placement is of short duration but if the student were enrolled on a training course with longer, more regular periods of contact, for example nursery nursing, then a check would be required at the start of the course. Supervision of students and children should of course be in place and the selection and recruitment of students should ensure that they are well matched with a placement.

Does the '*in loco parentis*' principle transfer from school to college?

This concept refers to a standard of care not set down in law but recognised and upheld in courts. It holds, as most people understand, that adults in charge of children would act in the same way as any reasonably prudent parent would in the same circumstances. This means that when a school pupil is on a placement or programme at a college or in a workplace and therefore in the care of the college or provider the school must ensure that they provide that standard of care to the pupil. Effectively this means that the answer is 'yes', the college or provider is agreeing to assume responsibility, but the school still retains responsibility for making and monitoring their choice.

What happens about insurance cover for the younger learners in colleges and work placements?

Existing insurance, even for a college that regularly has children and occasional young learners on the site, perhaps supervised by staff from their own institution, does not always cover for regular new provision with the younger learners, especially in a range of contexts. Employers and colleges should check with their insurers about taking out additional insurance to cover 14–19-year-olds on extended placement as this is sometimes necessary, in which case adjustment to premiums may increase the costs. Travel to and from placement may not be covered and parents must be made aware of this.

What happens if a school pupil has an accident while on a placement?

Arrangements must be in place to ensure that the school is immediately informed. If accidents do occur the school should discuss the implications with the college/provider. Employers should be aware of their duty to report accidents to the HSE/Local Authority under the Reporting of Injuries, Diseases and Dangerous Occurrences Regulations (RIDDOR) 1995. If there is a question mark over health and safety standards then the placements may need to be suspended for checks, or stopped altogether.

A contract previously agreed should be in place such that the employer is obliged to report immediately full details of any accident involving a student. All assaults and serious and fatal accidents must be reported immediately by telephone to the LSC National Health and Safety Team (02476-823-239).

How much information about the profile of the student being placed can be disclosed to the college?

Given the consent of the pupil or, in some cases, the parent, it is legitimate for schools to release certain data on attendance, behaviour, prior attainment and other relevant information to the college. Without this consent, release of data may not be possible. Parents and pupils should always be told that the school is sharing personal data for the purpose of carrying out educational functions. Intentions behind the disclosure should always be carefully explained.

Having said this, there are circumstances where information will be deemed 'sensitive personal data' under the Data Protection Act. This could be SEN or behaviour issues. In such a case the school must obtain explicit consent for disclosure from the pupil or, in some circumstances, the parents/guardians. An overall set of permissions, information and regulations may be the easiest route. Schools and colleges should certainly take advice on disclosures and permissions as to their obligations under the Data Protection Act.

What are the post-16 chances for those who do not get five or more GCSEs at grade C or above?

Many pupils who prefer practical, hands-on learning and would benefit from applied studies of some kind, are offered no choice in conventional education until they reach the age of 16. Even then, because of the widespread view in this country that specialised occupational and general vocational programmes are second best, the young person may well find that parents, well-meaning teachers, friends and even some advisers discourage their interest and steer them towards a 'safer' mainstream academic alternative. This kind of failure to meet the needs of the 14–19 age group is far less visible than the drop-out statistics or low-attainment levels in the tables since many of these intelligent individuals will achieve, just not what they wanted.

The aims of post-compulsory education and training to cater for the needs of all learners, especially those needing second chances, changing career and developing their skills, are usually clearly stated within a lifelong learning ethos or mission. Contrary to the belief of some, even within the sector, the recovery of the very young learner who has previously failed is not always the norm. It is often a long-term process involving false starts, attempts to build basic skills, struggles with behaviour and learning how to learn. New flexibility and collaboration may remove the pressure sometimes placed on colleges of FE to provide quick fixes and retakes, which in many cases may be inappropriate and not well suited to the needs of the individual. In fact statistics show that retakes tend not to be a successful route and most students do not raise their grades.

Don't students go to college for a second chance to retake GCSEs?

The motivation for students entering college is not just related to retakes. Many 16-year-olds make a positive choice to change their environment and to study in what they perceive to be a less restrictive environment. FE has spent huge amounts of time and resources and built up expertise in student support not just from choice but from the necessity of having to deal with so many learners in a remedial way. Often these efforts are too little and too late or the resources available prevent staff from supporting students to achieve what is defined as a recognised achievement.

In fact much progress may have been made and eventually, through working at a more appropriate pace, an individual may emerge with some formal qualification and acknowledged success. The difficulty for the lecturers and other professionals concerned is that for each achievement there are many who cannot be retained in a system so rigidly constrained and accountable in the very short term for approved results. The student must be eligible in all respects for funding and the whole educational package must conform to strict recruitment, retention, achievement and quality parameters in order to be acceptable. These constraints and barriers to flexible teaching are not only a problem in FE colleges but they have historically been felt in this sector as a consequence of learner profiles and the nature of the programmes.

What does 'The strong core 14–19' mean in PCET?

As a result of their experience with post-16 learners lacking in core skills and the learning skills and motivation to deal with the deficit, FE lecturers and other staff feel very strongly about early and effective provision of the basics to as many young learners as possible. They do recognise the obstacles facing schools, not least those of non-attendance and external pressures which are so evident in the same individuals throughout their FE careers.

For PCET the strong core would ideally mean a reduction in the necessity to redress skills deficits and demoralisation among young learners. The expectation, however, is that there will be considerable work to be done with the increasing numbers of new entrants to the sector to enable the difficult process of linking diverse experiences and settings into a coherent programme of learning.

What concerns can be heard within the sector about the new Diplomas?

The Diplomas will have a profound effect on PCET generally and especially on the colleges currently involved in the partnerships which will be delivering new entitlements to young learners. The plan is that the 3,500 plus vocational qualifications will remain in place during the early stages of implementation as new units are introduced. Existing qualifications and their components will be combined and offered within the new Diploma lines and this will initially take place in a limited and tightly regulated way. Meanwhile the QCA will work with employers and awarding bodies to develop and commission the new Diplomas.

The concerns are obvious since, even with a date of 2015 for implementation of the full 14-line entitlement, there should be four by 2008 and eight by 2010. This incremental approach to introduction is criticised on the grounds that it is potentially more disruptive and confusing for those involved than a total new system implementation. Having worked with parallel and even conflicting systems throughout their careers, and with all the issues raised by partial reform, the slow and steady approach to a new construct is the stuff of nightmares for some managers and practitioners. They immediately quote key skills, Curriculum 2000 and GNVQs as examples of poor curriculum innovation.

If the changes, however limited, are to stand any chance of avoiding past failures and providing a genuine increase in the status of vocational learning, significant resources will need to be dedicated not only to the systems, structures and support of learners but to the prior development of staff involved. As experience has shown, without the full understanding and co-operation of key personnel, new partnerships and qualifications will not be implemented successfully.

Throughout the whole process, the main aim is to ensure that those who gain a Diploma, made up of whatever units, will have been fully stretched so as to bring out the best of their abilities, and that it will be accepted at the best universities and for the most desirable career paths on the basis of the qualification being good currency and their other recorded skills and experiences. The new Diplomas should prepare successful students for progression from one level to another and this journey should be a logical and easily comprehensible process. For this purpose, the notion of interlocking levels and components, proposed originally by the Working Party, has been accepted.

How does this integrate with the National Curriculum?

For Key Stage 4 (see also Chapter 5) the full National Curriculum will be followed and so all 14–16-year-olds will be expected to achieve the broad underpinning foundation. This should give them a basis for future specialisation and ensure that even though they have had access to challenging and exciting new vocational options during this stage, they should not have lost any of the basics which allow them to retain a full range of choices and changes later in their learning career.

In other words, a student who spent considerable time on the work-based route 14–16 should not be disadvantaged if they shift to a fully academic A-level path from 16–19 any more than a student travelling the other way or one who 'mixes and matches' their options. It sounds ideal, at least within a certain given set of values and aims for education, but, that aside, the practical achievement of this state of affairs will be a very tall order.

What happens to those students who fail to complete or achieve their programme of study?

The increased collaboration between sectors and the focus on the individual learner's programme tailored to suit their needs over time, should result in better communication and a reduction in the barriers to success in learning. This is the theory, and in practice what the government intends is to enable any student with a partial Diploma to move almost seamlessly into the adult qualifications framework and gain credit for units. The background to this is the current consultation on the Framework for Achievement of adult qualifications. It seems that this may inform the design of the Diplomas and this would provide a more coherent structure.

How will PCET be made accountable for the 14–19 learners?

There are many, very natural concerns regarding the influx of 14–16-year-olds into FE and work-based training contexts, and for some they outweigh the perceived benefits to young learners and the economy. In order to allay such fears and establish a robust yet sensitive accountability framework, the government have proposed new measures in the White Paper (DfES 2005a: 86). The location of the young person in terms of enrolment on a roll and the accountability of the 'home' institution will be a very significant element in the practical implementation of new initiatives. Many FE institutions would be less wary of innovative and collaborative programming if the school retained significant responsibility for the learner. This would not diminish the willingness of FE professionals to be fully involved in teaching, training, guiding and advising younger learners but would add an important sense of security to the process, especially in the early days as workforce training and development take shape. Of course, the accountability and the credit do need to be all the more 'sharp', accurate and yet sensitive if appropriate credit is to be given and if resources attached to success and appropriate action to follow where weakness is identified.

Achievement and Attainment Tables already contain value-added measures for 11–16 institutions. The government is now developing similar measures for post-16 learning to ensure continued progress for all young learners:

- A measure of value-added for 16–19 learners following level 3 qualifications. An institutional value-added measure will be introduced in the Achievement and Attainment Tables in 2006, after a pilot this year.

- A complementary measure of distance travelled for 16–19 learners, which is being developed by the LSC and the Inspectorates. This will measure learner progress on qualifications at level 1 and 2 and ungraded qualifications like NVQs at all levels.

- A measure of qualifications achieved by learners as a proportion of the qualifications they start with. This qualification success measure is already in use in colleges. Changes to the PLASC survey will mean that this measure can be applied in school sixth forms from around 2008. From September 2005, the qualification-success measure used for training providers will be brought into line with the measure used in colleges.

What is the Learner Achievement Tracker?

As a part of the drive to improve data and transparency as well as accountability, schools, colleges and training providers will be able to access the value-added and distance-travelled information through the Learner Achievement Tracker to be piloted from 2005. This will provide all participating institutions with information on national norms for 16–19-year-olds in terms of most subjects and qualifications. The measurement of learner achievement and progression in terms of value-added and distance-travelled measures has been an area of debate for many years. Full understanding of results as they relate to real people, their lives, efforts and potential can be significantly enhanced by the use of such measures as opposed to crude outcomes and results devoid of any context and can support targeted developments.

Will all the existing adult qualifications be available to 14–19-year-olds?

No, as the outline above shows there will be careful selection of appropriate and increasingly customised qualifications designed and adapted with this age group in mind, and the access to vocational education will eventually be limited to the specialised routes established. Their progression, however, will be considered and this will require real interlock with the framework and levels above so there will be guarantees that the Diplomas in full and in unit form will continue to be open to the adults leaving the 14–19 phase who need to complete or wish to continue.

What are the funding concerns?

Apart from the broader pay-differential concerns which are long-term issues still not adequately addressed, there is a sense of pressing problems inherent in the new qualifications arrangements. One such is related to the availability and funding situation. The departmental statement seems to suggest significant and imminent alterations to funding mechanisms which may indeed make colleges of FE and other training providers pause for thought. Unlike the school sector whose involvement with the vocational qualifications is far more limited and recent, and whose core curriculum business is fixed to the mainstream A level and GCSE, the PCET sector historically deals in all of the 3,500 or more vocational qualifications and must look with some anxiety at the prospect of any major overhaul:

> The qualifications that will be available to young people in future will be GCSEs, A levels and Apprenticeships and those that fall within one of the lines of the Diploma. We will progressively move to a position where we fund only those qualifications consistent with the programmes and Diplomas described in this document.
>
> (DfES 2005a)

The key message in the above statement is that funding will follow approved qualifications and that these will be adjusted and inevitably reduced to fit the new agenda.

The responsibility for development of the specialised lines above will be spread across the appropriate Sector Skills Councils who will use their industry links and expertise to ensure that the new qualifications are genuinely employer led. In order to realise the aim to integrate vocational and academic study and skills more closely, there is an expectation in the planning that the Skills Councils, QCA and other lead bodies will explore the inclusion of GCSEs and A levels where appropriate into the design of the vocational Diplomas. The responsibility for driving forward this difficult task is being shifted outside the remit of the mainstream professional educators. By leaving the traditional qualifications relatively unchanged, with their identity intact, and concentrating the reform outside schools and colleges in the skills and workplace context, the government has avoided some serious conflicts but may have missed opportunities for full-concept and partnership development.

What is meant by employment and work-based learning (WBL)?

This covers a very wide area of activity from private independent work to in-house training for companies and from public-sector work under contract to commercial

Table 6.1 Specialised learning lines

Specialised learning line	Relevant Sector Skills Councils
1 Health and social care	Skills for Health Skills for Care and Development
2 Public services	Central Government Skills for Justice
3 Land based and environmental	Lantra
4 Engineering	SEMTA Go Skills Energy & Utility Skills Cogent
5 Manufacturing	Skillsfast-UK ProSkills SEMTA Improve
6 Construction and the built environment	Construction Skills Summit Skills Asset Skills Energy & Utility Skills
7 Information and communication technology	e-skills UK
8 Retail	Skillsmart Skills for Logistics Automotive Skills Go Skills
9 Hospitality and catering	People 1st
10 Hair and beauty	People 1st SkillsActive
11 Sport and leisure	SkillsActive
12 Travel and tourism	People 1st
13 Creative and media	Creative and Cultural Skills Skillset
14 Business administration and finance	Financial Services Sector Council

Source: DfES 2005a

and industrial provider programmes. Clearly, much of this does not directly relate to the 14–19 area, though the term is now frequently used in relation to this group and confusion can arise. LLUK provides the following breakdown of the area:

- Commercial and publicly funded work-based learning through higher education institutions and business schools

- Commercial and publicly funded work-based learning provided by further education colleges on their own or on employers' premises

- Work-based learning in community settings, particularly that funded directly or indirectly through public-funding bodies

- Work-based learning delivered through independent learning providers on a commercial basis

- Corporate training provided by companies in their own premises, whether by their own staff or by external contractors

This demonstrates the scope and complexity of the area and the networks of relationships between the training providers, clients, learners and partners. Some colleges are work-based learning providers in their own right and have set up private companies. Funding bodies contract with these college companies, independent providers and local authorities to deliver training programmes.

Colleges are often used by independent training providers to deliver underpinning knowledge or specialist skills for their work-based trainees. This situation applies especially in the case of those on publicly funded apprenticeship courses. There are some independent training providers employing hundreds of staff in centres across the UK but the more usual model is for smaller enterprises with a specialised focus.

What are the key issues for post-compulsory education and training?

'Skills: Getting on in Business, Getting on in Work' builds on the government's 2003 Skills Strategy and is designed to continue the progress towards providing employees for business and industry with relevant skills. The sector is being reassured that significant new funding will be provided but there are concerns that these will be directed towards the new 14–19 phase. The older returners to learning are seen as vulnerable in terms of future resources as are programmes with no obvious or direct connection to employment and skills.

Training for staff is an area of increasing concern linked to the terms and conditions of contracts. Even more contentious is the issue of the continuing funding gap between the school and college sectors and there are no immediate signs that this will be addressed with any sense of urgency. The funding gap can be as high as 30 per cent and the introduction of specialist provision in school is liable to exacerbate this situation.

As colleges develop to provide more options for younger students the environment will alter and for staff the implications of new partnerships will be the extension of this into other locations.

Conclusion

Colleges of FE have been identified as key institutions in the reform of 14–19 education and training: 'Eighty-four per cent agree that successful FE colleges are as crucial to the competitiveness of businesses in the UK as are successful universities', wrote Jo Clancy in *The Times Educational Supplement* (8 April 2005). If this vision of effective education for younger learners is to be translated into some form of reality then the PCET staff involved will require action on fundamental issues relating to pay and conditions. Partnerships rely on a disposition towards co-operation, shared aims and effective working relationships producing benefits for all parties. In 14–19 terms FE and PCET generally cannot be allowed to remain the poor relation. No amount of initiatives or directives can substitute for genuine professional autonomy and negotiated engagement with others in a common purpose. For this state of affairs to be established there is an urgent need for more common professional cross-sector and phase frameworks to deliver parity, security and equal opportunities for new flexible professionals.

Partnerships

> It is our intention to work with the grain of existing organisational structures to achieve that change; and to build systems that are driven bottom-up by partnerships of independent, autonomous schools, colleges and training providers.
>
> (DfES 2005a)

The implementation of the ambitious proposals for vocational education and training 14–19 and the changes to existing academic qualifications will place new demands on all providers. If the combined resources and expertise of the sectors are to rise and meet the challenges, major increases in the rate and level of partnership building are required.

Background: where are the existing partnerships?

The different learning institutions have been working together over many years. Partnerships, built at the time of the LEA, became fragmented during the competitive period that followed incorporation in FE. The Conservative government, in keeping with its broad strategy, was set on reducing state intervention and establishing the new free-market approach with associated structures and funding across this and other public-sector areas. In conjunction with the decline of union power through the period, as increasingly tough legislation began to bite, this aggressive drive towards new managerialism was supposed to create a leaner, more efficient and demand-led FE sector.

Managers in FE colleges had to acclimatise themselves to running budgets based on outcomes, having performance measured in terms of fixed targets and facing the threat of redundancy if they did not achieve set indicators of performance. The results were far-reaching and the costs to some colleges and individuals were high. Not only were there significant staff cuts and closures in some areas but many established links were broken as some schools and colleges moved in on one another's business.

In the 1980s and 1990s, competition within the sector was the chosen route to delivering affordable, efficient and effective training. The Further and Higher Education Act of 1992 completed the separation and colleges became independently incorporated. The newly established Further Education Funding Council assumed responsibility for both funding and for a new inspection regime to oversee quality and standards. Colleges began to operate in this new climate and the priorities of their governing bodies and management teams were clearly very different from those of their predecessors. The FEFC had no planning remit so that although the funding mechanism in a range of evolving forms functioned as a kind of centralised directing mechanism, strategies employed were subject to the vagaries of local conditions. Some colleges proved to be adept at adjusting to the new context, moving in on a wide range of work, amalgamating and extending their base. Others struggled and failed to respond fast enough to the market forces. Of course, the new system culled poor provision in this way, but good teams and worthwhile projects also suffered.

Many of the victims of the severe downsizing of this period were the partnerships with existing institutions. Some very creative and productive work with the Adult Education Service and with schools failed to thrive in the changed climate. It might be claimed that partnerships were not deliberately cut, but the reformed system had such a strong focus on rapid return on investment and on meeting short-term targets that the slow development of learners and potential routes for learners certainly suffered in this period.

The responsibility for strategy resided with the governors of the newly incorporated colleges who were charged with responding to local need in a financially viable way. Their mission statements were very customer focused and their perspective far more local and regional than national. With new stakeholders to consider and previous partners, adult and community education services, sixth forms, colleges of HE, and many agents and private trainers transformed into competitors, the colleges were forced to make radical adjustments.

Some school links, that had previously allowed pupils regular access to the expertise of a local college without charge as a means of building interest in vocational training, were dropped in favour of short courses for adults paying to learn how to use their new computer or their digital camera. Leisure courses once invaluable in encouraging widening participation initiatives through gentle moves into the community had to show results within a financial year or they were axed.

The cumulative effect of a series of changes was to remove layers of local long-term initiatives without any accurate audit of their value. In certain areas, programmes that had begun the process of drawing whole families more closely into the education process were unable to survive because too many elements did not qualify for funding. The pressures of convergence on funding were huge, as the FEFC model was forcing up 'productivity', defined in unitary terms through incremental reduction-funding allocation over time and per capita. Volume, output and turnover inevitably replaced other goals in all areas of the sector. Subsequently, it has been interesting to see some of these early initiatives resurrected in the recent atmosphere of collaboration. Some colleges expanded very rapidly and became adept at taking advantage of loopholes in the funding mechanism, and they often grew at the expense of partners and occasionally with total disregard for legal niceties.

What is the current situation?

In order to deliver all of the promises to learners about improved choice, quality and innovation, there have been some significant and imaginative new collaborative ventures. Federations are one of the most developed and least tentative of the reactions to the changes occurring. They are at a more advanced stage in areas where increased co-operation was taking place prior to the headline reports and initiatives. Such proactive work had often been embarked upon in areas where conventional approaches had not had a great deal of success in raising achievements and extending opportunities. There are particular challenges present in some regions and concentrated clusters of expertise and experience in meeting complex educational, social and economic needs. These conditions have enabled an apparently speedier response to the new circumstances when, in fact, the infrastructure to permit the enterprise to go ahead was in place.

The pressure is now intense upon all institutions providing for 14–19 learners to become more involved in formal partnership agreements and the role of the local LSCs and other bodies is central to this planning. In order to deliver the new curriculum breadth and specifically the work-related learning elements of new entitlement, it will be vital to have well-structured collaborative arrangements at a local level and excellent national support systems. The collaborations, if managed with care, will ensure that learners have access to the necessary broad range of learning programmes suited to their interests, talents and aspirations. All this is designed to improve participation, engagement and achievement.

What is the new vision?

The implications of new partnerships are far-reaching since the most ambitious future visions detach the learner from the individual institution to a much greater extent than is usual at present. It involves the creation of easily accessible and flexible options for all students across the new age phase. In order for this to operate efficiently and really deliver there must be extensive collaboration to enable 'joined-up' curriculum planning to take place. The success of these enterprises will certainly depend on the quality of the transition phase. Many education practitioners, commenting throughout the consultation process, have emphasised the key significance of Key Stage 3 in the equation. Finally, the options, whether they are more traditional academic exams or vocational qualifications, will need to be supported by good guidance and underpinned with provision of all the necessary elements of student entitlement.

This new version of partnership is far wider than a schools/FE model. Both vocational and academic curriculum areas suffer from shortages of various kinds. In response to this, the partnership model could provide solutions through collaboration over resources and delivery. Potentially, this would include employers and training providers of all kinds and would draw in the independent sector where appropriate. There are no real limitations to the partnership concept in the minds of some planners. Some programme planners have not ruled out work experience abroad and other adventurous options. With the rapid removal of current obstacles to innovation, it is a question of waiting for ideas to take shape.

In some situations institutions may wish to keep a greater degree of autonomy and to retain more control within their context. Such schools and colleges may develop links and buy in expertise on a temporary basis while they establish their own strong specialism and identity. In other circumstances, the new opportunities and demands may trigger much more radical approaches and new hybrid institutions may emerge. Whether institutions simply want to contract provision from one another or to enter into more complex shared staffing or governance arrangements, there will be advice to assist in the process. Legislation will be introduced to increase the scope for joint governance arrangements to strengthen collaboration between schools and FE colleges.

And the new system configuration?

In order to deliver the ambitious vision for the future with all the challenges of retaining existing components and making them work together, it is generally accepted that there will need to be far more integration. One interesting reason for a less radical, more evolved approach is perhaps the demographic data. The next ten years will see a reduction in 14–19-year-olds, so a system configured to accommodate them but not totally built for them is obviously viewed as the most cost-effective approach.

The capacity for delivering the full range of choice is dependent on key parts of the system working in partnership. The first stage of the process to develop a new system includes the drawing up of a prospectus of options for all young people in this age range. LEAs and local LSCs will have this initial responsibility and will be required to audit existing provision and commission any additional resources and staff where they are required to fill any gaps. Regulations and guidance will ensure that all the relevant local providers are consulted and fully involved, including schools, LEAs, colleges and diocesan authorities. The LSC has planning and funding responsibility already and the extension of its powers into the management and supervision of partnerships is a natural move.

The real focus will be on the vocational education providers, both schools and colleges, and those already delivering successfully in this area can expect to receive more attention and support as the system is extended from strong partners. This process will include:

- Extending the role of CoVEs
- Developing new Skills Academies as national centres of excellence in skills
- Strengthening schools' vocational provision through specialism and opportunities to become leading schools by adopting a second specialism

The partnerships will be absolutely vital since all schools and colleges must ensure that the full range of choices is available to all students in the age phase on their roll.

Inspection will ensure that the obligations are met and in the early stages meeting the requirements in full will certainly be a tall order. The actual forms this 'configuration' will produce may well prove quite varied, though as Tomlinson rightly pointed out, there are some workable models in existence. Having emphasised the need for innovation there are limits set on the scope and scale of change. Wholesale change to the organisation and infrastructure of schools and colleges themselves is not on the agenda but the systems for funding and training may see adjustments to accommodate the new phase demands.

What are Learning Partnerships?

Learning Partnerships are non-statutory, voluntary groupings of local learning providers and actors across all sectors – HEIs, FE colleges, schools, employers, trade unions, faith groups, voluntary providers, local government and the Connexions/ Careers Service, to mention the more usual partners. They are directly relevant to the 14–19 phase in all its aspects because of their aims to promote a culture of provider collaboration across the sectors and to rationalise existing local partnership arrangements relating to post-16 learning. The core roles of the partnerships are defined as:

■ Promoting provider collaboration in support of lifelong learning
■ Maximising the contribution of learning to local regeneration

The involvement of Learning Partnerships in the phase does not end there. They are drawn into follow-ups to Area Inspections, 14–19 proposals and many other initiatives, including Basic Skills, progression into HE, workforce development and local regeneration strategies. They are funded through the LSC Local Intervention and Development Fund. Following LSC consultation using NIACE research, guidance on policy, planning and budgeting arrangements can be found on the website (www.lifelonglearning.co.uk/llp).

How will successful partnerships be established?

There will be a prospectus and advice regarding best practice through Education Improvement Partnerships. These should support schools, colleges and other providers to establish shared provision, especially in areas where there are no partnerships. There are many challenges ahead for schools and colleges, but the latter may face difficulties that are less obvious, for though they may have existing and long-established provision in place for vocational education this may well not be structured to accept and support the younger learner from the 14–16 age range.

The process of establishing partnerships or building on those that exist is one of careful negotiation and consideration of the strengths and weaknesses of the institutions involved. The DfES has set out a series of steps in this process:

■ Schools, colleges and other providers set out what they propose to offer both individually and collaboratively, on what scale and to which students.

- The local authority and the local LSC draw together this information to identify any gaps against the national standards, or barriers to effective collaboration.

- The LSC would hold a flexible funding pot (as it does now with the pathfinders and IFP), which would be used to commission additional provision and provide some additional funding for transport and partnership management, to ensure that the national standards are met for all young people in the area.

- The end product is a prospectus, jointly published by the local authority and the local LSC for all the providers, which sets out for each young person a clear picture of what is available in the area.

The whole partnership structure is aimed at widening choice for the 14–19 learner by opening up a more varied and relevant range of learning environments. It relies on all the local partners actively contributing to the process and supporting one another in order to improve the opportunities for this group of learners. The success in practical terms of the 14–19 pathfinder projects and other localised school and college initiatives have encouraged this commitment to a partnership model of delivery.

Where the partnerships work best there is often real innovation and a willingness to move away from conventional structures. This may mean that the school is not the location of theory teaching in a classroom context; instead the factory floor can be the classroom and large numbers of students from a range of schools and colleges can find themselves being taught as well as trained by an industry expert for part of their week. The West Kent Learning Federation consists of 15 schools and four specialist schools in a consortium attached to West Kent College. The aim is to increase the opportunities for younger pupils to take part in vocational learning. This kind of partnership is very interesting in the post-White Paper environment because some of the schools are offering GCSEs a year early and are making links with colleges to support their vocational teaching.

What are the financial implications of partnership?

Effective collaboration in a rapidly changing environment is very difficult to establish. The difficulties inherent in delivering the new strategy for 14–19 have been discussed in the sectors concerned and have been the subject of wide consultation on the part of government. The establishment of new bodies and structures was achieved fairly early with the LSC and SSCs, and all aspects of management and organisation have seen some change.

The DfES is still working on the development of the best ways to provide funding attached to young learners taking the new flexible range of entitlements and options so that funding follows them rather than dictating their pathways. What usually happens in many teaching and training situations is that the funding is, for good reasons, fairly rigidly controlled but is therefore unresponsive in situations where alternative or individual approaches are more suitable. The worst news of all for the proposals published for 14–19 would be a scenario where funding issues were so complex and restrictive or even uneconomic that institutions became disillusioned with the whole process. As some of the initiative, curriculum and examination fiascos of the past have demonstrated, leadership and public commitment are only a part of the package necessary for successful policy implementation.

There have always been mixed views on the most efficient funding mechanisms and the arguments relating to finance, especially in an education system which is full of inequities, can be very acrimonious. So it is not surprising that consultation did not produce a single obvious recommended approach. Perhaps wisely, there has been considerable use of piloting in this period of change and the 14–19 pathfinders are the most successful example of this.

Setting other matters aside, the pathfinders have been used to test means of funding collaborative working. Is it better to push all the funding through schools or to separately fund schools and colleges or should this be left open for local agreements? The 2005 White Paper makes reference to planned legislation to support changes which will affect and support this last approach. The DfES claims that they are absolutely committed to avoid additional bureaucracy and that they remain true to the drive to reduce the burden rather than increase it.

In spite of the downward trend in the 14–19 cohort, there has been significant pressure from all sides for additional investment. Raw numbers of individuals are not the only factor to be taken into account when funding since small groups of students still need technical support, materials still need writing, workshops must be found and, even with e-learning technologies, it is not usually possible for students in Nottingham to share a qualified teacher with others in Milton Keynes. The 14–19 pathfinders are being used to assess the scale and nature of the additional costs that might arise from new patterns of provision and the best funding solutions.

The LSC is responsible for post-16 recurrent funding and, following consultation, has agreed the core principles underpinning this funding, as well as an ongoing programme of converging methodologies for school sixth forms, further education and work-based learning. This is designed to reduce and eliminate unfair differences over time.

The funding is, as always, being used to drive forward change in the sectors involved. To support quality of provision, funding decisions take account of existing good-practice evidence from evaluation of 14–16 pathfinders. Any proposals for change to the 16–19 framework will be incorporated within existing LSC plans for development of new integrated funding arrangements. The DfES do not, however, plan to change the current arrangements for funding 14–16 provision through LEAs.

Capital funding arrangements are different for schools and post-16 institutions but as far as the provision of capital funds to support organisation and delivery of the 14–19 curriculum is concerned there are a number of different partners involved. These include local authorities, the national Learning and Skills Council and the local LSCs and the schools, colleges and providers themselves. The DfES allocate capital support for post-16 learning and skills to the LSC who then allocate to providers as they see fit. Capital funding for school sixth forms is still the responsibility of the local authorities although revenue funding of sixth forms is the responsibility of the

LSC so there is still a divide in the 14–19 conditions of operation. This is because it would be difficult to separate pre- and post-16 school capital as buildings are shared but the LSC does have revenue responsibility for school sixth-form students.

Many colleges have specialists working on the financing of programmes and capital projects from a range of different sources. Large and small sums and ongoing support can be drawn from a very wide range of public and private organisations. European funding can be given to institutions in certain areas of need, industry funding and sponsorship is not uncommon, and many other funding streams are regularly accessed to increase opportunities. It is important to realise from a partnership perspective that the 14–19 funding cannot be separated from the whole school spending and will vary as a result of individual school differences and decisions. The School Capital Programme includes just over £5 billion for 2005–6, an increase of over half a billion pounds each year since 2003. This funding is shared over 21,000 schools (3,500 secondary schools) and this big picture is not so widely understood in the PCET sector, just as the schools' side of partnerships lacks knowledge of post-compulsory education and training.

Local decision-making structures mean that there is no set amount allocated for the needs of 16–19-year-olds in school sixth forms or for 14–16 learners below that level. There is a needs-related formula dictating the allocation of funds to LEAs and schools and this is linked to locally agreed asset-management plans just as the colleges have to agree development plans with the LSC. All schools receive a devolved formula allocation and, in addition, the DfES runs a targeted capital bidding round for projects meeting key government criteria. This is not large in scale and is designed to complement Building Schools for the Future (BSF) on stream for 2005–6. This ambitious programme and the Academies programme are discussed elsewhere.

The LSC administers the capital programme for post-16, including over 400 FE colleges, and has a £408.5 million allocation for 2005–6. This comprises capital funding for FE and the Adult and Community Learning sectors as well as funding to develop the Information and Learning Technology infrastructure, the Centres of Vocational Excellence and the Neighbourhood Learning in Deprived Communities programme. The current priorities of this programme include the raising of standards using the outcomes of the Area Inspections and the Strategic Area Reviews (StAR) process. This is now complete and will be used to identify and rationalise patterns of provision.

The LSC uses both formula and bid mechanisms to allocate its capital and, at present, these funds are given in response to bids from colleges. The major difference between capital funding for schools and colleges is the fact that the LSC usually funds only a proportion of the investment cost and the benchmark is not high (around 35 per cent).

How can schools and the post-16 sector work together on projects requiring capital funding?

Given the separate funding arrangements, the DfES has taken steps to promote joint working as follows:

- LSC guidance to local LSCs has been amended so that all bids for capital funding must cover discussions with LEAs

- Guidance on Asset Management Planning requires LEAs to consult with local LSCs

- Proposals for BSF projects require that all local partners are signed up to the local vision of secondary provision – delivery can be by Local Education Partnership LEP joint ventures

- Guidance for local LSCs on taking forward StARs

There are also specific plans being made to support collaboration in the other ways:

- Looking at how to forge closer links between the LSC and the new Partnerships for Schools (PfS) body to help take the BSF programme forward

- Improving the synergy between BSF and funding allocations for FE colleges in the light of the spending review

- Supporting the prioritisation of LSC funding for 16–19 provision and BSF roll-out to 400-plus FE colleges

How do Skills Academies fit with partnership?

The new national Skills Academies will each have close links with employers and the relevant Sector Skills Councils. Eventually there will be at least one Skills Academy for every vocational area. Their aim is to challenge educational under-attainment in areas of disadvantage by raising the standard of education to match the best available in the maintained sector. They should have a very broad community focus and have an impact on whole families and on the locality rather than just on the pupils.

As the Academies become established, the intention is that they will share expertise with other schools and the wider community. The other, more controversial, aspect of partnership involvement is the sponsorship angle with each using the particular expertise of the sponsor to develop a distinctive ethos and mission. Like the Business Academy in Bexley, with its enterprise curriculum, city firms links, teaching of the International Baccalaureate, 'City Trading Floor' in the centre of a new building and active project-based Business Fridays, the new Academy model should demonstrate timetable innovation, creative and flexible approaches to teaching and learning and a 'technology-rich', work-focused environment.

The objections, quite strongly voiced, to the Academies are that the partnerships allow individuals or groups too much influence. For what are relatively small capital sums the sponsors gain a significant controlling influence over multi-million pound institutions. They can effectively buy the right to dictate the curriculum, strategy and business interests within the school, and such 'partnerships' are the object of suspicion because of the opportunity they provide for inappropriate interference in education by groups and individuals whose motivation may be questionable or whose views, imposed on children, may be considered harmful by others.

Other objections centre on issues of quality improvement and will not be settled in the short term. Results in the Academies established so far have not seen significant improvements and there have been some headline-grabbing stories about the personalities and the financial implications of the new schools. However, since most educationalists would agree that to turn around a school in one of the most disadvantaged areas is a long-term project, the jury will have to stay out for a while longer.

What were Connexions Partnerships?

Connexions (see also Chapter 2) was the government service for supporting 13–19-year-olds in England. It was designed to be very responsive and to provide impartial, individual advice, guidance and access to personal development and opportunities but is now to be largely superseded by an integrated youth advice service and college and school-based careers work. The approach linked six government departments and their resources, agencies and organisations with many other groups and youth/career services. The breadth of agency involvement was intended to join up the expertise and support that the target group would need throughout their teenage years.

The help offered was very practical and designed to take the young person through the career and training options and personal-development opportunities, including sports, creative and voluntary activities. There were also considerable resources available to refer young people for help on issues like homelessness, substance abuse and other problems. The service was being delivered through local Partnerships covering the same geographical areas as the Learning Skills Councils. National guidance was supplied but flexibility was allowed in order to improve the service's ability to meet local needs and in places like Merseyside, Nottingham and Manchester this has been very successful in helping the 'at risk' groups and cutting NEETs. Delivery was organised through local management committees covering the same areas as local authorities.

All young people should have been given a personal adviser, these being prepared to work in a wide range of settings including colleges, schools, one-stop shops, outreach and community centres. There were around 8,000 personal advisers, many of whom are based within secondary schools. However, in reality, the numbers of advisers never reached more than half those required and the National Audit Office reported that the combined service was under-funded. In the eyes of advocates of the multi-agency partnership approach, the idea of targeted, impartial and expert advice and guidance was always the best approach and they believe it has produced a good-quality service for many learners. Others consider that funds will be better spent directly by schools, colleges and related providers.

In what ways are the federations different from other partnerships?

School federations are more extreme and permanent forms of partnership. Groups of schools collaborate under joint governance arrangements and/or having a formal written agreement to work together on raising standards. These joint governance arrangements could involve working under the collaboration and federation provisions of the 2002 Education Act which made possible the formation of single governing bodies, overarching strategic committees or joint strategic committees. There are other models, including school groups with non-executive joint governance or management arrangements (outside the provisions of the Act), and these may perhaps include head teachers working across more than one school.

The federations work at providing the broader curriculum opportunities and addressing identified skills shortages in an area but they also focus on quality and some have been using peer observation and mentoring strategies. Other examples of the successful use of shared resources and expertise can be found in shortage accommodation, behaviour management, ICT and e-learning and joint materials production.

Example of Learning Partnership: the London pledge

In order to widen the experiences and vision of young people in London, the local authority and schools in each borough are working with all kinds of organisations to increase the opportunities for young people in a range of significant learning areas.

This collaborative initiative is a very positive example of the advantages for students of creative work with partners. The detail of the wider opportunities and guarantees for individual students provided within the pledge are given in Chapter 5, as they relate to schools. Of wider interest, is the breadth of the enterprise and the scope of activities which can be provided as a result of employing a large number of co-operating bodies. Once such a network has been established it can be extended and harnessed in many ways, as is the case here.

What national support is there for new partnerships?

The Department for Education and Skills provides support for institutions willing to become involved in new partnership initiatives. This includes the education–business links partnerships (EBLCs) with local employers and with the Regional Development Agencies and Government Offices. The Learning and Skills Council as well as the Sector Skills Councils and local authorities have all been involved in the development of 14–19 policy and are central to the new networking and to building collaboration over provision.

The Increased Flexibility for 14–16 Programmes exists specifically to support the formation of school and FE college/training provider partnerships. This is intended to supply a framework for coherent joint delivery of a more relevant and attractive curriculum offer. In three years nearly 2,000 partnerships have been set up between colleges, schools and some other providers. They provide the opportunity for young learners to combine school and college situations and to access vocational courses and work-based or work-related learning options. Study might be for one or two days per week and a proportion of this will be off site and ideally in a real work environment.

On the whole, the students involved in this programme are studying for at least one of the vocational GCSE subjects. The evaluation of this work in terms of quality has produced some mixed judgements but partnerships of this kind are still relatively new and need time to settle and develop in order to overcome initial problems. There has been considerable interest in the roles of schools in their communities and the impact of the school/community relationship on performance and the school environment. One important study is the Extended Schools Pathfinder Project.

The Specialist Schools Trust provides support for leading and Specialist Schools in vocational education and so has a key role in support of the reforms. The New Relationship with Schools is another important lever for quality as is the LSC's relationship with colleges through the development planning cycle. There is also a new national quality improvement body – QuILL – being established for the post-16 sector and this will assist the development of advice, materials and best practice across the area. Even quite radical proposals for partnership, federation and joint working are achievable within the existing legislation. There are pioneering versions working well all over the country with support and assistance from national and local bodies.

What is the Strategic Area Review?

The Learning and Skills Council, as described earlier, is responsible for fostering and supporting the development of partnerships. The 'Success for All' strategy, described in Chapter 1, has generated new Strategic Area Reviews (StARs). These reviews are designed to use local LSCs and build real links between providers of post-16 education and training across the country. This will obviously impact on the whole area 14–19 provision. Through a process of discussion and regular contact, the idea of StARs is to identify local needs. At the next stage, the reviews are intended to promote capacity building in the wider context of the local and regional economy. They should also benefit from national collaboration and pooling of good effective practice. 14–19 pathfinders have been established to play this kind of role.

How do the 14–19 pathfinders work?

Areas designated as 14–19 pathfinder areas contain schools, colleges and training providers collaborating and supported by the LSC and the local authorities to offer a wider range of options than a single institution can deliver. In some cases new sixth forms and colleges are being established to extend choice and participation. In 2002–3 the first 25 pathfinders were set up to test the feasibility of the policy changes put forward in '14–19: Opportunity and Excellence' (DfES 2003a). The purpose of pathfinders is to establish a base to meet the demands being made on the education system for new flexibility. Without some carefully structured relationships the necessary collaborations in a diverse range of settings with a variety of teams and learners just would not work. Goodwill and enthusiasm will not be sufficient in itself to ensure successful delivery in complex environments. While there are some cutting-edge cross-phase partnerships in existence, the majority of professionals are inexperienced in the field and already overloaded, so additional assistance is essential.

Schools, colleges and other training providers have usually developed specialisms and the government strategy involves maximising access to these resources for more learners. In addition the pathfinder approach aims to disseminate good practice and to build local support networks. The potential national costs of the changes in provision can be assessed from the small-scale pilot areas. This is a local-area approach based on the development of strengths and specialisms of individual institutions. The pathfinders were expected to work alongside other initiatives like Enterprise and Diversity Pathfinders, the Increased Flexibility for 14–19-year-olds Programme, Entry to Employment, Excellence in Cities, the Excellence Challenge and others.

For the new partnerships to work there must be new and different routes created for students and for staff building new collaborative teams. The second year of operation (2003–4) brought another 14 on board and initiated some more radical ideas:

■ Employers were drawn into the mix in order to expand work-based training for the phase

■ E-learning received more attention in line with flexible access targets and the need to build appropriate ICT skills for future employees

■ More specific vocationally targeted pathways to occupations were designed with key skills included in the offer

Up till 2004–5 the LSC is matching funding to that of the DfES to provide a total of £46 million over the three-year scheme. From 2005–6, identified examples of good practice will be disseminated as a result of trail pathfinders. The links with employers are a key element of the work being undertaken. This kind of engagement is time consuming to establish and maintain and even where one institution has created a set of productive relationships it may be hard to introduce a partner. In one instance an engineering company that had been very satisfied with its long-term links with a local college and 16-plus students was not prepared to move down the age phase and admit 14–16-year-olds on to their workshop floor. Not only did they feel that the risks of working with younger learners were too high but that they were not necessary in commercial terms since the older group supplied an adequate stream of tested apprentices.

The pathfinders are designed to pilot and assess a variety of models of collaborative working. Key issues such as finance for providers and learners, cross- and multi-site management of learning, and provision in rural areas where there are transport issues are among those being examined for future developments. Whereas phase one tested the medium-term changes, phase two looked at more radical approaches and the most effective best practice can now be disseminated more widely.

As early as the evaluation of the first year there were some interesting findings and the experience of providers in all kinds of partnerships beyond pathfinders seems to support some of these initial indications (Higham 2004).

- The 14–19 age range tends to be prioritised and the sense of a coherent 14–19 phase is less clear
- The focus is strongly on the disaffected and low achievers where positive work is done but the majority of middle-range achievers are less affected
- The complexity of local environments require a more consensual and persuasive kind of leadership to build effective collaboration
- Sustainability does require constancy in national policy and adequate funding but also an embedding of principles within the values and practices of all those involved
- Student engagement on all levels is essential
- Expert, accessible and dedicated advice and guidance is a key element
- Provision of work-based learning is one of the toughest tasks

What are the ideal factors required for establishing and maintaining good employer links?

These factors and others are often already in place in the FE college and the new arrangements and student groups can access the existing opportunities:

- Time and resources for relationship building – qualified and experienced staff should be involved in activities such as risk assessment, and legal advice is also necessary
- Clear and effective communication channels to deal with issues and forward planning – e.g. the implications of accepting younger learners for insurance
- High-level institutional support to give status among employers and in the community – college and school senior team and governor level involvement
- Qualified and energetic support staff to administer partnerships and maintain good quality communication which is so vital to success
- Institutional marketing to build a profile and attract participants
- Utilisation of the external sources of support available – e.g. LSC, DfES projects, HEI involvement, TTA initiatives and local/national government development and regeneration funds and support

Over the past four years since the Green Paper 'Schools: Building on Success', the rationale for greater vocational and specifically employer-led elements has remained the same. The White Paper (DfES 2005a) offers an upbeat picture of achievements and emphasises the key role of partnerships for future progress:

> In some parts of the country, designated as 14–19 pathfinder areas, the process has gone even further. Schools and colleges have worked with local authorities and the Learning and Skills Council (LSC) to offer young people a range of options that extend beyond those any single institution can provide and which will succeed in attracting many more young people to learning. In other places, new sixth forms and colleges are being opened, boosting participation and choice.
>
> (DfES 2005a: 10)

What problems do providers anticipate in relation to partnership?

Some problems being anticipated are operational and it is probable that the detailed frameworks and procedures for handling specific delivery issues will gradually evolve. The process of implementing partnerships in practice and testing effective working practice through the establishment of precedents, and the testing of cases as problems arise, will be painful, but those who are optimistic feel that increased consultation, communication and joint operation towards shared goals will be beneficial for all partners, especially learners. (Chapters 4, 5 and 6 explore many of these issues in more detail in relation to the demands and risks involved when working with new learners.) The key issues include:

- Lack of clarity over roles and responsibilities for learners
- Additional invisible costs for providing institutions
- Practical considerations associated with transport
- Supervision, staffing, team operation
- Legal considerations
- Health and safety issues

The aspects of partnership that present the greatest challenges concern leadership and funding. To avoid dissent and raise the trust between partners, it seems imperative that the structures provide willing participants with a level playing field. Even before these partnerships are fully established, there is a disinclination on the part of some potential players to commit themselves to what they perceive is an inequitable enterprise.

Credit in collaboration – which institution benefits from students' success?

When institutional partnerships form in order to improve student opportunities through collaboration, the initial discussions tend to focus on management of the process but eventually the question of reporting must be considered. The issue produces some sensitive questions. There may be a spirit of collaboration but if one institution is deprived of published acknowledgement or there is confusion because of 'double counting', then some of the evolving benefits of such partnerships will be lost.

In recognition of the complexity of some of these problems, the DfES is taking a slow route towards potential resolutions. Options may well include more changes to the structure of performance tables (see Chapter 5). Possible mechanisms to support collaboration need to take account of the joint efforts of the partners, and to credit, for example, the work of the school in the case of a student who progresses slowly but finally achieves in a college. The dimensions of partnership are increasing and becoming more diverse as the DfES encourages all those involved to participate in consultation and evaluation.

What could employers offer to the 14–19 learners?

- Provide direct long- and short-term access to structured work experiences
- Build the LSC Enterprise Adviser Service through Education Business link Consortia
- Real opportunities for enterprise projects can be designed for the workplace
- Workplace materials can be adapted to provide contemporary and realistic training resources – for example, case studies using documentation and actual events, including marketing campaigns and their outcomes, product development and launch
- Contact with individuals who serve as mentors, role models and sources of advice for groups and individual young people
- Sources of labour-market information for the schools and colleges and closer access to employers and therefore to employment opportunities for the learners
- Visit the classrooms and other learning environments to help reduce the barriers between work and learning and increase their relevance to each other

What do employers gain from the partnership?

- Potential new recruits – students who may transfer from interested students directly to apprenticeship or who may return at a later date following higher education
- As a result post-employment training costs can be reduced
  Positive raised profile in the community with associated benefits
- Stimulating new business ideas, market intelligence and opportunities from wider networking contacts with young people, parents, professionals in several institutions and links with external agencies

- Increased contacts through agencies such as the LSC, with other like-minded employers
- With the development of collaborative arrangements employers gain a stronger voice in local-education planning, and this means that colleges and schools can assist with expertise and that curricula can be adjusted where agreed to meet local labour-market needs

Employees can also gain from the partnership in terms of staff development if they contribute to the process. Of course the advantages inherent in these outcomes are debatable. Not everyone subscribes to the view that a good education should aim to match and pre-train young people to meet local labour-market needs, nor that it is desirable for employers to have a strong voice in local-education planning.

What can partnership really achieve?

Crossways Academy, Brockley

Taking the lead in the 14–19 federation initiatives is a group around the Lewisham area from which the major Crossways Academy initiative has emerged. In December 2002, following area-wide inspection, Lewisham submitted its action plan on post-16 education to the DfES. This Area Wide Action Plan was constructed with key partners from the borough, including schools, sixth-form and FE colleges, Connexions, London East LSC, HE and work-based learning providers.

The strategic objectives in the plan are in line with the government's 14–19 agenda:

- Raising attainment
- Improving work-based learning provision
- Increasing participation, retention and progression
- Providing quality support and guidance for students choosing post-16 options

Specifically, the Crossways Academy is federated to four secondary schools: Catford Girls, Addey and Stanhope, Crofton and Deptford Green. Other schools, including Haberdashers' Aske and Malory, Christ the King College and the Hillsyde Sixth Form consortium of schools are participating by forming 14–19 partnerships. The plan is for the Academy to become the destination for year 11 pupils from the group of schools. In preparation for this formal co-operation, the members of the federation are beginning the process of integrating their strategies and sharing activities and structures.

In concert the institutions will be able to:

- Offer a wider curriculum at 14–16 that feeds into the Academy
- Provide opportunities for gifted and talented students to extend their curriculum

- Provide extra-curricula activities to students across the federation
- Share best practice
- Share data and establish benchmarks across the schools
- Provide support and assistance to each other when the need arises

What are post-16 e-learning partnerships?

The national learning network (NLN) is a national partnership network working to increase the levels of expertise and use of Information and Learning Technology across the learning and skills sector. This network is supported by working groups dealing with a range of issues. One of the groups is the 14–19 ILT Development Group. This was set up to create a sector ILT strategy for integrating ILT into all 14–19 learning practices.

What is meant by Learning and Skills Beacon status?

This is awarded to LSC funding providers with outstanding inspection reports who have been assessed as suitable by the LSC. In return they become responsible for the dissemination of good practice and constructive collaboration on behalf of other local providers.

Location of provision for 14–19-year-olds – where does the learning take place?

The majority of 14–19-year-olds are school based and there are no plans to alter this state of affairs in a major way. It is possible, under current arrangements, for FE to provide secondary education and the changes will lead to some increase in the numbers of 14–16-year-olds based in colleges. Some examples of new organisational models for integrated working include:

- Establishing a jointly managed sixth form, perhaps in a separate centre, which may eventually facilitate curriculum development for the 14–19 phase across a wider community
- Opening a community learning centre incorporating (all, or a selection of) pre-school, primary, secondary, FE, learner support, social and other services on a single site
- More informal collaboration between schools, colleges and training providers to jointly plan and provide a 14–19 curriculum for their area, supported by ICT networks and a common approach to student guidance
- New developments and approaches to deliver high-quality provision within the existing legislation

How will initial issues of funding be handled in this fluid partnership environment?

Questions such as this are fundamental and, though, as here, they are not always considered first, this is misleading since they are in fact the deal breakers. Unless there are clear lines for transferring appropriate levels of funding, and a reasonably fast response time, as well as an absence of complicated and restrictive advance bidding for contracts, there will be widespread resistance among key players. Schools and colleges sometimes feel disempowered but over time they have demonstrated their muscle to good effect. While they can be led and coerced to some extent, the funding mechanisms so frequently employed for this purpose must be in place. As a result of some problems with school funding the DfES has published a consultation document on proposals for a simplified school-funding system from 2006. This would give schools a three-year budget and enhanced planning opportunities. The Learning Skills Council will also be directing more resources to the needs of this age phase.

Funding for 14–16-year-olds currently flows through the LEAs and for 16–19-year-olds through the LSC. Capital investment is also under consideration, with priorities to include increased and improved facilities, support for training and flexible provision and upgrading in areas where 'transformation' is needed. There is a growing recognition of the financial and other disincentives to collaboration. The following were identified in the White Paper (DfES 2005a: 73):

- In the past, there has been no expectation that schools and colleges might buy from other providers in order to increase quality or breadth. If we are to take advantage of existing specialist staff and facilities, that will need to change.
- The systems exist for institutions to purchase places on courses from other providers, but there is a visible marginal cost. A school sending a few learners to study at college will have to pay for their course places, but will not see a reduction in its requirements for staff and facilities.
- There are 'start-up' costs to collaborative working. Institutions working together to meet the needs of young people in an area will need to analyse what provision is needed, agree which institutions will deliver it and organise it so that all young people in the area can access it.
- There are substantial logistical challenges to collaboration to enable young people to learn at more than one institution at the same time. For example, schools and colleges will need to co-ordinate their timetables and arrange transport between them.

The Increased Flexibilty Programme (IFP): who is involved and how does it work?

Over 300 local partnerships are involved in the IFP and more than 90,000 learners have benefited from the programme to date. The participants include schools, colleges and training providers, and they are all working to extend vocational education and training in the new group of 14–16-year-olds. This means that expertise in the multi-site, multi-experience is being developed. Students get to study out of school in an FE college or with another training provider for one or two days a week during Key Stage 4. The support for this works out at around £100,000 per year.

Concrete examples are the best way to understand this kind of programme: at its best, the initiative should remove barriers and allow imaginative and innovative solutions to the problems of providing high-quality vocational education to the maximum number of students. Young people involved in the programme will:

- Study off site at a college or with a training provider for one or two days per week during Key Stage 4
- Have opportunities to work towards vocational and work-related qualifications
- Be given the opportunity to develop knowledge and understanding in a work context

The IFP is not just about course delivery but about staff development across the sectors. Over time the school professionals in the best-practice examples are building up their experience of vocational courses and the industrially trained and experienced college and workplace staff are gaining knowledge and skills as they work with school colleagues and younger learners 14–16.

Each LSC area has at least one partnership and there are positive indications of successful operation. There are targets and objectives for the programme:

Targets/Aims:

- One-third of young people in the programme should gain at least one GCSE in a vocational subject at level 2 (over and above their predicted GCSEs)
- One-third should gain at least one NVQ at level 1 (over and above their predicted GCSEs)
- Three-quarters of the young people involved should progress to further learning
- Attendance rates of the young people involved should match that of the average for the Key Stage 4 group (age 14–16)

Objectives:

- To raise the attainment in national qualifications of participating pupils
- To increase their skills and knowledge
- To improve social learning and development
- To increase retention in learning after 16

The difficulty does not lie in finding examples of good practice but in capacity building to make certain that the entitlement is consistently provided on a national basis.

Who are the key partners in the IFP?

The LSC is the main funding route for such partnerships and supports the partners from the development stage, facilitating the relations through representation on the strategic steering groups through to monitoring and evaluating the programme. The Learning and Skills Development Agency provide the training and support, including regional conferences, training for placement co-ordinators, consultancy support, and the production and distribution of materials. The National Federation for Educational Research are researching the overall impact of the programme and early indications are that good progress is being made. Attendance and behaviour seems good and the drop-out rates are low. The vocational GCSEs are being studied, with ICT proving most popular.

How will the necessary levels of vocational provision be offered to young learners?

The responsibility for this provision is being passed to the local area partners. While vocational provision is the key area, academic courses and any options of interest to individual young learners could form part of a wide offer. Each institution would open its strongest specialised provision to students and all the participating institutions should collaborate to ensure that practical arrangements are put in place to enable individuals to take advantage of the opportunities. Arrangements for younger learners would be made as follows:

- Up to the age of 16 the pupil would be based in school but could spend up to two days per week in alternative settings
- The learner's home institution is responsible for finding the provision and for pastoral support
- Schools are responsible for buying in provision from colleges and training providers for the 14–16 age group
- Schools should also take steps to develop their own capacity to provide/contribute to vocational education in the future

Does the vocational, work-related emphasis show bias towards the FE sector?

There is a degree of sensitivity in dealing with all these developments. FE has been called a 'cinderella service' but the new policy visions seem to present opportunities to address historical problems. Realistically, the shift towards broader, vocationally focused approaches will only create a revitalised sector if the funding gap is closed and the status implications of studying in the sector are successfully addressed.

Conclusion

Finally, if new and less elitist and divisive qualifications and curricula are to be created, all parties must be involved and the hard-won consensus among stakeholders so clear at the time of the Tomlinson Working Group must be regained. If the funding methodology, pay and conditions issues are addressed in time then productive partnerships my well develop, especially in areas where structures and the will to collaborate already exist. Without these measures the barriers to change may well prove insurmountable.

CHAPTER 8

Qualifications and assessment

There is a huge and very confusing range of qualifications available in the UK. The main academic qualifications, GCSEs and A levels, whose survival or demise provoked such controversy and emotion during the 14–19 Working Party consultations, have now been reprieved at least in the medium term. Tomlinson's proposed cull of the public exams would have replaced the vast number of existing vocational qualifications with an overarching Diploma in one radical step. Now, we have instead proposals for new Diplomas in 14 vocational subjects and a promise to improve standards in English and maths. These would, as previously proposed, reflect key areas of the economy and replace the 3,500 vocational qualifications on offer at present. This new vocational system would operate in four subject areas from 2008. The four-level Diploma may have been shelved but it is not totally ruled out. The government has said that the final decision will rest on a review in 2008. For the immediate future the government has announced a new general Diploma for all 14–16-year-olds who achieve 5 GCSEs A*–C including English and maths.

The history of vocational qualifications

The introduction of National Vocational Qualifications (NVQs) was a significant element of curriculum development in the 1980s. They were not cast in the same mould as previous vocational qualifications but brought a new kind of occupational focus to education and training. Like the National Curriculum emerging in the later 1980s, the approach taken assumed measurable, quantifiable knowledge and skills sets. In such models, the contextualisation of occupational or any other kind of learning in its real social, economic and political setting is marginalised or ignored.

In the early 1990s the General National Vocational Qualification (GNVQ) was a new introduction. Designed to be a replacement for the existing BTEC National Diplomas and Certificates, this qualification was far more prescriptive. The standards issues were never fully resolved, outcomes-based courses and assessments were mechanistic and very limiting, validity and reliability and other principles were all called into question, and the process of implementation was very badly managed (Ecclestone 2000: 2002).

Many teaching teams in FE who had worked with the BTEC qualifications over the years, contributing to their development and building stimulating learner-centred projects and assignments, resisted the movement towards what they perceived to be an over-complex, poorly planned and confusing new product. Sets of highly prescribed information and detailed yet fragmented tasks were provided and subsequently tested as change followed change. The specifications were complex, removed choice and creativity, and, rather than encouraging learner autonomy, they actively limited any individual approaches or interpretations.

In terms of assessment in workplace and training settings, NVQs and VQs are governed by the QCA Code of Practice, which covers the operation of awarding bodies and other organisations involved in their delivery. These bodies do not think and act in harmonious concert. The same conflicts and internal strife that beset other curriculum developments from the National Curriculum to the GNVQs were evident here. At the centre of these debates are long-standing arguments over assessment ideology and standards definition (Black 1997; Burke 1995; Raggatt and Williams 1999).

Curriculum 2000 was not a success in spite of serious pressures on professionals to make it work. In principle, there were ideas within this new post-16 structure that seemed to promise a more flexible future for post-16 learners.

Notions of choice, destined to become more common, were introduced at this stage but the failure of the Curriculum 2000 innovation to deliver promised improvements to the structure, content and opportunities for the post-16 group was widely criticised.

Examinations and modernisation

It is generally acknowledged that the exam system, at least in England, is in need of a significant overhaul to improve efficiency. The government has allowed £100 million for this task over two years and, as additional support, some of the burden for exam administration will be reduced. The National Assessment Authority (NAA), part of the Qualifications and Curriculum Authority (QCA), works with the exam boards to review and overhaul the system. This process includes:

- A recruitment campaign to increase the supply and quality of examiners
- Better support for exam officers in schools
- Improvements in the transfer of information between schools and colleges and exam bodies through an electronic portal
- Pilots schemes for e-marking exam papers

The QCA, awarding bodies and the National Assessment Agency will collaborate with HE, SSCs and employers on the development of programmes, syllabuses and assessment criteria for the new qualifications.

In order to minimise disruption and administrative burdens, the intention is to work with existing bodies and systems in a carefully managed modernisation process. However, the reputation of the NAA was hit by the 2003–4 disastrous test process. The QCA itself reported on the Key Stage 3 testing process in very critical terms and the head of the agency resigned as a result. Considering the equally scandalous A-level exam fiasco only two years previously and the fact that new appointments and changes had been made to address the issues in the examination system, this failure was all the more shocking.

In this instance all the key targets for 2003–4 were missed in reading, writing and understanding of Shakespeare at 14. More than 500,000 pupils waited more than three months to receive their results due to IT and marking systems failures. In the end, the results website crashed causing unacceptable delays for individuals and for the publication of performance tables. This kind of quality issue must be addressed if any qualifications and assessment systems are to have credibility and public confidence.

In future, awarding bodies should work from a set of principles agreed with the QCA with the emphasis on:

- focusing on the needs of learners;
- maintaining and improving public confidence in standards;
- reducing costs and bureaucratic burdens on schools, colleges and other providers, in particular through developing common systems; and
- actively consulting with employers, HE and subject bodies.

Even with the announced retention of GCSE and A-level qualifications, there are still many changes and an ambitious strategy proposed for vocational education. To implement this strategy and integrate it within the existing frameworks within the 14–19 phase, significant resources and structural changes will be required. The government has already committed around £100 million to be made available over the next two years in order to support improvements in the efficiency of the examination systems.

Mike (now Sir Mike) Tomlinson was the chairman of the A-level standards inquiry following the 2002 grading crisis. He then became the chairman of the Working Group on 14–19 Reform, with its 15-member group representing the interests of further- and higher-education professionals, schools, employers and young people. This group was tasked with helping to design the future structures capable of contributing to the, 'lasting transformation of 14–19 learning'. The October report recommended subsuming A levels and GCSEs into a new Diploma containing more vocational opportunities and providing a range of skills:

> The status quo is simply not an option. Nor do we believe further piecemeal changes are desirable. The way ahead is through evolution rather than revolution. Our recommendations build upon the best of the current system to strengthen and deepen existing qualifications.
>
> (Press Launch, 18 October 2005)

There is to be a general Diploma (GCSE) and increased flexibility for learners to achieve earlier or later than 16 but in many respects the status quo has been preserved. Without rebranding and improvement it is hard to change the image of a product, and there is a strongly held view that the road to raising the perceived value of vocational education will be a long one.

Why does the current curriculum fail so many learners?

If you are lucky enough as a student to choose the well-trodden academic route in an established supportive school, to have a stable home and no external problems, you will join the growing numbers successfully entering higher education with the prospect of a better than average salary to look forward to. On the other hand, if your background is not so standard, you face more barriers to learning in your environment and personal life, and if you aspire to and prefer a more practical and applied education, you may well become lost and disillusioned in the system and fail to fulfil your potential.

Such students may take GCSEs without success (i.e. not get 5 or more A*–C GCSEs at 16) and this will reduce their chances of going on to study at level 3. The success rate for retaking GCSEs is low, and only appoximately 20 per cent of those retaking get a higher grade than they did first time around. This gives a scandalous figure of 80 per cent of retakes being a waste of time and resources and a terrible source of demoralisation. With this behind them young people may well slip further into a cycle of failure and disengagement. Even when receiving advice and further opportunities there is every chance that students with bad experiences in public examinations will opt for soft or superficially easy courses rather than the right, challenging course, for themselves. Nearly all FE professionals will testify to having encountered such students. In the current system there is really no space for flexibility to allow a student to work at a slower pace towards GCSEs.

What is wrong with the existing vocational qualifications on offer?

- They are not widely available at 14 and there are gaps at post-16
- They are not set within a simple enough framework – levels, sizes are very different
- There are too many of them
- Transfer between routes is not easy
- They are not widely understood and accepted
- The system does not compare favourably with that in other industrial countries
- Only traditional apprenticeships are commonly understood and their new form is still being disseminated
- Success rates are poor

From a learner perspective the existing qualifications, around 3,500 at present, are not only confusing but can disadvantage learners in situations where progression is

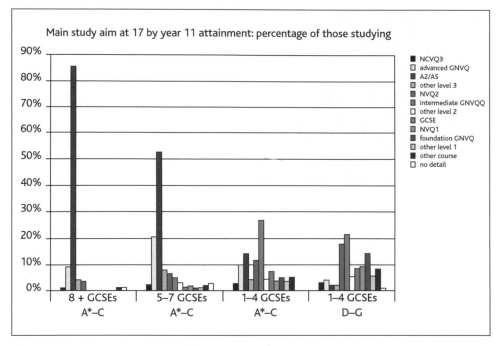

Figure 8.1 Post-16 courses pursued by young people

Source: DfES 2005a: 18

difficult or where transfer of learning credit is not possible. Some are well respected and have currency but only in a limited sector of the economy. Apart from the difficulty presented to an older learner who may want to alter their career path, this factor is a serious cause for concern if younger learners are to be allowed to build vocational experience and qualifications, and to bank this for future flexible careers in a shifting economy.

What implications did the publication of the White Paper of February 2005 have for qualifications?

This is an important question but the response is far from straightforward. With an election imminent, there were all kinds of public image and party political issues at stake, and a real sense in which those immediate factors could be seen to drive both policy and its presentation. However there has been a long debate within and beyond education and there are strong vested interests and camps established in the field. This means that even for those who fundamentally disagree with the direction chosen, there is an acknowledgement that a considered position is being adopted and for those who support this position the main argument is with the lack of courage they identify in the pre-election clinging to tried-and-tested exams. To this cohort the tried-and-tested element of the existing exam system should read tried and found wanting.

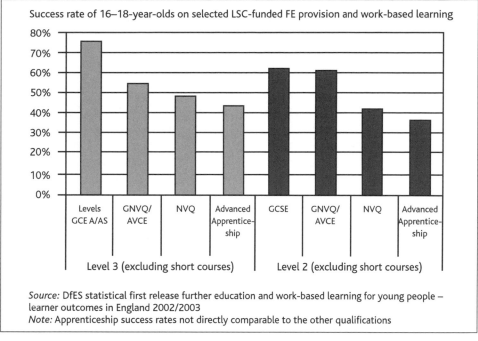

Source: DfES statistical first release further education and work-based learning for young people – learner outcomes in England 2002/2003
Note: Apprenticeship success rates not directly comparable to the other qualifications

Figure 8.2 Comparison of young people's rates of success on different courses

Source: DfES 2005a: 18

The most obvious impact of the initial press announcements on the White Paper publication was the news that there would be no radical reform to the existing GCSEs and A levels. These are being retained as 'cornerstones' within the new system, although a Diploma is being introduced in a more limited sense. The White Paper talks about 'routes to success for all' (page 3 of the executive summary) as a means to create a system where individual needs are leading the design of the learner's programme. This vision of a system where learners mix and match individual components is not new nor is it particularly controversial. It is, as anyone involved in Curriculum 2000 will testify, just very difficult to deliver.

So what is new in the qualifications framework?

The Diploma

A general (GCSE) Diploma will be awarded when the individual achieves 5 A*–C grade GCSEs including English and maths. In order to complete this new qualification successfully, pupils must achieve functional qualifications in maths and English, and complete relevant GCSE or A-level courses and suitable work-based learning.

New specialised Diplomas are being introduced, covering each occupational sector of the economy and containing academic and vocational material. These will be available at levels 1 (foundation), 2 (GCSE) and 3 (advanced), and the level 2 Diploma will require functional English and maths at level 2. Employers are being given a leading role through the Sector Skills Councils and, supported by HE and the QCA, they will be closely involved in the design of the specialised Diplomas as qualifications, providing an appropriate grounding for work and further study in the given sector.

The new level 1 Diploma should provide opportunities for learners at an achievable level and allow for skills to be developed as a sound basis for progression up the levels. QCA will continue to develop the alternatives to achieving functional skills within the GCSE for those unable to gain the full award, e.g. Skills for Life qualifications to be studied alongside the KS4 programmes. According to the minister, Ruth Kelly, there is a guarantee that employers will be involved in the design of the new vocational diplomas from the outset.

What about entry-level qualifications?

The entry-level qualifications are particularly important in that they provide a step to achievement for, among others, young people with special educational needs. In May 2004, QCA reported on these in 'An Evaluation of Entry Level Qualifications'. Progress is now being made on the recommendations from the report in order to develop a coherent framework of provision below level 2 as part of the new Framework for Achievement. The results should enable a more practical set of qualification units to be created and these could be incorporated into personalised learning programmes, building on the SEN framework. In this way, the inequities of 'one size fits all' qualification design can be addressed. The continuation of study in functional English and maths to level 2 post-16 will be an important feature of the entitlements for some students.

How will the new specialised Diplomas be introduced?

The Diplomas are designed to replace significant elements of the current system of around 3,500 separate qualifications and the hope is that they will provide a credible and practical alternative gateway to higher education and skilled employment destinations.

- To achieve a Diploma, young people will need to achieve appropriate standards in English and maths, specialised material, relevant GCSEs and A levels, and have work experience.
- Diplomas will be introduced in 14 lines and make these a national entitlement by 2015. The first four Diplomas in information and communication technology, engineering, health and social care and creative and media studies will be available in 2008. Eight will be available by 2010, including construction, and the Sector Skills Councils will work with other relevant bodies to pilot and subsequently roll out the full set of Diploma lines.
- Employers will be involved to offer more opportunities to young people to learn at work and outside school.

- Improvements will continue regarding the quality and number of employment-based training places through apprenticeships, bringing them within the Diploma framework.

As a young person progresses through the Diploma route, their study programme will become increasingly specialised. They will be able to choose an occupational area and their study and experience will be focused on this, though the coverage of basics and the breadth which might enable subsequent change of direction will be preserved. The final diploma will reflect the specialism in the title so in theory, once the Diploma brand has established itself, it should function as a straightforward and recognisable currency, as well as a relevant and constructive learning experience.

Is there any illustration of the new model for proposed Diplomas?

Diploma in Engineering

Level	Age	Core			Main vocational learning			Optional specialised units taken from within...		
Intermediate	14–17	GCSE Maths	GCSE English	GCSE Applied ICT	GCSE Double Award or BTEC[1] First Certificate Engineering	GCSE Design Technology	GCSE Science	City and Guilds[2] Progression Award in Applying Engineering Principles		
								GCSE Electronics		
								EMTA[3] NVQ[4] Performing Engineering Operations		
Advanced	16–19	A Level Maths			A Level Double Award or BTEC National Certificate Engineering			AS Physics	AS Design Technology	BTEC National Award or OCR[5] Certificate for IT Practitioners

Diploma in Creative and Media

Level	Age	Core				Main vocational learning		Optional specialised units taken from within...		
Intermediate	14–17	GCSE Maths	GCSE English	GCSE Key Skills	GCSE Science	Applied GCSE Art and Design	OCR Level 2 National Certificate in IT or BTEC First Diploma for IT Practitioners	GCSE Spanish	GCSE Film Studies	BTEC First Certificate in Media
Advanced	16–19	A Level Art and Design				BTEC National Certificate in Media or OCR National Diploma in Media		AS Business Studies	ABC[6] Award in Online Media Production Skills	City and Guilds Diploma in Media Techniques

Figure 8.3 Models of the proposed diplomas

Source: DfES 2005a: 56

1 BTEC is a qualification brand.
2 City and Guilds is an awarding body.
3 EMTA Awards Limited is the industry awarding body for engineering and technology.
4 National Vocational Qualification.
5 Oxford, Cambridge and RSA Examinations is an awarding body.
6 Awarding Body Consortium (ABC) is an awarding body.

The award of a Diploma will require the achievement of a minimum volume of qualifications; for example, at intermediate, the qualifications achieved must be equivalent to a minimum 5 A*–C at GCSE and include functional English and maths. The relevant SSCs and HE institutions may determine content that is greater than the national minimum. In designing the detailed specifications of Diplomas, Sector Skills Councils may also ensure that new Diplomas really stretch the candidates through the inclusion of additional components and possibly some A-level study as a requirement.

How will the introduction work?

At first, Diplomas will consist mainly of the existing qualifications and their units forming what should be realistic options and combinations acceptable to employers and universities. This stage will present numerous obstacles since there are thousands of existing qualifications and the White Paper warns providers that initially there will have to be strict constraints placed on potential combinations. Of course, this means that the advertised flexibility and choice aspects of reform will not materialise initially and perhaps not for a number of years.

It must be understood that the Diploma route includes A levels and GCSE. For example, a level 3 Diploma could include a double-award vocational A level and an A level plus any additional qualifications attached and credited. The possibilities for individual students should be increased, especially in terms of the potential for mixing the vocational and academic from level 2 onwards. The real strength of the Diploma if it can be realised will be the opening up of opportunities to take qualifications outside current conventional time constraints. Some of the pilot projects at both level 2 and 3 have allowed 14-year-olds to access routes once exclusively available only to the 16-year-old school leaver. Apprenticeships, in particular, will be developed in this way with the work experience and vocational GCSE options opening up pre-apprenticeship routes that will permit a subsequent fast track at 16.

The Diplomas will not be designed to narrow students down too early and, for this reason, although they will credit and make reference to the specialised occupational achievement and recognise this in the Diploma title, all units will be recorded and this will assist in any future process that might help the individual to transfer their learning credit.

Common Knowledge, Skills and Attributes

As described earlier, the Common Knowledge, Skills and Attributes will be included in new developments. The QCA will be working with employers and others to develop an outline description of the skills and eventually a single framework covering all abilities. These are linked with the outcomes for young people set out in 'Every Child Matters':

- Be healthy
- Stay safe
- Enjoy and achieve
- Make a positive contribution
- Economic well-being

How do young apprenticeships fit in?

Apprenticeships are open to young people in the 16–24 age range and currently operate with 130,000 employers and around 250,000 trainees. An apprenticeship is level 2 NVQ or Advanced, level 3. Young people also gain a technical certificate and Key Skills qualifications. This level of enrolment in apprenticeships is low by comparison to other countries and, following the Cassell's Committee review of the area, targets are more ambitious: 28 per cent (175,000) of all 16–21-year-olds to start an apprenticeship in 2005–6 and, by 2010, at least 35 per cent of the age group to be signed up. Apprenticeships have traditionally had reasonable status with employers and entry into this form of training has been competitive. The idea in extending this route is not to devalue the qualification or dilute the value of apprenticeships as currency but to develop genuine expansion of high-quality employment spaces.

The training is demanding and, in the past, trainees have sometimes entered the workplace context without a real understanding or any experience of the demands and expectations. The suitability of the candidate for apprenticeship can be hard to judge if they have only ever been in a traditional educational environment. In order to address this important area and improve retention and completion rates, the 14–16 phase will offer significant, innovative solutions. The work-experience entitlement and other preparation for work will improve the preparation for apprenticeship and the opportunities to assess and guide learners in making the most appropriate choice for their future. Information and guidance should in future be more about tasting and testing than reading and talking about options. The existing apprenticeships contain many features considered desirable for the new Diploma (academic and vocational content, core functional skills, employer direction and real work experience since apprentices are employed) and integration of the kind recommended by the Working Group 14–19 is planned to enable apprentices to receive Diplomas.

The new Diplomas are supposed to draw in serious employer involvement. The learning will not be seen as real vocational experience without this connection. The Young Apprenticeship model provides this with 50 days learning alongside skilled workers with an employer. Young Apprenticeships form a part of the qualifications structure as one of the ways in which 14–16-year-olds can follow new Diplomas. There is an individual learning plan which will include any GCSEs: vocational GCSEs are designed to fit with the occupational lines and other relevant qualifications can be taken as part of the overall package. Throughout the work-based elements of the vocational learning programme the young person will have a workplace supervisor.

If a 14-year-old is already showing interest in and an aptitude for a more practical, vocationally focused route then they may be considered an appropriate candidate for a 14–19 programme with a greater proportion of work-based learning. This would be seen as preparation for a full apprenticeship and the idea would be to keep the learner interested and committed. The concerns about these extended routes focus on the quality issues. A real apprenticeship had value because it was challenging, extended and required commitment and the demonstration of real aptitude and relevant skill and knowledge on the part of the trainee. These programmes were never meant to be about part-time attendance on a low-level work-based learning option. At their best they select well-prepared and keen applicants and put them through an intense and testing set of experiences. If these opportunities are genuinely extended then learners would benefit but if the apprenticeship label is used to cover a diluted and poor-quality new provision then the hard work of many professionals will be jeopardised.

Does the extended project, proposed by the Working Group, disappear?

Extended projects will be included in the options for learning. On vocational and/or academic routes this piece of work is considered both relevant and valuable. The original concept contains much to recommend it to education professionals and it is a real asset to learners who continue to study at degree level. Work undertaken in the past as A/AS level coursework achieved high standards and certainly engaged traditional and non-traditional students in a very special way. Many teachers hope that the best of previous examinations will be incorporated in the new structures.

Are there any changes to A levels and GCSEs?

These familiar qualifications remain but the plan is to strengthen them with GCSE English and maths being made more difficult to ensure that the functional foundation in the subject is secure. These improvements are intended to strengthen the credibility of a grade C GCSE as demonstrating a real working understanding of the subject. At GCSE the following will apply:

- English and maths GCSEs will be restructured to make sure it is impossible to get a grade C or above without the ability to use functional English and maths.
- Coursework will be reviewed to reduce the assessment burden.
- Work to reform maths will continue as proposed by Professor Adrian Smith, improving motivation and progression to advanced level. This is likely to include a new double maths GCSE.
- The promotion of science will continue and include the implemention of the new science GCSEs with expectation that young people should do two science GCSEs up to the age of 16.

One of the problems currently encountered with GCSEs is the insecurity of achievement across the functional core because, as they stand, strengths in one area can compensate for weaknesses in another. These measures are intended to address the issue of basic skills grounding and provide a better guarantee that students have achieved the functional core of maths and English. GCSE maths changes, designed to raise achievement at level 2 and 3, will continue to emerge from the developments following the Smith report, 'Making Mathematics Count'. They will provide answers to some specific problems and address issues identified as important for future learner success and progression. We will see the following changes in maths:

- development of a two-tier GCSE which will mean that no-one walks into the exam room knowing that a grade C is impossible; and no-one gets a B or above without being assessed on the most testing parts of the syllabus
- a review of the content and size of GCSE maths, including the role of ICT in the curriculum, teaching and learning, and assessment, and the content and teaching of statistics and data-handling
- development of a curriculum and assessment model for maths provision setting out clear pathways from National Qualifications Framework (NQF) entry level to level 3

English GCSE will alter only enough to permit the delivery of functional English requirements and will keep its existing range. Science for KS4 is discussed in more detail in Chapter 5 and the new GCSEs will be available across the board in 2006 following successful pilots. It is of course compulsory and the new entitlement for learners in the phase is to a course that leads to the equivalent of two science GCSEs.

What is offered for the most able pupils/students at A level?

We have been promised that the most able learners will be 'stretched' and this is to be achieved by the introduction of the more difficult questions at the end of exam papers. These learners will also be encouraged to take HE modules while they are studying at sixth-form level and to complete the extended project. Of course, the number of assessed A-level modules will be reduced from six to four with no change in content. There are also plans for the QCA to examine the possibility of introducing at least one more higher grade for A-levels.

How will the assessment burden be reduced?

In addition to the reduction in assessed A-level modules, there will be a review of GCSE coursework in order to plan some reduction in the burden of assessment currently placed on teachers. Overall the balance will not be radically changed.

Will GCSEs be unitised and are there further plans for change?

Not all GCSEs will be unitised and there will be future changes, that are already in the pilot stage. Although greater flexibility is an aim, full unitisation of all GCSE qualifications is not proposed. The applied GCSEs have been given a unit value of 3, and the QCA is proceeding with the development of a common core within GCSEs accompanied by a vocational or general element of choice. These new flexible GCSEs are being evaluated through pilots; science and history are the first to go through this process.

How will coursework be reduced?

The QCA will be reviewing the use of coursework with the following three areas of focus:

- Ensuring fairness
- Reducing the overall burden on learners
- Ensuring that the approach to coursework in similar subjects is consistent and appropriate – that it tests skills and attributes that cannot be tested in terminal examination

The principles for best practice in assessment are reiterated in the White Paper and these are directly applied to the question of coursework.

A levels

A levels have been retained and are perceived to be a strong-branded product. This is not to say that they will remain unchanged; although it is the fear of disruption through change, and public, though not professional, resistance, which has led to this decision. The recent history of the qualification is a contributory factor in this safest-known option approach. Curriculum 2000 attempted to introduce breadth through the AS exams for the year 12 learners and the vocational A level. It is true that the four AS and general studies combination is now common with a three A2 and general studies follow-on in year 13. However, this pattern only applies to far less than half the age cohort since under 40 per cent take even one A level and less than a third pass two or more.

The popular press view of A levels is that they must be worth less since so many now achieve and so many achieve high grades. Apart from the way this perception contradicts arguments about the high esteem in which the qualification is held, it is not really borne out in reality. The percentage of high achievers is not, in fact, so great and the government wants to increase the numbers achieving three or more grade As beyond the 3.5 per cent recorded for 2004. In this, they are at one with the findings of the Working Group but they are choosing to approach the issue of extending the test and the challenge for this group in a different way. In order to help universities differentiate between the highest performing candidates and to provide the 'stretch' for this group in their studies, a new section will be introduced to A-level papers covering AEA material. The strengthened A level will:

- increase stretch for the most able by introducing optional harder questions into separate sections at the end of A-level papers (Advance Extension Award)
- introduce an 'extended project' to stretch all young people and test a wider range of higher-level skills – this would be undertaken in an individually chosen subject area and would tend to replace the fourth or fifth AS level
- enable the most able teenagers to take HE modules while in the sixth form
- ensure that universities have more information on which to make judgements about candidates by ensuring that they have access to the grades achieved by young people in individual modules by 2006; there will also be support for those universities who wish to have marks as well as grades
- the assessment burden at A level will be reduced by reducing the numbers of assessments in an A level from six to four but without reducing the standard or changing the overall content of A levels

The 'Inquiry into A level Standards' (Tomlinson) and the findings of the Working Group proposed a reduction in the number of assessment units, though no change to content. The reduction to four rather than six units with only four rather than the current minimum of six exam papers is significant. It provides one-third less assessment, reduces costs and assists the process of exam scheduling. These changes will be introduced over time as each subject examination is re-accredited. Coursework at A level will not be replaced as it is mainly subject specific but QCA will be considering the cumulative effect of coursework across A levels.

So how will all this work together and will choice really be improved?

The most difficult questions are often given the briefest and least specific answers, and this is no exception. To be fair, the White Paper is setting out the framework without claiming to address implementation and operation but, still, there is a great deal left unsaid in the following;

> We will ensure that there are natural progression routes both through the levels of the Diploma and between GCSEs and A levels and the different levels of the Diploma. By doing so, we will secure for all teenagers routes that avoid early narrowing down, but provide real choice of what to learn and in what setting.

(DfES 2005a)

The delivery issues so evident in this are examined in more detail in Chapters 5, 6 and 7.)

There is some discussion of CoVEs, Skills Academies and partnerships led by institutions and monitored by the local authorities and the LSC but much is left for further discussion:

- We will be consulting in detail on our proposals, set out in our 5-year plan, for a presumption in favour of high-performing 11–16 schools engaging in post-16 provision.

- We will also develop new Skills Academies as national centres of excellence in skills.

- We will support the workforce to deliver. We will ensure that the right staff are in place, including those who have the necessary experience of the workplace to deliver vocational education, and that they have the professional development, qualifications and support that they need.

- Schools, colleges and other providers will take the lead in each local area. A prospectus of options will be made available to all young people, setting out what is on offer to them.

- Inspection will ensure that this is delivered.

- Each school and college will be expected to make the full range of choices available to young people on its roll, though perhaps at other institutions.

(DfES 2005a:58)

The last point suggests government commitment and the ambitious nature of these reforms since it is unequivocal in the demands it places on providers. The most important questions for managers will relate to the levels of support and adequate resourcing to deliver this extended choice. It is clearly stated that there will be support for staffing and training and that, where there are any gaps, it will be the responsibility of local authorities and the local Learning and Skills Councils to commission provision to fill them. The delivery of such promises may well be a less clear-cut operation.

Any news on flexible approaches to the age at which young people take exams?

This remains quite open in that the wording of the White Paper is not prescriptive, nor prohibitive. The aim is to

challenge and support schools and colleges to ensure that young people take qualifications when they are ready, not at a fixed age, encouraging acceleration to level 2 and ensuring early achievement at advanced level is recognised in Achievement and Attainment Tables and elsewhere.

(DfES 2005a)

So, it is a question of rewarding those institutions able to stretch the learner without placing unrealistic demands on the schools and colleges who focus on their more pressing targets.

Who provides the approved qualifications for the 14–19 phase?

The awarding bodies have been amalgamated over recent years and this has reduced the number of main providers. AQA, OCR and Edexcel are chief among these. The

Learning and Skills Act 2000 ensures that schools, colleges and employers can offer to students under-19 courses leading to external qualifications which are LSC or LEA funded only if they are approved. This means any qualification accredited and recommended for approval by the QCA (Qualification Curriculum Authority) under Section 96 of the Act 2000 according to specified criteria.

Will we all understand the new routes and qualifications?

It may be true that the existing qualifications framework is over-complex and illogical in many respects but serious effort will be required to introduce change. Work is needed to ensure that all parties, from schools and colleges to employers and universities, really understand the new routes and qualifications. Subject specialists, particularly those working with the core or the entitlement areas at KS3 and 4 where extra space is required, will have to make sense of the new demands and expectations for enrichment, support and integration.

What are the existing main qualifications for the 14–19 phase?

National Qualifications Framework

Entry level

These qualifications provide progression to foundation-level qualifications across the national qualifications framework.

GCSE

The main qualification for assessing attainment at the close of Key Stage 4.

Vocational GCSEs

These cover both the new vocationally related subjects like Applied Business and Applied ICT. The 'hybrid' GCSEs incorporate elements of both vocational and traditional learning.

Key skills

Communication, Application of Number and Information Technology have been identified as the essential generic skills judged to underpin success in education, personal development and long-term employment and lifelong learning. These qualifications are established in their own right and are taken alongside others as part of the learner's full programme of study. In addition to these three, there are a further three wider key skills of Improving Own Learning and Performance, Problem Solving and Working with Others. Students work in an integrated way and are assessed through a portfolio of evidence.

National Qualifications Framework		Framework for Higher Education Qualification levels (FHEQ)
Original levels	**Revised levels**	
5 Level 5 NVQ in Construction Project Management* Level 5 Diploma in Translation	**8** Specialist awards	**D** (doctoral) doctorates
	7 Level 7 Diploma in Translation	**M** (masters) master's degrees, postgraduate certificates and diplomas
4 Level 4 NVQ in Advice and Guidance* Level 4 Diploma in Management Level 4 BTEC Higher National Diploma in 3D Design Level 4 Certificate in Early Years Practice	**6** Level 6 Diploma in Management	**H** (honours) bachelor's degrees, graduate certificates and diplomas
	5 Level 5 BTEC Higher National Diploma in 3D Design	**I** (intermediate) diplomas of higher education and further education, foundation degrees, higher national diplomas
	4 Level 4 Certificate in Early Years Practice	**C** (certificate) certificates of higher education
3 (There is no change to level 3 in the revised NQF) Level 3 Certificate in Small Animal Care Level 3 NVQ in Aeronautical Engineering A levels		
2 (There is no change to level 3 in the revised NQF) Level 2 Diploma for Beauty Specialists Level 2 NVQ in Agricultural Crop Production GCSEs Grades A*–C		
1 (There is no change to level 3 in the revised NQF) Level 1 Certificate in Motor Vehicle Studies Level 1 NVQ in Bakery GCSEs Grades D–G		
Entry (There is no change to level 3 in the revised NQF) Entry Level Certificate in Adult Literacy		

Figure 8.4 National Qualifications Framework

GNVQ

This General National Vocational Qualification began life as a three-level Advanced GCSE and has been replaced by the VCE. The six unit GNVQs that have not attracted large numbers will be withdrawn in 2005 and the larger entry subjects in 2007.

NVQs

Are designed to demonstrate competence in a specific vocational area. Vocational Qualifications – relate more broadly to a wider occupational area. These were traditionally taught in FE colleges but are increasingly available in schools especially where specialisms and partnerships are being developed. They include BTEC, City and Guilds and RSA awarding-body qualifications.

GCE A levels and AEAs

These include the AS which is a stand-alone qualification equivalent to the first half of an A level and the A2 which does not stand alone as a qualification in its own right but added to an AS provides a full A level.

The Advanced Extension Awards are designed to stretch and credit the most able candidates and can be taken in any school or college.

VCEs

These Vocational A levels were originally introduced as an element of Curriculum 2000 to provide a viable vocational alternative to the A level and from September 2005 it was planned that they became known as GCE A levels to signal their equal value.

What improvements were originally proposed for the system?

The reformed framework, as stated earlier, would:

- Introduce a new diploma qualification awarded at four levels: entry, foundation, intermediate and advanced.
- Consist of two parts – core and main learning. Core learning would focus on developing basic skills. Main learning would comprise a young person's subject study (including the KS4 requirements).
- Replace the large quantity of externally set coursework with an extended project. This demanding piece of work would develop research, analysis and presentation skills and allow a young person to study a chosen subject or subjects in depth.
- Offer all learners access to programmes that would ensure they had every component necessary to achieve their full potential.

The group claimed that the changes would address the systemic and long-term problems currently plaguing this key phase of education and the transition to employment and higher education. These include low post-16 participation, low levels of basic skills, an over-burdensome assessment system and a generally poor vocational offer.

If fully implemented the new structures would establish the following improvements:

- be more rigorous than the current system;
- place literacy and numeracy at its centre;
- stretch and challenge all young people;
- reduce the burden of assessment;
- offer high-quality vocational education; and
- encourage more people to stay in education and achieve highly.

The key aims are all present here: stretch, participation, skills, relevance, standards rigour and assessment efficiency and effectiveness. While there is considerable consensus on the broad sweep of policy, the devil is in the detail. Qualifications are the bread and butter of students and of those who teach and assess but they are also invested with historical and emotional significance beyond their immediate currency value. In the end the proposed changes were met with greater resistance and more outright public opposition than even the most pessimistic reformers anticipated.

Has there been a U-turn?

Most of these aims can still be found in the 2005 White Paper and the minister insists that the spirit and much of the detail of the Working Party recommendations have been heeded and taken up. The issues in terms of qualifications are the retention of the traditional academic route and the decision not to make significant changes in the balance of external and internal assessment. Both of these were always going to be close calls since stakeholder pressures were intense and though there is a sense for some that the outcome was a safe (pre-election) choice, there was never a promise to go for radical reform. It is also a simplification to see the way forward from the White Paper as safe. Although total qualifications redesign and roll-out would have been risky and very disruptive for several years, the shift in public perception of vocational and academic qualifications would have been made easier from a clean-sheet start.

Without this fresh start, all kinds of difficulties seem likely to emerge in the process of integrating reformed vocational qualifications with existing, established provision.

Which reforms affect assessment?

Over the two years following the general election, reduction of the burden of examination administration on colleges and schools and increased efficiency of the system as a whole are twin goals for the DfES. They have made over £100 million available to further these aims. With this in mind, the new National Assessment Agency integrated within the Qualifications and Curriculum Authority is charged with working towards a complete overhaul of the examinations system. The plan is for this to be achieved under the auspices of the current regulatory regime. The NAA will also have responsibility for the delivery of National Curriculum tests. There is still a certain amount of structural tension in provider regulator roles being located in one place.

Key areas of concern include the quality and supply of examiners, development of electronic portals to improve exam information transfer, e-marking pilots and improved support for school examination officers. The quality improvements in these mechanisms should address some of the efficiency and modernisation issues raised in previous years. Issues of security relating to the marking, movement and moderation of examination papers and scripts between centres, examiners and awarding bodies have been the subject of allegations and inquiries over recent years. This has led to review and reform of some of the key processes in this area. In particular there has been work on streamlining the processes involved to prevent the unacceptable delays experienced in some quarters. QCA is introducing a limited amount of second marking and improving the pay of examiners as well as increasing recruitment in some shortage areas. The establishment of an institute for examiners and a professional framework for examiners will be a component part of these improvements.

Will the assessment burden be reduced as originally proposed?

Reducing the complexity and the weight of the burden on both students and staff in the 14–19 phase was a stated aim of Tomlinson. To cut the quantity of externally marked exams and draw teachers into more assessments would, of course, have a great impact on the workload of staff in schools and colleges. The profession was unlikely to accept the reforms unless there were credible plans for additional resources to be injected prior to implementation. The plan was to instigate these improvements in advance to ensure that whatever the outcome of the Tomlinson recommendations there will be a quality improvement in the processes surrounding the operation of examinations. Following all the consultation and recommendations this issue has been laid aside:

> Finally, some people argue that the overall amount of assessment in the system is now too great. At different times, the concern has been about the burden on students, the burden on teachers or the burden on the examination system of the volume of scripts. This was a particularly important issue following the introduction of the Curriculum 2000 A level reforms. The latest evaluation reports on Curriculum 2000, however, suggest that the system has bedded down and that students and teachers are generally more comfortable with the amount and type of assessment in most cases. And in the post-16 sector, our measures to reduce bureaucracy, led by Sir Andrew Foster, have sought to eradicate inappropriate assessment arrangements...We believe that the current balance between internal and external assessment is essentially the right one to

secure public confidence in the examinations system. We therefore do not propose major change here.

(DfES 2005a: 7)

The Independent Committee on Examination Standards found that 'no examination system at the school level is better managed', and the government therefore decided not to accept the Tomlinson proposals for radical change. Above all they have rejected the shift in balance from external to internal teacher assessment. From 16-18 there will be reductions in the overall burden as a result of the changes to GCSE, AS and A2. Since the number of units in the AS/A2 will be cut by one third and the coursework for GCSE is reduced there will be a definite lightening of the assessment load. As for the vocational qualifications the adjustments will be to the form of practical assessment moderation, including e-portfolio use.

Does this mean there will be no change for teachers in the phase?

Not quite. The Department takes the position that more 'robust' teacher assessment will improve teaching and learning. They do agree that the burden of assessment on learners, teachers and the system in general should be reduced. In practical terms it is the KS3 stage below that will see the real change rather than the 14–19 phase. The White Paper (DfES 2005a) sets out the following:

- Externally set and marked National Curriculum tests will continue in the core subjects of English, maths and science. From 2008, subject to successful piloting, we will also introduce an external online examination in ICT. The remaining foundation subjects of history, geography, citizenship, design and technology, modern foreign languages, PE, music and art and design will continue to be assessed by teachers, but we will do more to improve the effectiveness of assessment.
- A focus on teacher assessment supports the professionalism of teachers developing their skills to employ teaching strategies, curriculum and assessment to personalise education to each learner's needs and aptitudes. We will provide training and guidance for teaching staff to develop their assessment skills and provide them with materials to help them accurately assess student performance. This will include a bank of nationally-developed standardised tests and activities, which teachers can use to support their professional judgement.

Are there changes to the assessment of vocational qualifications?

Existing qualifications have a range of different internal and external assessment methods but, once again, there are no plans to alter the balance and the approach remains light and distanced. The combinations and proportions of internal and external are deemed to be suitable and well matched to the requirements, especially in terms of competence demonstration and workplace performance. Systems for validation, verification and moderation will not be changed. They are supervised by respected, approved awarding bodies who work effectively to assure quality.

How will the new vocational qualifications be given improved status in the labour market?

This really is a burning question since the academic qualifications will not be radically reformed. The new Diplomas will be assessed to internationally approved standards and fit within the developing European Qualifications Framework and European Credit Transfer system for vocational training. This is a new framework based on the NARIC and NRP systems currently in place which will clarify and credit the relationships between the qualifications across EU countries. In addition there is the Europass, launched in January 2005, which provides a standardised portfolio of documents constituting a record of qualifications, competences and related work experience intended for widespread use throughout the EU.

None of this will help during the time public perception continues to regard the vocational routes as having lower status. Efforts to engineer a shift in this area are made very difficult by the existing strong correlation between attainment and family background and by the continuing predominance of middle-class students at universities. There are poor retention and achievement rates on vocational courses and those most at risk of dropping out are the students from low-skilled parental backgrounds, males and previous low achievers. The danger for the 14–19 age range is that once they have experienced failure the chances of later achievements are severely reduced even when additional funding and support are supplied. In terms of the status of vocational qualifications as currency, there seems little incentive for students with good early academic achievements to undertake such programmes since the returns in employability are minimal.

Will e-assessment really play a key role?

Many professionals have a rather jaded view of the e-solutions. There have been fiascos with past systems for assessment and tracking of achievement where they have been introduced too early and with insufficient testing, evaluation and de-bugging. When awarding bodies have suffered from high-profile difficulties they are inevitably associated with the e-systems in place having to deal with large numbers and tight deadlines. On a smaller scale, the schools and colleges are very aware of the time and training required to enable all concerned to familiarise themselves with the demands and restrictions of new systems. While real streamlining and advances in quality are welcomed, the sense of foreboding frequently expressed is understandable.

There is a real commitment to the use of e-assessment and a sense that it will enable learners to access both practice and real testing at times and at a pace that suits them. This would be an advantage for both slower and faster learners. QCA will be involved in moving towards e-assessment of the functional maths and English elements of GCSE. Interest in other aspects of technology and assessment is quite high and there will no doubt be monitoring and evaluation of projects. Innovation will certainly not be welcomed unless there is a genuine improvement in quality and learner experience/support or in the processes surrounding marking, moderation and reporting of results.

How would the proposed qualifications have been structured?

Among the key components of the new Diploma were the central core of skills, the vocational route and the challenges for the more able students. The recommendation was that A grades be split into three with additional, more stretching questions giving students the chance for the highest of these.

Would the proposed Diploma system mean that all the familiar qualifications disappeared?

The four new Diploma levels fitted the existing levels of the National Qualifications Framework but the intention was that the manner of progression would be more individualised and less compartmentalised as each level will be interlocked with the next. It would also be possible to enter the framework at the most appropriate level and to progress without getting the Diploma qualification at each level, so enabling 'fast-track' movement.

What is the place of the Vocational GCSE and A levels in the future?

Aside from the debates surrounding the qualification titles, there are key questions to be answered in this area. At present, in spite of previous reform attempts, the vocational and academic routes remain very separate and the reforms over five years and longer are designed to produce more of a continuum. It is hoped that this will result in improved vocational and work-based routes for 14–19-year-olds and that these could be combined with modules of an academic nature. The qualifications should have equal status and be as challenging as their academic equivalents but enable learners to gain more involvement with employment contexts at an earlier stage.

In March 2004 Ofsted reported on Vocational A levels and, in July 2004, on vocational pathway development through the new vocational GCSEs. The findings are obviously significant for the 14–19 phase and the following key principles were identified. High-quality vocational courses should:

- Engage students in real workplace issues
- Develop investigative, creative and business skills

Table 8.2 How the proposed qualifications would have been structured

Age Range	14–16 most 16-year-olds on next level	14–16	14–16	16–19	14–19
Equivalence	At pre-GCSE level	GCSE: D–G NVQ level 1	GCSE A–C NVQ level 2 Intermediate GNVQ	A, AS NVQ level 3 (Top A grades = A–1st year degree)	All students throughout
Title	ENTRY DIPLOMA	FOUNDATION DIPLOMA	INTERMEDIATE DIPLOMA	ADVANCED DIPLOMA	CORE SUBJECTS
Status	Minimum 'leaving' qualification	Students choose open or specialised lines	Continue with open or specialised diploma	Diploma continues to Advanced level	Compulsory
Content	**National Curriculum** Maths English Science	**Open** Students own combination of modules	**Open**		**Functional Learning:** Basic Maths Communication IT
		Specialised Up to 20 subject 'lines' pre-combined modules Academic and Vocational	**Specialised** Some lines exclusively academic or vocational, some mixed		**Extended Piece** Any subjects Any form
			Lines include: health, science and maths, philosophy and theology, public services and care		**Wider Activities** Work, sports, art experiences, etc. (recorded – unassessed)
All students leaving any stage take a transcript detailing: Pass/Merit/Distinction, Module marks and Record of all activities					

- Provide progression routes to general and vocational courses at higher levels or to modern apprenticeships
- Provide learning in vocational settings
- Emphasise practical and work related, over theoretical learning

The view of Ofsted and of most practitioners and employers is that good-quality vocational education of any kind should link relevant subject and vocational expertise to real experience in industry. Methods used should be appropriate to the context and learners should spend time applying new skills within such settings. There are many practical problems associated with placements and with learning in real rather than simulated work environments but the genuine experience is widely held to be superior.

Within Ofsted reporting there is a clear move towards learning with a more applied and practical bias, especially regarding these new vocational routes as it would improve even the satisfactory examples. The findings can be summarised as follows:

- Teaching is generally satisfactory or better but the proportion of unsatisfactory teaching is higher than for comparable courses
- Students/pupils' achievements are generally lower than comparable courses, but are better once prior attainment and added value are taken into account
- In both teaching and students/pupils' achievements there are significant variations across the vocational subjects

Among the findings there was a sense that the range of teaching and learning approaches was quite limited and that the vocational approach was inadequate. From the point of view of those involved in teacher education and development for this phase, this may not be a surprise. There are many providers in both the school and the FE sectors who have, for a wide range of reasons, introduced vocational courses without adequately qualified and specialised staff.

These deficits inevitably lead to the weaknesses described in the Ofsted reports. Courses designated vocational were often too theoretical, lacked suitable practical activities and were insufficiently related to vocational contexts. There was also far too little effective work experience included and this was particularly noted in relation to the advanced courses.

Vocational GCSEs

These qualifications were established in vocational subjects in September 2002 to enable younger learners to experience a more work-related course at an earlier stage.

There are ten double-award GCSEs (eight of which are applied) currently on offer and two pilots:

- Applied Science
- Applied Business
- Applied Art and Design
- Manufacturing
- Leisure and Tourism
- Applied Information and Communication Technology
- Health and Social Care
- Engineering

- Applied Physical Education (pilot)
- Performing Arts (pilot)
- Construction and the Built Environment
- Hospitality and Catering

Each is equivalent to two other GCSEs and an institution must invest considerable time, planning, staff expertise and resources in order to deliver them effectively. They should appeal to both school and college students of all ability levels and are designed to run in conjunction with existing qualifications in any institution and alongside the core National Curriculum in schools. They provide an early opportunity for students to explore vocationally relevant study and to link it with real work experiences in order to sample career paths.

Transferability and progression

The equivalence of the qualifications and their place within an accepted qualification framework are intended to provide young learners and their families with a safeguard since learners receive accreditation, which enables them to continue in education if they wish or to return later. The transferability of the qualifications provided has always been a significant issue. Learners and their families, carers and advisers may well be either risk averse when faced with an untested qualification or unwilling to base their life chances on an unfamiliar package.

The obvious progression routes include the vocational A levels and students may also enrol on other vocational qualifications such as the BTEC Nationals or take other AS and A2 courses and use the early GCSE in vocational areas as a taster experience and an opportunity to work in different ways. The advantages of such qualifications might in some cases be their direct relevance to a chosen occupational/career path but for other, undecided learners they may just provide a more generally stimulating environment which maintains a learner's interest at a vulnerable point.

Learner engagement in some groups, for example young males, can be a real issue and the motivation gained by the employer links and work-related activities of a good vocational GCSE or BTEC level 2 certificate can be very powerful. Other students might progress on to a Modern Apprenticeship at 16 and so into skilled employment. This kind of route should not prevent the learner from accessing relevant higher education opportunities at an appropriate time. The frameworks and the development of foundation degrees in vocational areas have been designed to provide progression routes containing greater flexibility.

What is the difference between a general and specific vocational course?

General vocational courses like the vocational GCSE, the AVCEs and the GNVQ introduce learners to a sector. They take a broad view of industry or business, its key concepts and theories, the structure and operation of its industry and management, and they promote the development of skills relevant to this world of work and an understanding of the wider context. Specific vocational or occupational courses like the City and Guilds schemes, NVQs and HNCs have a direct link to particular industry standards. They develop a particular set of skills and build single-industry knowledge of occupational theories and practices. Essentially they are preparation to qualify for an identified job in a vocational area and their titles will reflect this. (See Annex A, 'Work-related Learning at Key Stage 4', DfES/0132/2003d).

How should providers ensure a good-quality vocational course?

The lesson from Ofsted reports has been quite explicit. However, it is easier to understand the criticisms than to propose and implement appropriate improvements. If a provider is aiming to introduce a high-quality vocational course then the work experience, work-related content and appropriate teaching and learning strategies, combined with industry aware and qualified staff, are the key elements. The vocational approach means links with local industry/commerce or public-sector employers. It indicates recent and relevant materials and potential contacts to enable progression into real employment, further experience or genuine advanced courses of a similar high quality.

Planning and networking are often the victims of workload pressures on staff and it can be very tempting to fulfil the minimum requirements of specifications when introducing a new vocational course into a school or college especially when those involved have little experience. The ideal future scenario would involve providers more closely in established networks and partnerships with the local employers, LSC, awarding bodies and with one another in federations. As things stand, there is still a very fragmented and patchy offering and the best practice is not always effectively disseminated. According to Ofsted, too few teachers possess or have access to recent, relevant industrial experience. In the short term this makes the potential support and contribution of employers even more valuable to the young learners and in the longer term the contacts may even provide interesting staff-development opportunities.

What support is available for those trying to establish such provision?

One of the advantages of the longer lead times in this phase of educational reform should be the availability of a more developed set of support networks and agencies. Government has had time to establish and fund new bodies to build and consolidate the structures and relationships required to implement policy most effectively. This gives schools and colleges access through LSC and LSDA to established local partnerships with the Educational Business Links Consortia and the LEAs.

What are the new apprenticeships?

Everyone understood the traditional apprenticeships in years gone by and, in spite of or perhaps because of their strong working-class identity, they were both successful and well respected. Their decline was the result of economic, political and social changes outside the scope of this text but their reputation combined with the recent shortage of skilled craftspeople in some sectors of the workforce has led to a resurrected and redesigned version of the concept.

The new apprenticeships offer a work-based learning route that allows young people to achieve qualifications at both level 2 and 3. They have been fitted into a new national framework in which there is progression towards a vocational area foundation degree as a higher-education goal. The rebuilt apprenticeships are wide ranging and they contain a strong emphasis on core skills in addition to the acquisition and practice of specialised vocational knowledge and skills. Apprenticeships can be undertaken in engineering, social care and IT.

Who are the new apprentices?

These are no longer exclusively taken up by boys. On the contrary, around 50 per cent of those undertaking apprenticed training are girls. They are currently available as an entitlement for all students who reach the required standard and the numbers of places are set to expand. The plan is to increase this work-based route and to link it to the wider national structures.

What status and prospects does an apprentice have?

There are Apprenticeships and Advanced Apprenticeships and the majority of those enrolled on the latter are actually employed. Nearly 90 per cent of those who leave are employed within six months, so there is a sense that the reintroduction of this qualification route has been very successful. Elsewhere fears that the reputation of apprenticeships may be affected by poor-quality schemes have been expressed.

In the debate about the quality of new apprenticeship provision, the fundamental importance of the relationship with employers cannot be emphasised enough. If employers are fully committed and take responsibility for the learning, and if they are given the necessary resources and authority to ensure that standards are maintained then the qualifications have a high currency value in the employment market.

When young people with a good standard of education choose vocational routes in significant numbers, we may begin to assume that conventional attitudes have begun to change.

What is a Young Apprenticeship?

This is a far more radical development at Key Stage 4, enabling some 14–16-year-olds to follow a new industry-specific route towards a vocational qualification in an employment situation. This extension of the existing post-16 apprenticeship uses the same structures and components and so provides the young learner with prior experience of the context and early exposure to components of the apprenticeship with the opportunity to achieve parts of the qualification ahead of the standard time. The progression for a successful young learner would then be to a fast-track version of the apprenticeship.

Will other existing qualifications continue to hold their value?

The National Certificates and National Diplomas awarded since the end of the First World War are still in place and valued today. They are a fascinating example of the endurance of a qualification in the face of several attempts to reform the system and abolish a qualification. It seems that, for the medium term at least, the GCSEs and A levels will join them as survivors of the qualifications and curriculum environment. In spite of the shifts away from the Tomlinson proposals and their emphasis on the reduction and rationalisation of the vocational offer, the plethora of qualifications currently available will undoubtedly face cuts.

Work-based training

In many respects the move towards new versions of the apprenticeship is a revisiting of previous initiatives. Every single decade has seen its own harvest of innovation in this area as the traditional apprenticeship declined. This constant cycle of reinvention and collapse has inevitably left many sections of education with a deep sense of cynicism. It is hardly surprising that enthusiasm is difficult to find when there are plenty of professionals with personal memories of the time and effort they invested in various schemes and young people who participated without the promised high-value outcomes. For many, all such schemes seem to be no more than artificial means to address poor employment prospects for the young.

The 1970s gave us the Youth Opportunities Programme and New Training Initiative, themselves designed to improve existing apprenticeships. Further attempts to push the vocational training area forward occurred in the 1980s with the whole TVEI (Technical Vocational Educational Initiative) movement to establish, support and accredit Youth Training Schemes in various forms.

Apprenticeships – background

From the 1990s the apprenticeships themselves were addressed through the introduction of the Modern Apprenticeships. The intention was to upgrade and improve the qualifications, giving them mainstream acceptance and raised status. However, the nature of the changes had the opposite effect, leading to a reduction in the work-based training and a shift away from employer supervision as the agency providers assumed more responsibility. Without sufficient real work-based apprenticeship places, many trainees were given simulated work experience either in colleges or centres. Given the broad nature of the work areas that came under this umbrella there was often a lack of suitable places in local areas and the substitution of artificial and sometimes fragmented alternatives led to a devaluing of the experience and of the schemes.

The new Modern Apprenticeships are a key part of the framework reforms. In order to shift attitudes and perceptions, the redesign of such an important area is surely crucial. In terms of providing real work-based experience supervised within an industry sector the relationships between employers and educational institutions are very important. For more discussion of this key area see Chapter 7.

What is the role of the new National Assessment Agency?

The new National Assessment Agency (NAA) created by the QCA has been given a modernisation brief alongside responsibility for the delivery of National Curriculum tests. It has a more general responsibility for the oversight of the delivery of public exams and the administration of Key Stage tests. QCA will retain the regulatory role and continue to monitor standards. In the past, the regulator and test provider functions were too close and this restructuring has addressed the issue.

Conclusion

The widespread support for the Tomlinson reform has not dissipated and now that the general election is well past and the status quo on traditional qualifications appears to have been preserved there is time for the sectors to reconsider the situation. There seems to be a sense of hope that the planned review by Sir Andrew Foster and other post-election shifts and tasks will enable the desired evolution to continue. After a period of respite and regrouping there are significant moves to continue applying pressure on government for a more coherent reformed framework. As things stand, even the positive elements incorporated within the White Paper will not address the need for increased clarity and simplicity nor for real equalisation and integration of the academic and vocational routes. The now perennial achievement improvements will only serve to heighten the debate surrounding level 3 qualifications.

Useful websites/links

Table 8.3 Websites/links for information on qualifications

Area	Site	Focus
Key skills	www.keyskillssupport.net	Main gateway to programme initiatives, resources, support
	www.qca.org.uk/nq/ks	QCA site with examples of tests, proxy qualifications and guidance
	www.qca.org.uk/14-19	Comprehensive site for 14–19 providers, learners and supporters
	www.aqa.org.uk/qual/keyskills/com.html	Largest unitary awarding body – guidance and specific information
	www.dfee.gov.uk/key	Government policy information/ guidance
	www.dfes.gov.uk/learning&skills	Key providers – colleges, sixth forms, private, adult and voluntary, etc.
	www.key-skills.org	City and Guilds site
	www.asdan.co.uk	Award Scheme Development and Accreditation Network programmes
Awarding bodies	www.aqa.org.uk	
	www.edexcel.org	Awarding body information
	www.ocr.org.uk	Information on OCR qualifications – levels 1–4
Vocational GCSE/A level	www.vocationallearning.org.uk	
Design and Technology	www.dtonline.org	Mainly KS 3&4
	www.design-technology.org	Free materials for schools and colleges
Leisure and Tourism	www.vocationallearning.org.uk	Contains L&T vocational GCSE resource
	www.tourismsociety.org	Professional site
MFL	www.bbc.co.uk /11 16 /languages	Useful resources and links
ICT	www.becta.org.uk	
	www.techsmith.com	
	www.ttsonline.net	
	www.ngfl.gov.uk	
General	www.dfes.gov.uk	Main site with links Standards
	www.thestandardssite.gov.uk	
	www.teachernet.gov.uk	Excellent comprehensive site
	www.lsda.org.uk	Learning and Skills Development Agency
Work-related learning	www.vocationallearning.org.uk	LSDA site
	www.dfes.gov.uk/nvq	Background and detail on
	www.dfes.gov.uk/qualifications	vocational qualifications – see also main awarding body sites
	www.leacan.org.uk	For work-related learning toolkit

CHAPTER 9

Where next?

In an educational environment where things rarely stand still, where the very nature of the work ensures sector involvement at the centre of most policy shifts, there is always a sense that any investment of time, effort and other resources may be wasted and overtaken by the next round of change. One task of the recent White Papers has been to provide some reassurance that the need for consolidation, long-term development and stability has been recognised. Following the 2005 General Election Ruth Kelly, the new minister, has launched the White Paper. The announcement that the government will not be implementing the full range of reforms recommended in the Tomlinson's final report was met with widespread disappointment.

In their own terms, the government claims to have demonstrated determination to implement 'far reaching reforms to the 14–19 phase over the next decade' (DfES Standards Unit (2004)). For ministers, the test will be whether the UK can move itself from the position of equal 27th out of 30 OECD countries in the league table of participation in education for 17-year-olds. On the foundation of an improved system of education and raised achievements, high hopes are being built for crime reduction, better economic performance and greater personal fulfilment for all members of a more equal society. Is the optimistic vision shared by all?

What are the wider responses to the publication of the White Paper: 14–19 Education and Skills?

It remains to be seen whether the chosen approach will fulfil the claims made by government and satisfy the majority of stakeholders but key figures are already expressing their disappointment and disapproval. Dr Ann Hodgson and Dr Ken Spours both served on committees for the Tomlinson inquiry:

> The sense of betrayal is heightened by the fact that there was a carefully constructed consensus for a unified and inclusive diploma system for all learners, built up by Mike Tomlinson and his colleagues over 18 months of consultation. They [the thousands involved in the review process] will see their document and some of its terminology

used to support proposals for a divided, elitist, complex and tedious 14–19 phase – the opposite of what they had in mind.

(http://education.guardian.co.uk, 1 March 2005)

Hodgson and Spours' disagreement with retaining existing academic qualifications as 'cornerstones' of a system is that this crucial compromise sabotages the whole effort. They criticise most elements of the White Paper, from the elitism of the notion of stretch without similar attention to inclusion to the new general diploma (5 GCSEs A*–C including maths and English), which they point out will mean that 'Learners who cannot reach this level will be channelled into vocational programmes because there are no general foundation or entry level diplomas in this "new system". This has introduced a cut off point which the Tomlinson proposals would have avoided' (ibid.). Along with many others they express fears about the appeal and weight of the 14–16 curriculum with its additional maths, and science on top of an existing set of GCSEs and have serious concerns regarding the increased complexity the proposals will introduce. They condemn the 'complacency' and 'disrespect' shown and feel that unless the many outstanding issues are addressed, learners and professionals will all suffer. They predict that efforts to maintain the momentum for a unified Diploma will continue.

QCA

The QCA response to the White Paper is far more supportive. The tone of their response emphasises the slow movement towards radical change by talking about the publication of the proposals as an 'important step' in this direction. The terms used are still quite measured but, while not denying the levels of work required, they believe that opportunities are now available to allow assessment loads to be reduced, they welcome the new Diplomas and call for long-term piloting and evaluation.

TUC and CBI

TUC General Secretary Brendan Barber, commenting on the unacceptable yet long-standing, second-class position of vocational education, made the following demand: 'We have to turn that around and in the process open up new routes to learning for all those our system has been failing. If we can make that difference new generations of learners and our economy will both derive immense benefit.'

For some, the right choices were made in the White Paper and they would not agree that the success of reformed vocational education is compromised by the retention of the traditional academic qualifications. Sir Digby Jones, Director-General of the CBI, said:

Employers have been urging governments for years to accentuate and prioritise vocational training so young people, parents and teachers do not feel their efforts in this direction are inferior to Higher Education initiatives. Keeping GCSEs and A-levels is essential for employers who depend on recognisable standards when employing young people and stretching the brightest pupils is vital if we are to win as a nation in the globally competitive race.

Such views are not based solely on European and North American comparisons but, increasingly, comparison with emerging nations such as China and on the demands of international global corporations.

The White Paper does acknowledge aspects of the complexity and intractability of some of the problems faced in the sectors concerned.

> We understand and appreciate the argument that we should challenge our A level students further, by demanding more breadth. But there is no clear consensus amongst pupils, parents, employers or universities on whether or not it should be done. We also believe that so soon after the introduction of Curriculum 2000, stability is important. We will therefore work with employers and universities to see if we can identify what, if anything, would add value to existing courses and we will review progress in 2008.
>
> (DfES 2005a)

Association of Colleges

Although it gives a qualified welcome to the positive measures set out in the White Paper, the Association of Colleges has strong words of warning on the post-16 aspects and says that skills and education for adults and employers in England in 2006–7 is 'a disaster waiting to happen'. The detailed warning is that:

- Money has run out in many parts of the country for 16–19-year-old college places despite a government pledge to guarantee their funding
- Colleges are being told to return money to the funding council even though they have met targets for young people and adult training
- Colleges are facing cuts to skills courses for adults
- Substantial fee hikes or cuts to courses for older adults are looming as these are outside the government's priorities

The clear fear expressed here is that the shift in priorities to the younger learner will strip resources from other areas of work and ultimately have a serious detrimental effect on the quality of all provision. The AoC does not see sufficient incentives for employers to invest more in training, especially in the area of adult skills. This kind of claim and any actual evidence that the 14–19 area is in competition with the 19-plus provision is extremely counter-productive. The idea that all partners collaborate in a constructive way relies upon reducing cynicism and self-interest between the sectors and the real or perceived existence of disadvantage and further inequities in funding would destroy much good work and goodwill (see http://www.aoc.co.uk).

Learning Skills Council

The LSC has responded to the White Paper, and in particular to its own central role in the shape of things to come, in a measured way. It emphasises the obvious importance of partnership, sufficient funding and innovative thinking, and Caroline Neville, the National Director of Learning, said:

> A key challenge will be to ensure that the proposed specialised diplomas are – and are acknowledged to be – of equal status and rigour as GCSEs and A levels. We believe that challenge must be met. We will meet that challenge. We will drive the 14–19 agenda, working with local authorities, the Department for Education and Skills, and with schools, colleges and training providers, and we will very quickly begin to see a positive impact on the achievement and aspirations of young people.

The LSC summarises its role as one of ensuring 100 per cent support and access opportunities for 100 per cent of the country's young people. The four current key priorities are:

- Learning entitlement for all young people with the right courses available locally and the opportunity to progress to further learning and into higher education
- Wider choice of vocational routes with more employer involvement
- More apprenticeships and opportunities for learning at work
- More school, college and training provider collaboration to improve the individualised offer to young learners

Further development work is clearly identified and, for many, this suggests that in the longer term, the way has been left open for future changes to the design of the system. The comments from the LSC demonstrate a recognition of the concerns across all the sectors involved and suggest that there may well be genuine efforts to work on these and to find avenues to achieve the central aims. The PCET sector has been subject to such large-scale change in recent years that a sense of insecurity is endemic in many quarters. It is a time of challenging reforms and huge operational upheaval, affecting not only the innovators who have chosen to be involved in new projects, but those faced with the prospect of their own roles being altered.

On a local level, the LSC asked colleges for their views and received very positive and quite practical responses. Colleges, which have participated, have found both the Increased Flexibility and the E2E programmes beneficial and seem to welcome the emphasis within the White Paper on utilising the expertise and facilities located within colleges. They are willing to shoulder the leadership responsibilities suggested for CoVEs and are keen to develop existing work with schools, employers and other providers in partnership.

Most colleges are already playing a significant role in local strategic planning through LSCs and in association with others in productive Learning Partnerships. They see the dangers less in terms of the overall offer than as a question of inappropriate provision in unsuitable contexts: 'There are dangers that schools may attempt to try these things at a small level and find that not only is it too expensive, it is also difficult to recruit specialist staff' (Fearon 2005).

According to the LSC a key area of work is the establishment of agreed core times which enable students to move between colleges, schools and other providers to offer maximum curriculum breadth. As a balance to the enthusiasm and commitment there is still the sense of 'missed opportunity' in the face of the government's decision not to implement the proposal for an overarching vocational and academic Diploma.

Vocational provider response

The vocational awarding bodies have expressed their sense of frustration at the government's failure to implement the full Tomlinson proposals. Their concern is that the entrenched prejudices in favour of academic routes are so deeply fixed in our society that partial measures to broaden real opportunities will not suffice. Many believe that factors such as class and misinformation on vocational education and training will continue to uphold the elitist status quo. The Director-General of City and Guilds, Chris Humphries, said,

> City and Guilds is thus extremely disappointed by the government's overall response to the proposals of the Tomlinson review. We believe it has failed to grasp the real opportunity for positive and beneficial change for future generations that was created by the 14–19 review, and would call on ministers to reconsider their position.
>
> (http://education.guardian.co.uk, 12 April 2005)

Specialist Schools Trust response

As the lead body for this important programme the Trust has responded very positively to the proposals in the White Paper. They are currently working with other expert bodies to support schools and to develop vocational education. They see their role, as described in the proposals, as central to the development of improvements in joint sixth-form developments to assist in the provision of increased places.

What is the response outside England?

The Welsh Assembly has examined the English proposals in comparison with their own 14–19 learning Pathways and the Welsh Baccalaureate developments. In spite of the different paths being taken in Wales, Northern Ireland and Scotland, there is a commitment to UK involvement and increased joint working. The Welsh response welcomes the leading role to be played by the Sector Skills Councils in the development of new vocational qualifications and states their willingness to include them on an equal basis within their 14–19 framework. Amid the positive comments, it is hard not to notice the contrast between the proposals for England and the flexible Welsh Baccalaureate, with its ability to accommodate both vocational and academic routes at both levels 2 and 3 (with a level 1 Foundation Diploma under development).

In Scotland the rejection of the core of the Tomlinson proposals was widely viewed as a missed opportunity and recent Scottish experiences intensify the response. In 1992 the Howie Committee proposed a Scotcert vocational qualification and an academic baccalaureate but the dual-qualification approach was not accepted as it was believed that it would simply reinforce the division between the routes. The alternative produced by the Scottish Office was a new model diploma with five levels very similar to the Tomlinson system. Ultimately the group awards were not allowed to replace the Highers, though the voluntary Scottish Group Awards were launched as an attempt to develop a new unified qualification structure in a gradual and consensual way. Scotland knows that this approach has not worked and this colours and informs the response.

How will the engagement of all learners be continued?

This has been a headline element of policy because it is so central to the wider agendas of social justice, inclusion and foresight in workforce planning. There have been some successes in what is historically an intractable area but there is still a great deal to be done. The messages are therefore related to continued development and building on good practice.

The government has taken the line that early intervention is vital. This belief has informed the strategy of starting at the beginning with 'Every Child Matters', a programme aimed at removing the personal barriers to learning which exist in the background and home environment of the individual child. It is a part of the long-term perspective being taken and there is some evidence of the success of programmes like this which rely on building contexts and enabling in a positive and preventative sense rather than intervening in a reactive way once young people have failed. There is widespread support for the principles informing such efforts if not for the methods employed.

Among 14–19-year-olds, one key group targeted in the present round and for the future is the cohort labelled disaffected. They are, of course, diverse but the belief in the effectiveness of motivation and re-engagement through employment contact informs many of the strategies being implemented. In order to build on the E2E programme with 14–16 in mind, a programme for those with serious barriers to re-engagement is planned. It will, of course, contain a significant work-focused component of up to two days per week. The now familiar intensive advice and support will be incorporated and this will extend to workplace support and mentoring. The model for this support will be informed in part by those voluntary sector organisations which possess considerable experience in alternative approaches with 14–19-year-olds.

The initial stages of the programme will involve goal setting with an adviser, at which point the short- and long-term targets and aspirations will be discussed. Over time the plan constructed will be reviewed in the light of progress or problems and the young person will continue to engage with the Key Stage 4 curriculum and with the achievement of functional skills. The level 1 Diploma is likely to be the main qualification aim where appropriate, though a tailored progression leading to this or an alternative programme at a higher level may be more suitable for some individuals. The central aim to stretch and challenge each young person should not be compromised by the personal difficulties which should be viewed as barriers to be overcome.

All young people involved would be given a personal development programme aimed at providing them with skills for employment and life. The usual progression routes would open up in due course and hopefully they would find themselves moving on to Apprenticeships or other work-based learning. The transition to academic routes and perhaps HE is not emphasised and this might suggest a continuation of the view that certain routes are more suitable for those learners who make slower progress. This new model would be piloted from 2006 and should then be available from 2007/8 to around 10,000 learners. Following satisfactory results from evaluation of participation and achievement rates and wider social benefits it will be extended and given a higher profile.

Realistically, some will say that this kind of aim sets the bar too high but there is certainly evidence that, in spite of tremendous disadvantages, some learners and their teachers working in environments that are hugely obstructive to their efforts do succeed in improving life chances through good planning and sound, consistent, principled approaches. It really does remain to be seen whether the evidence will support this strongly held new establishment belief in the effectiveness of relevance credo.

What are the new FE skills academies?

The academy programme has proved controversial in schools and will certainly raise questions and divide opinion as it is introduced into the FE sector. Twelve new skills academies are planned for completion by 2008. These new academies for post-16 students were signposted by the minister as 'centres of excellence providing a new benchmark in the design and delivery of skills training to young people' (http://education.guardian.co.uk, 22 March 2005).

The sponsorship element is, predictably, the most criticised aspect of the proposals. Just as the sponsor's control is subject to suspicion in the school sector, there are concerns in FE that such ideas are about innovation for its own sake. The entrepreneurs involved may provide publicity, minimum start-up stakes and some expertise but they may interfere too much or lose interest fairly early on and generally do more harm to learners than good. All the classroom unions, including the ATL, representing teachers in schools and colleges have opposed the academies in principle.

How will the 2005 budget funding support learners in colleges and work?

At least £20 million will be spent to encourage work-related education for the 14–16 group of learners from 2006–8. In addition, a key group of 16–17-year-olds in work but not training will be offered possibilities for negotiated learning agreements with their employers and funding will be provided to support this. £80 million is being made available to test the scheme in eight areas through financial initiatives which have been designed to enable these teenagers to work and study or to enrol on apprenticeships. New CoVEs are also being established in city colleges where there are large ethnic minority populations.

What is the situation for schools?

So much has been achieved in schools that an insider might be forgiven for assuming that there would be general celebration of achievement but media attention prefers a crisis and 'good news is no news'. Hardly surprising that the poor literacy results are a headline while it is hard to find members of the public who are aware of the improvements in college success rates and the rise in test results for 14-year-olds. Even the good news that does emerge becomes a matter of questionable interpretation. For instance, since 1997, GCSE results have improved until those gaining five or more GCSEs at grade C or above has risen nearly 10 per cent. The fact is that raised achievement at both GCSE and A level is often read as a dilution in standards and attributed to too soft an assessment regime. For teachers and students it can be a difficult period, especially if potential employers reflect these views.

Why are secondary heads calling the White Paper 'a lost opportunity'?

Since the 1980s, the Secondary Heads Association has been campaigning for a unified system of 14–19 qualifictions. Their support for the Tomlinson proposals was neither sudden nor unexpected but based on long-held principles and extensive consultation. These views mean that the Association has serious reservations about the continuation of the present system of academic qualifications. Secondary heads had expressed real concerns about the burden of external examinations and were fully supportive of the original Tomlinson proposals to introduce a system of chartered assessors accredited to carry out internal assessment to external standards.

Dr John Dunford added to the strong and emotional responses to the White Paper when he said, 'The Tomlinson diploma is carefully crafted with the support of employers.' He regrets the government's failure to reduce the 'bloated external examination system, which is costing schools and colleges £610 million per year. The failure to adopt the Tomlinson recommendation for chartered assessors is a severe blow and suggests a lack of confidence on the part of government in the professionalism of teachers to carry out internal assessment to external standards universities, colleges and schools, has been strangled at birth' (http://www.sha.org.uk). These issues are very sensitive professional matters which will affect the relationship of the workforce, the Secretary of State and the DfES in the future. However, he praised the following elements.

- The slimming of the curriculum for 11–14-year-olds which will provide space for secondary schools to prepare pupils better for the start of the 14–19 phase
- The emphasis on English and maths in the White Paper
- Employer involvement in the design of the specialised diplomas
- The renewed commitment to introduce a post-qualifications applications process to university

What will happen to the unified, coherent system of 14–19 qualifications?

This concept of coherence and unification, supported by so many stakeholders, has not been abandoned. Many see the setback as rather less than permanent. Dr John Dunford highlighted an area noticed by many commentators: 'I welcome the hint in the White Paper that the government is prepared to look again at the question of a diploma in 2008' (http://www.sha.org.uk).

How will 14–19-year-olds receive quality impartial advice on their future?

With Connexions being integrated within local services and new arrangements (see Chapter 4) for college- and schools-based advice being introduced, there are fears that impartiality and multi-agency expertise will be lost. Partnerships had been developed which may well now be lost along with successful approaches, especially those responsible for re-engaging NEETs. There may have been insufficient advisers but without increased funding the quality will not necessarily improve and the impartiality could be a casualty of the restructured and split service. After all there is an incentive for schools under pressure to encourage pupils to stay on even where it is not the most appropriate choice for them.

The more vulnerable young people already outside the school system will no longer access the same support routes and may well feel stigmatised. Many teenagers do not know what they want to do after leaving school or college and even those with aspirations and those who enter HE can be unhappy with the advice they received. The new systems will have a great deal to prove, especially in view of wider changes.

Progression to HE: how will this be supported?

Extended projects, additional AEA materials as a new section in A level, similar developments for Diplomas, proposals for HE modules to be made available in schools are all measures designed to stretch learners and to demonstrate their achievements more clearly to universities and employers. It is well known that universities have been calling for additional means to allow them to differentiate between the high-achieving candidates for places.

The provision of clearer and more specific information on students' profiles and the detail of their results is a way forward. The UCAS consultation on introducing information on unit grades is an important part of this and will provide high-quality, reliable information for all concerned. The Joint Council for Qualifications will work with UCAS to provide the unit grade information in advance of the 2006 admissions round. Some might see this as quite optimistic but they seem confident that this can be achieved. In order to avoid an increase in re-sits following the introduction of PQA (post-qualification application) there will be a review of the rules with safeguards introduced to prevent this. The use of a single aptitude test is also a possibility and research is being carried out in this area. A system of post-qualification application is currently under consideration and consultation. This should simplify and increase the fairness of the admissions procedure for all concerned.

How do universities view the future?

The university sector was very supportive of the 2003 Tomlinson Review and was keen to see all the key recommendations implemented, from the core skills focus and overarching diploma to their own particular need for the means to differentiate between the best applicants. The immediate response of Universities UK to the White Paper reflects their concerns and a relatively positive view of the future:

> In the absence of an overarching diploma at Level 3, it is all the more important that in the implementation of the reforms, the Government makes every effort to ensure that the vocational and academic routes have parity of esteem. The introduction of an overarching diploma at Level 2 to encapsulate GCSEs is a positive step, which we hope will lead in time to the wider acceptance of overarching diploma proposals at Level 3.
>
> (http://www.universitiesuk.ac.uk, 24 February 2005)

The university sector has always voiced its support for a broader and more inclusive HE offering. They will be involved in the design of both core functional skills and the new vocational routes and FE level providers must hope that the warm endorsements of 'multiple opportunities for cross-over between academic and vocational routes' and new recognition for vocational learning as a viable route into HE will indeed be translated into more openings for applicants.

Universities are pleased with the assistance given to their admissions process by the provision of A level unit marks. They also welcomed the new more stretching optional questions at A-level and the extended project pilot. As far as the proposals on functional literacy and numeracy within GCSE and the core skills for all learners are concerned, there is widespread support. The principle of more universally accredited work and life skills has survived, though not fully intact, from the Tomlinson Report.

How will quality improvements be achieved in FE?

According to inspection reports, there is a great deal of good post-16 provision, which is not to say that improvements are unnecessary, just that in order to make good use of such information it is vital to establish what was measured/assessed. One worrying aspect of poor practice was the identification of work-based provision with low-quality teaching and learning. Inspections in the area began in 2001 and, in spite of some significant areas of weakness, the college- and work-based learning contexts are on the whole judged to be satisfactory. The colleges performed better than the work-based learning provision – the former scoring 90 per cent and the latter only 61 per cent in the satisfactory or better categories. It is to these areas that resources and strategic attention are being directed through a range of reforms under the 'Success for All' umbrella.

How will Initial Teacher Training change?

As an important element in the delivery of Success for All in the learning and skills sector, initial training should support the strategies for 14–19 and skills improvement. Among the 'works in progress' are the Standards Unit ITT Reform Pilots. In the policy document 'Equipping our Teachers for the Future: Reforming Initial Teacher Training for the Learning and Skills Sector', notice was given of proposed pilots connected to aspects of reform. The first phase of these were initiated in September 2004 with a focus on mentoring. From January 2005 proposals have been invited for Phase Two pilots. These can be undertaken by eligible, individual and group providers including HEIs, FE colleges and adult, community and work-based providers. They must be completed by July 2006. There are two areas of work sought:

- Individual Learning Plans (ILPs), including initial assessment, support offered, documentation and tracking systems, staffing, links with HR systems and processes, etc.

- Teaching Observation and Practice, including methods used, documentation, staffing requirements, staff support, trainee support, links with HR systems and processes, etc.

'Equipping our Teachers for the Future' (DfES 2004b) sets out the reforms for implementation over the next three years. The key elements are:

- Revision of standards by LLUK – by spring 2006

- Piloting of mentoring began in 2004 and evaluation should be completed by 2007 in time for national roll-out.
- Systems to register trainee and qualified teachers and to award QTS (set up by the Institute for Learning) in time for first trainees to register in passport courses in 2007
- Necessary changes to legislation by June 2007
- Full HEI and awarding-body course leading to QTLS to be delivered from September 2007
- Funding for development throughout the period to flow from 2005

Future training models

Ideally CPD should be a continuum. Many people believe that there could be a great deal of potential in a model that takes a wider view of training. This might consist of a beginning teacher phase and more structured additional components for subsequent years, some compulsory and dictated by career progression as responsibility roles develop in the current system, and some optional and related to interest and personal research with a longer-term focus.

There is room for the views of education professionals far more open than any of those currently being discussed. The conventional structures, which now separate individuals into very fixed areas for the duration of their career, are already being eroded as a result of pressing needs. So there are routes for the non-graduate FE lecturers to become graduate teaching professionals by way of foundation degrees and the Certificate in Education teaching qualification. Learning Support Assistants can now achieve formal qualifications and take a route into teaching and the same applies to technicians and instructors in the post-compulsory sector.

What development of progression measures is planned?

There is also a drive to build and develop data on the qualifications achieved by learners in the period 11–19. The purpose of many of the new accountability measures is to improve participation and achievement to 19 and beyond and this data will contribute to the development of a progression measure to show how successful pupils in each school have been in gaining qualifications in post-compulsory education and training. This will move the tables forward from the current position which provides data on the 11–16 phase. Data collected in this way will be used to improve progression and enhanced by the information collected by Connexions regarding destinations. The LSCs and LEAs at local level as well as the inspectorate will all have access to this data source (see also Chapter 6).

What will happen to the LEAs?

Recent initiatives and shifts in policy are likely to reduce the role of councils education department. The increase in the number of foundation schools and the changes in 14–19 education are factors affecting the survival of the authorities as they function at present.

What did the party manifestos promise?

All three main parties gave FE and the vocational and skills agenda much more space than in previous elections. They seemed to agree that 14 was the new key age and that, by whatever means, new combinations of academic and vocational learning should be made available from this point onwards.

Labour has always been the most engaged with the sector and its issues, and have raised their game significantly in spite of the collapse of the more radical version of policy. They will continue the expansion and improvement of vocational training opportunities and of skills acquisition and enhancement before and during the phase. The extension of the Centres of Vocational Excellence to include every FE college was anticipated and the overall number of high-quality vocational places will be increased. There is an acknowledgement in the manifesto of the need to find increased resources for the reform of the FE colleges but, in spite of expressed intentions to work towards closing the school and college funding gap, there is no written commitment. It has also been observed that despite pre-election care over areas of perceived sensitivity, government attitudes to the more radical elements of Tomlinson's proposals are not set in stone.

Conservative support for such developments was both new and unexpected. After many years during which the party effectively ignored the PCET sector, they have joined the rush to focus attention on the area of youth opportunity. Their preferred approach, as outlined in the manifesto, includes greater 'freedom to manage budgets', support for innovation and new 'super colleges'. They promise to make a third of a million grants of £1,000 each available to 14–16-year-olds who wish to combine conventional school courses with college and work-based vocational study. These promises will not be achieved through existing structures since they have announced that they would abolish the LSCs and ensure that money follows the student. Those who have worked in the sector for long enough recall the detrimental effects of the funding mechanisms created to achieve such results. They led to colleges prioritising raw student numbers over quality and real employment and progression prospects. Without detail, it is difficult to establish how some aspects of the proposals are significantly different or how others could be achieved.

The Liberal Democrats picked up the baton of the diploma system and claimed that they would adopt the Tomlinson proposals in full and replace GCSEs and A levels. The system they suggested would be a post-14 mix of academic and vocational education incorporating the stretch component. Their promises to drop tuition fees and to cut class sizes have received more attention than other policy statements but it is worth noting that they have announced an intention to completely replace the National Curriculum with a minimum curriculum entitlement that stipulates children's study in five key areas – maths, science, ICT, English and languages.

What significant changes are planned for the next ten years?

The government's change programme is now well under way and the following outline timetable of the major changes was published in the White Paper with a promise of a full version to come.

2005

- More GCSEs in vocational subjects
- More Young Apprenticeships
- Roll-out enterprise education
- Pilot English and maths GCSE changes
- Agreement on Diploma lines
- Skills Academy establishment
- First vocational leading schools announced

2006

- A-level differentiation data to HEIs
- Extended project pilot
- New science KS4 and GCSEs
- Upgrade CoVE network

2007

- Legislation to free up local governance
- Start of major CPD for school and college staff

2008

- KS3 curriculum and assessment changes
- First four Diploma lines available
- 12 Skills Academies open
- 200 vocational leading schools in place

2010

- All vocational lines available
- Eight Diploma lines a nationwide entitlement
- Further 13 Skills Academies

2015

- All Diplomas a nationwide entitlement

A Regulatory Impact Assessment, setting out some more detail of likely organisational effects over time, has been published alongside this and is available on the DfES website. Specialised Diplomas, learning from successful qualification systems in other countries, will be designed. As far as possible reforms will be compatible with arrangements in other countries. In order to continue and 'shape the reform process', Sir Andrew Foster will be conducting a review of the sector. This process is likely to have a significant impact on colleges in the sector.

In conclusion

Any new, broad structural reforms or positive and creative individual projects require similar supportive circumstances. Lead times must be extended to allow for real experimentation and evaluation, for mistakes, successes and revisions. The process of design, especially in an area as complex as curriculum and qualification reform was never going to be straightforward; it presents significant implications for students and teachers in terms of recent policy. Increasingly imaginative and brave solutions are sought if the current issues in education relating to these marginal phases are to be addressed centrally. The system has always suited conventional achievers, students who are successful and those who are satisfactory. The school sector appears to have had incredible success in recent years but critics can still point to large minorities who do not benefit from all the improvements.

Concern about the balance between the ambitious demands and the time and space available in the curriculum

The intention has always been to increase choice from an earlier age, providing good 'grounding' and the space to 'catch up'. There is indeed a central requirement for a broad curriculum but there is also a tension between the avoidance of narrowing down and the making of space for stretch, experience and specific preparation of skills for employment. The White Paper made this clear:

In opening up these wider opportunities, we will address the risks. We cannot have young people making such narrow choices at the age of 14 that they cannot later change tack. So all the pathways must remain broad, at least until the age of 16 and must give young people transferable skills. We cannot have young people ignorant of what is available or unable to make choices that are good for them. We cannot return to the days before the National Curriculum when boys and girls sometimes had little opportunity to study in areas which had been the traditional preserve of the other sex. So good quality and impartial information, advice and guidance are crucial.

(DfES 2005a: 23)

The ambition is clearly stated, though the real practical difficulties inherent in implementing this vision are not fully addressed.

Development of new routes

Once more young people have been through different routes into employment and higher education and the assumption that every 18-year-old will still be in education or training is common, the acceptance of such routes will grow. Two of the main weaknesses in the current qualifications offer are inextricably linked: poor understanding and acceptance of vocational qualifications by employers and HE, and therefore a poor reputation and take up among learners. Where we do have well-respected and recognised pathways there is competition, commitment and family and social support for them; medicine, the law and engineering are among those established in the UK.

Beyond the functional

The point made elsewhere about the overlap between phases, their dependence on each other and their interaction is at the heart of this endeavour. Adults as well as young people, parents as well as teenagers and the pre-school children being taught by parents who have recently returned to education are all named in the various new initiatives and policy documents.

There are economic drivers which often receive the greatest attention in public pronouncements but the social and personal incentives for change are equally significant. While it can seem logical to begin with the basics it is very important not to ignore the individuality of those concerned. What might seem to some to be the soft packaging of the White Paper, the emphasis on personalised approaches and the importance of choices, abilities and preferences on the part of each learner, is in fact the real potential for change. It is only through this kind of engagement achieved by professionals who feel themselves valued and whose work with individual learners is validated by the system that real progress will be made in terms of those most ambitious aims for improved social cohesion and greater contentment, stability and quality of life.

An overarching Diploma by 2008?

Even if the passage of time does allow for a gradual move towards a unified qualification structure, there will still be many obstacles. An overarching Diploma system in the near future is unlikely and would not necessarily remove the prejudice against vocational learning nor is it easy to find a common approach to assessment for a very wide range of programmes. Methods designed for one area of learning can be entirely inappropriate for another. The drive towards uniformity may be based on some admirable principles but the practicalities of implementation and the social changes required could prove insurmountable. Diplomas may be constructed to be equivalent in terms of volume across all levels but the nature of the learning puts real equivalence much further from reach. Internal assessment can be a vital feature in some vocational programmes where students must build and demonstrate competence. External written examinations are cost effective and can be more easily administered but are totally unsuited to many vocational contexts. The public are however always more inclined to trust externally rather than internally assessed qualifications.

Some schools fear that the vocational focus and other curriculum change may damage their hard-won strengths. Within the PCET sector there are equivalent fears that the 14–19 focus on level 2 work may be under-funded and achieve results at the expense of higher-level programmes and adult provision. If there is to be a coherent system it must address such issues and allow for the individuality of the different areas and contexts for learning. These steps have already proved too much for the current climate and without wider reform and shifts in attitude there will be no significant change. The elusive parity of esteem will not be achieved simply through qualifications and curriculum reform.

References

Armitage *et al.* (2003) *Teaching and Training in Post-Compulsory Education* (2nd edn), Maidenhead: Open University Press.

Association of Teachers and Lecturers Conference April 2005 (www.atl.org.uk/atl_en/news/conferences/annual 2005/default.asp).

Becta (2005) *Using Technology to Support the 14–19 Agenda* (http://www.becta.org.uk/corporate/publications/documents/14-19 Agenda.pdf).

Black, A. (1997) *Transitions, Work and Learning: Implications for Assessment*, National Academy Press (www.nap.edu).

Burke, J. (ed.) (1995) *Outcomes, Learning and the Curriculum: Implications for NVQs, GNVQs and Other Qualifications*, London: RoutledgeFalmer.

Coles, A. (ed.) (2004) *Teaching in Post-Compulsory Education*, London: David Fulton Publishers.

Dearing, R. (1996) *Review of Qualifications for 16-19 Year Olds*, London: SCAA (http://www.dfes.gov. uk/14 19).

Delors, J. (1996) *Learning: The Treasure Within – Report to UNESCO of the International Commission*, Paris: UNESCO.

DfEE (1992) 'The Further and Higher Education Act', London: DfEE.

DfEE (1999) 'Learning to Succeed: A New Framework for Post-16 Learning', London: DfEE.

DfEE (2000) 'Consultation Paper on the Introduction of Compulsory Teaching Qualifications for FE College Teachers', London: DfEE.

DfEE (2001a) 'Schools: Building on Success', London: DfEE.

DfEE (2001b) 'Special Educational Needs Disability Act (SENDA)', London: DfEE.

DfES (2001a) 'Further Education Teachers' Qualifications (England) Regulations 2001', London: DfES.

DfES (2001b) 'Modern Apprenticeships: The Way to Work', London: DfES.

DfES (2001c) Schools: Achieving Success' (White Paper), London: DfES.

DfES (2001d) 'Skills for Life: The National Strategy for Improving Adult Literacy and Numeracy Skills', London: DfES.

DfES (2002a) '14–19: Extending Opportunities, Raising Standards' (Green Paper), London: DfES.

DfES (2002b) 'Languages for All: Languages for Life – A Strategy for England', London: DfES.

DfES (2002c) 'Success for All: Reforming Further Education and Training', London: DfES.

DfES (2002d) 'Transforming Youth Work: Resourcing Excellent Youth Services', London: DfES.

DfES (2003a) '14–19: Opportunity and Excellence', London: DfES.

DfES (2003b) 'Consultation on ITT in Further Education', London: DfES.

DfES (2003c) 'The Future of Initial Teacher Education for the Learning and Skills Sector: An Agenda for Reform', London: DfES.

DfES (2003d) 'Removing Barriers to Achievement: The Government's Strategy for SEN', London: DfES.

DfES (2003e) 'Work-related Learning at Key Stage 4', London: DfES.

DfES (2004a) '14–19 Curriculum and Qualifications Reform: Final Report of the Working Group on 14–19 Reform', London: DfES.

DfES (2004b) 'Equipping our Teachers for the Future', London: DfES.

DfES (2004c) 'Every Child Matters', London: DfES.

DfES (2004d) 'Work-related Learning at Key Stage 4', London: DfES.

DfES (2005a) '14–19 Education and Skills' (White Paper), London: DfES.

DfES (2005b) 'Building Schools for Success' (http://www.bsf.gov.uk/).

DfES (2005c) 'Disapplication of the National Curriculum' (http://www.dfes.gov.uk/disapply).

DfES (2005d) 'The Increased Flexibility for 14–16 Year Olds Programme', London: DfES.

DfES (2005e) Skills: Getting on in Business, Getting on at Work' (Green Paper), London: DfES. *Guardian*, 19 October 2004, p. 1 (www.education.guardian.co.uk).

DfES/TTA (2003) 'Qualifying to Teach: Professional Standards for Qualified Teacher Status and Requirements for Initial Teacher Training', London: DfES/TTA.

Ecclestone, K. (2000) 'Bewitched, Bothered and Bewildered: A Policy Analysis of the GNVQ Assessment Regime', *Journal of Education Policy*, 15, 3, 539–58.

Ecclestone, K. (2002) *Learning Autonomy in Post-16 Education*, London: RoutledgeFalmer.

Ecclestone, K. (2004) 'The Rise of Low Self Esteem and the Lowering of Educational Expectations', in Hayes, D. (ed.) *The RoutledgeFalmer Guide to Key Debates in Education*, London: RoutledgeFalmer.

Fearon, B. (2005) 'The 14–19 White Paper: What's in it for Colleges?' (www.senet.lsc.gov.uk).

FENTO (1999) *Standards for Teaching and Learning in Further Education in England and Wales*, London: DfES/FENTO.

FENTO (2004a) *Initial Teacher Education in the Learning and Skills Sector*, London: FENTO.

FENTO (2004b) *A Licence to Practice*, London: FENTO.

FENTO (2004c) Wider Sector: Wider Perspectives. *Securing an Initial Teacher Education Framework to Underpin Effective Teaching*, London: FENTO.

Hargreaves, D. (2004) *Learning for Life: The Foundations of Lifelong Learning*, Bristol: Policy Press.

Hayes, D. (ed.) (2004) *The RoutledgeFalmer Guide to Key Debates in Education*, London: RoutledgeFalmer.

Health and Safety Executive (1995) Reporting of Injuries, Diseases and Dangerous Occurrences Regulations (RIDDOR), London: HSE.

Higham, J. (2004) *Curriculum Change: GNVQ*, Leeds: University of Leeds, School of Education.

HMSO (1999) *Management of Health and Safety at Work Regulations*, London: HMSO.

HM Treasury/Department for Work and Pensions/DfES (2004) *Supporting Young People to Achieve: Towards a new Deal for Skills*, London: HM Treasury.

Hodgson, A. and Spours, K. (2003) *Beyond A Levels: Curriculum 2000 and the Reform of 14–19 Qualifications*, London: RoutledgeFalmer.

Hodgson, A. and Spours, K. (1997) *Dearing and Beyond: 14–19 Qualifications, Frameworks and Systems*, London: RoutledgeFalmer.

Hyland, T. (1994) *Competence, Education and NVQs: Dissenting Voices*, London: Cassell.

Kirk, G. *et al.* (2004) 'Towards a unified teaching profession', *TES* Online, 22 October.

LSC (2003) *Success for All: Implementation of the Framework for Quality and Success*.

McKenzie, P. and Wurzburg, G. (1998) 'Lifelong learning and employability', *The OECD Observer*, 209, December 1997/January 1998.

Neef, D. (1998) *The Economic Impact of Knowledge*, Butterworth Heinemann: Oxford.

Ofsted (2003) *The Initial Training of Further Education Teachers*, London: Ofsted.

Ofsted (2004a) *Developing New Vocational Pathways: Final Report on the Introduction of New GCSEs*, London: Ofsted.

Ofsted (2004b) *The Future of Inspection Consultation Paper*, London: Ofsted.

Ofsted (2004c) *Vocational A Levels: The First Two Years*, London: Ofsted.

Ofsted (2005) 'Developing New Vocational Pathways', London: HMI.

Raffe, D. (2002) *The Scope, Feasibility and Organisation of a Nuffeld Annual Review of 14–19 Education*, Oxford: Nuffield Foundation.

Raggatt, P and Williams, S. (1999) *Government, Markets and Qualifications: An Anatomy of Policy*, London: RoutledgeFalmer.

Seltzer, K. and Bentley, T. (1999) *The Creative Age: Knowledge and Skills for New Economy*, London: Demos.

Smith Report (2004) 'Making Mathematics Count' (http://www.mathsinquiry.org.uk/report/).

Taubman, D. (2000) 'Staff Relations', in Smithers, A. and Robinson, P. (eds) *Further Education Re-Formed*, London: RoutledgeFalmer.

Tomlinson, M. (2002) *Inquiry into A Level Standards*, London: DfES.

Tomlinson, M. (2004) '14–19 Working Group press notice' (http://www.14-19reform.gov.uk).

Websites

www.standards.dfes.gov.uk/academies/what_are_academies/innovation
www.educationguardian.co.uk
www.ofsted.gov.uk
www.tes.co.uk
www.dfes.gov.uk/section/96
www.lsda.org.uk/programmes/e2e/index.asp
www.ofsted.gov.uk
www.tes.co.uk
www.dfes.gov.uk/qualifications
www.inclusion.ngfi.gov.uk
www.learning-partnership.co.uk
www.lifelonglearning.co.uk
www.nc.uk.net
www.qca.org.uk
www.lluk.ac.uk
www.nc.uk.net
www.tes.co.uk
www.tta.gov.uk
www.lsc.gov.uk
www.lsda.gov.uk
www.niace.org.uk
www.qca.org.uk
www.sha.org .uk
www.standards.dfes.gov.uk
www.universitiesuk.ac.uk

Index